MUD SHOW

MUD SHOW:

BY FRED POWLEDGE

A Circus Season

Harcourt Brace Jovanovich   New York and London

Printed in the United States of America

Library of Congress Cataloging in Publication Data

Powledge, Fred.
  Mud show: a circus season.

  1. Hoxie Brothers Circus. 2. Circus—United States. I. Title.
GV1821.H69P68   791.3′0973   75-12691
ISBN 0-15-163212-X

First edition
B C D E

TO HOXIE TUCKER

CONTENTS

1 LEAVING

WINTER QUARTERS

In the North it was a mid-March of the worst kind. Something that looked like spring had come, warming the earth for a few days, and with it people's bones and spirits. But the spring had been untrue. Behind it, another cold storm had moved in from the west. This was inevitable, because in the North no spring can come in mid-March and hope to survive. The storm had moved down out of the Rockies and across the plains, where a late-winter storm was no news. It had hit Chicago, as almost all of them do, and it was no news there, either. When it got to the East it was a mixture of cold water, snow, sleet, and black, dirty air, and overnight it put an end to the false spring.

From Philadelphia northward, it was still very definitely winter, and the moment of warmth served only to remind people that the real spring would come this year, as usual, but that it was still a long way off. Immediately south of Philadelphia, though, there were isolated and lonely signs that perhaps the worst was over for another year. If you drove down the toll roads through Delaware and Maryland, you could be aware of a faint color to the banks of seemingly naked trees alongside the road. The trees had no leaves (that was still far away), but the impression you got, from a vehicle moving past them, was one of subtle faint reds and oranges, yellows and blues, and greens. You could stop and examine an individual tree and find no explanation for this phenomenon; you would see only brown limbs and trunks. But start the motion again and the total effect was one of faint color.

It was, of course, the hundreds of thousands of almost microscopic buds that provided the color. Individually they could not be seen, but when viewed as a mass, and in motion, they gave their world a cast that meant, among other things, that spring was coming. If you were going south along the mid-Atlantic states in that mid-March, the color seemed to intensify until it was almost possible to pick out individual buds. But then Washington intervened. The highways that get you around, and past, the capital became so wide, so grey, and so busy, so full of hurrying people and their vehicles, that you no longer could afford to look at the scenery. And then, below Washington, several miles into Virginia, when the traffic had spaced itself out, all of a sudden there was forsythia in bloom, and you knew that there was a spring this year, too; that the season had started. And the more southward you went from that point on, the more certain you became of spring. And when you passed central Florida and started the last long run toward Miami, you almost forgot that there had been, and in some places there still was, a winter.

Winter quarters was part of a dairy farm outside Miami, leased from a man who had put up signs saying NO TRESPASSING —SURVIVORS WILL BE PROSECUTED. It was a dismal place, partly because the Big Top was not set up and partly because ten or fifteen men and a lot of animals had been living there all winter, since the last season ended, and they had let their garbage fall on the ground. There were trucks, randomly parked and painted purple and white and with the lettering "Hoxie Bros. Circus" on their sides. Most of the men lived in one of those trucks, a tractor-trailer as big as a moving van that had been divided into three compartments. Bunk beds, four high, had been squeezed into the compartments, and the resulting dormitory was called a "sleeper." Other men slept in the cabs of trucks, and some of them slept on torn foam pads on the ground.

There were ten elephants, four of them mammoth grey

adults and six of them babies, and they were shackled at intervals along a chain. They swayed incessantly. There was a practice ring for the animals, and a well-worn rut ran around its inside perimeter. There was a well and a pump, its tank and motor and wiring exposed to the elements, looking like part of a moonshine still. A green plastic garden hose extended from the bottom of the tank, and every once in a while someone would walk over to it and turn it on and kink the hose a little so that only a small stream of water, for drinking, would come out.

In a pen next to the dairy sheds there were horses, a pair of zebras, a camel, a couple of llamas, all of them nuzzling at the small clumps of grass that were left. Two baby pigs ran wild, and in tandem, around the grounds, rooting constantly in the garbage and moving aside without even looking up when a human approached. A small donkey and a tiny horse ran free, too, looking for food. The cooktent was up, blue-and-white-striped canvas with orange tables and seats under it, and it was placed beside the truck that served as the kitchen. Most of the men kept themselves close to the cooktent; it was the central object in winter quarters.

In an open space between the office wagon and the cooktent there was a small green cage with wire walls. Its door was open, and attached to the cage by a long chain was a young baboon. Her name was Wahoo. She had been born the previous spring, and she had spent almost all of her time with the workmen, so she was exceedingly at ease with people. Whenever someone walked past her cage Wahoo would rush out and try to play, unless the person who walked by was one of those who teased her. In such cases Wahoo hurried inside the cage and tried to make herself small in a corner so she would not be seen.

Most of the workmen were kind to Wahoo, and they brought her bits of food from the cooktent. Some of them even came back from Sweetwater with whole bananas and apples for her, and she carefully peeled these and ate them lovingly. Wahoo also liked to drink Busch Bavarian beer, which was a favorite among the workmen. When she was on good terms

with you, Wahoo would groom you—that is, she would carefully pick at the hair on your arms and chest, using her slim,
delicate pink fingers to rid you of tiny bits of dirt and insects
and other foreign matter. It was a sign that she liked you. It
was something baboons did. If you groomed Wahoo in return,
she would become almost ecstatic.

It was warm at winter quarters in mid-March; during
the day it was even hot. Spring had not come here at all,
because it had never gone away. It and summer, in combination with each other, were the only seasons in this part of
Florida. The land was tropical, but, unlike much of the territory around Miami, there were no palm trees here; just pines
and scrubby bushes and a dark sand floor. The best way to
tell the season, perhaps, was to recognize the frequency with
which jets strafed the place. Winter quarters was just west of
the Miami airport, and all day and until late at night in mid-
March the big jets came close to the ground on their final
approaches, delivering late-winter vacationers to the beaches.
If you looked hard you could actually see the pale faces at
the windows.

The address of winter quarters was a normal-sounding one
—1500 Northwest 97th Avenue—but it was hard to get to. Jeff
Woosnam, who had come to the show in March to play in the
band, had ridden a bus from his home in Ohio to Miami, and
then he had caught a cab to the lot. He and the cab driver
had gotten lost several times, and it had ended up costing Jeff
twenty-eight dollars just to get to the dairy farm. Fifteen-
hundred Northwest 97th Avenue was not on an avenue at all,
but in the boondocks. They were, however, temporary boondocks. All around Miami, and especially to the west of the
city, where there was still room for expansion, workmen and
huge machines were filling the Everglades and building condominiums of doubtful quality and beauty. The construction
was not frantic but steady, and at the end of any given day
there had appeared, on top of the swamp, several thousand
more square feet of housing for retired cops from Manhattan
and former schoolteachers from Cleveland.

Hoxie used to have his winter quarters a few miles away,

in Sweetwater, close to the main road that ran into Miami, but that land had become valuable, and now it was covered with building blocks and asphalt and the forms for swimming pools and holes to receive transplanted palm trees. So he had moved a little farther away. But the sound of the construction was almost audible from the dairy farm, and you knew that soon this land, too, would change. The SURVIVORS WILL BE PROSECUTED sign would come down and a new one would go up—one proclaiming the place to be named La Barcelona or Boca Palmas—and Hoxie would have to move his elephants and zebras and llamas and men again.

A lot of the activity at winter quarters seemed to have to do with carrying things from one place to another. In one corner, workmen were painting thick boards on a modified assembly line. A young man with red-blond hair brought them huge piles of lumber on a fork-lift, two men slapped orange paint on them, and someone else took them away to dry in the sun. They were seats. A man went from one truck's engine compartment to another, testing something. To one side, a huge black man in dungarees and no shirt was using a cutting torch to make tent stakes out of long pieces of steel. He looked different from the other workmen. He seemed to be actually working hard—the sweat was collecting on his body in indigo pools—while everyone else was exerting himself as little as possible, in the manner of KPs in the army.

The big black man was one of the principal stars of Hoxie Brothers Circus. He was its boss canvasman—the person responsible for getting the Big Top up and down every day when the show was on the road—and he was the most skilled and handy person around winter quarters. He was also the lion-trainer. His name was Manuel Ruffin, and he was also known, in his role as lion-trainer, as Prince Bogino. He was *really* known as Junior. Now, in March of 1974, Junior was in his mid-thirties. Twenty-some years before, when he was twelve, he had left home in Los Angeles and gone to work for Clyde Beatty, the famous cat-trainer, as one of Beatty's assistants. Beatty had nicknamed him Junior.

That was when Manuel was small. Now he weighed close

to two hundred and fifty pounds, and you felt a little funny calling him "Junior," but that was his name. Junior's job, when the circus was on the road, consisted of spending eleven minutes, more or less, in a steel arena full of lions and tigers. The act opened the show. It came right after the Spec, in which all the performers and some of the animals walked around the track. Junior would walk around with the elephants in Spec, then rush outside to get his whip and pistol, and run back into the Big Top, where King Charles was already into the lion-taming music, and then he would dash into the steel arena.

There are some cat acts in which the trainer makes fools of his animals; he sticks his head into their mouths and generally demonstrates how tame they are, although he knows they can never be counted on to be really tame. Junior learned the other way from Clyde Beatty. He would bound into the arena with his whip cracking, and he occasionally fired off his blank pistol, and the cats frequently lunged and growled at him as if they really wanted to do him harm.

The act was so good that the workmen and other performers sometimes paid Junior their supreme compliment and gathered just inside the Big Top's back door (although performers are not supposed to do that) to watch those eleven minutes. Sometimes it turned out not too well. Exactly one year before, when the show opened its season in Sweetwater, on a lot a few miles away, Junior had been clawed terribly by his cats. It had taken his wounds a long time to heal, and when he went into the arena again several weeks later, when the show was in the Midwest, he had gotten attacked again.

Junior had had more than his share of bad luck. A couple of years before, he and his wife, a fine-looking woman who lived in the Bronx, had decided to try to get together again. She visited the lot when the show was playing in New Jersey and she saw her husband's performance for the first time, and she was amazed, she said, at his courage. Junior had worked a long time for Hoxie, and Hoxie knew Junior was good for loans, and Junior was planning to borrow some money and build a home—a proper one, not just a trailer—in Florida. His

Junior

wife would come down to live, and they would pick up their marriage again. But a few days after that performance in New Jersey Mrs. Manuel Ruffin was stabbed to death in the Bronx, apparently by a thief. The family didn't have the show's route card, so they didn't know how to get in touch with Junior. By the time he found out about his wife's death, she was in the ground. He called the police and asked what they knew, but in New York the murder of a black woman is not likely to keep the police more than routinely occupied. The assailant was never found, and Junior forgot about his plans to build a home in Florida.

Now he worked steadily with the cutting torch, snipping off stakes with apparent ease, although he was sweating a lot. Not far away from him was the steel arena, set up for practice. The cat truck was nearby, and inside it the beautiful cats prowled and slept. Its cages could be interconnected, and with the addition of a chute the cats would be prodded out of their truck and down the chute and into the arena. There were tall weeds growing in the big silver cage.

I asked Junior why he hadn't been rehearsing the cats more. "Too much else to do," he said. I asked why the circus always seemed to wait until the last minute to do such things as cutting stakes. "Because it's only *important* at the last minute," he said with a grin. Besides, he said, the cats didn't really get into their routine until they had performed a few times before a real audience. Junior seemed not disturbed by the fact that the opening show, now less than a week away, would be in Sweetwater, the scene of his injury one year before.

Jeff Woosnam had arrived in winter quarters on March 19. He had heard that the circus band needed musicians, and he had packed up his huge sousaphone and ridden the bus to Miami to work with the show. He had not known that the band didn't get together until the last possible minute, so he was left with a lot of time on his hands. He quickly befriended Joe Hamilton, a young man who had seen an advertisement in the Miami papers for circus help and who had come on the lot about the same time. Jeff, a large and open fellow, with a red-

dish blond curly beard, was gregarious and intelligent and
articulate, unlike many of the people who were at winter quarters, and he seemed to think of the circus not as just another
tiring job to be done, but as an experience to be cherished.
While he was waiting for the band to get together, he helped
with the animals, especially the elephants, and he also worked
in the cooktent.

Jeff had been born twenty-six years before, in Cleveland.
His father had been in numerous businesses; at the time of
Jeff's birth it was construction. The family moved around a lot
in Jeff's early years, but by the time he was in the first grade
they had settled on a farm near Seville, Ohio, which is not too
far from Cleveland. When Jeff finished high school he entered
Northwood Institute, in Midland, Michigan. Two years later
he had an associate degree in journalism and a lot of practical
experience.

He served as editor of the campus newspaper, worked at
the school's radio station, played bass in a local jazz trio, and
worked on the town's FM station. He was also a reporter on the
town's newspaper. In November of 1969 he accepted a girlfriend's invitation to move to New York City. There he worked
at various jobs while his draft status was being clarified. Jeff
was a conscientious objector. Later he went to Michigan and
played in a band; he went back to the farm; he moved to Ann
Arbor, Michigan, with another girlfriend; then he found himself in upstate New York as the news director of another radio
station. But he returned once more to the farm in April of 1972.

"I wanted to go back to the farm," said Jeff, there in winter
quarters, "because whenever I run into some problems and I
have to get my head back together, that's where I go. I sometimes get emotional about it. But that place means so much to
me, those ninety-five acres." He gazed up at the sky and smiled
through his curly beard.

I asked him why he was with the circus.

"The circus is here to be done," he said. "The main reason
I came to the circus is to get back into music. Music is one of
the important things in my life. I have quite a few important
things, and music is near the top of the list. And for three years
I haven't had a chance to play music."

Jeff said he planned to stay the whole season. In the circus life, it is not at all unusual for someone to leave the show abruptly. It is called "blowing the show." Workmen do it all the time. Musicians do it every once in a while. Performers, who are professional show people, usually stay the whole season unless some disaster occurs. Jeff said he was aware of all this and that he planned to stay. After the season ended in October, he said, he might try to join a Mexican circus for a winter tour, or maybe go to a show in Europe. "My main motive is to get some traveling done," he said. "To see some of the rest of the world."

Jeff also planned to do a little writing during the season. Once, when he had been a fledgling newspaper reporter in Michigan, King Brothers Circus had come through, and Jeff and a photographer had gone out to do a feature story. Jeff's story was different from the ordinary "the circus is in town" piece; he sought out not only the performers but also the workmen, and he tried to look behind the facade that the circus always holds between itself and the real world. Later, he showed me the story. Part of it went like this.

A hush falls over the crowd as the beautiful lady enters from the wings, is helped off with her cloak and is given a helping hand for the first jump to climb the rope hanging next to the trapeze.

She's very pretty, from a distance. But get a closer look. The age is beginning to show in her heavily made-up face. The act gets a little tougher each time she does it, she puffs a bit afterwards, but the smile, the "never let the crowd know what's really going on in your mind" smile is there, always.

Get close to the rest of the troupe. Notice that many of them are offhand about the entire affair, the circus which causes so many small boys (and not so small boys, too) to see visions of grandeur. And this is the nut of the whole thing. The circus is just a job, not glamorous, not exciting, but dreary. . . .

Joe Hamilton shared a couple of qualities with Jeff. He liked music (he had played the drums in rock and country bands in Georgia), and he had been opposed to the Vietnam War. He said he was born and reared on a five-hundred-acre farm outside Atlanta. When he dropped out of West Georgia

College the army took him. Because of his pacifist beliefs, he became an infantry medic in Vietnam. One day the platoon's point man was wounded by a wire-detonated mine, and Joe ran forward to help him. He tripped a mine himself, and the shrapnel went into his back and his chest. He stayed in the hospital for more than fifty days. In October of 1971 he got out of the army.

"I went home for a while," he said, "and I was going to try the living-off-the-land thing. But my father and I disagreed too much politically for me to get along there. He's conservative, and I consider myself a liberal. Of course, what's liberal for one person is conservative to another. But *he* considers me a radical."

Early in 1972 Joe moved off the farm and into Atlanta. He worked a while, took off traveling, first on a motorcycle, then by hitchhiking, then in a friend's Volkswagen bus. The bus broke down in Key West, and Joe started looking at the classified ads. One of them said that Hoxie Brothers Circus was looking for people who wanted to work and to travel, and Joe hitchhiked to winter quarters. He got to the main gate, and he saw the sign that said survivors would be prosecuted, and he turned around and started walking back to Miami. But the show's cook came along then and showed Joe how to get to the lot without being shot.

Joe was twenty-four years old. He was six feet, three inches tall, and he weighed two hundred and ten pounds, but he acted like the most peace-loving person on the lot. He was, in fact, a gentle person, a truly nice guy, and most of the other inhabitants of winter quarters seemed to recognize that and treated him with consideration and maybe a little awe. Joe described himself as something of a loner and an individualist. "I miss my privacy," he said one day, after he had been at winter quarters about a week. "Privacy and cleanliness. When I was home I sometimes took two showers a day. Here, it's kind of a strain."

There were none of the standard sanitary facilities for the men who stayed at winter quarters (and there would be none on the road, either). Someone had discovered a faucet several feet up the wall of one of the cattle barns, and it was possible to take a cold shower there. There were no toilets, or donnikers, as they are called in the circus business. If you had to urinate or defecate, you had to wander out through the weeds and do it there. If you had no toilet paper you used a newspaper, or nothing. In a sense, this was like being in the wilderness, but the wilderness disappeared when it came to sleeping conditions. Both Joe and Jeff disliked the cramped quarters of the sleeper.

"Being raised on a farm," said Joe, "you get used to being alone a lot. At least I did. On a five-hundred-acre farm, I could be out two days mending fences. And I'd come home at night, naturally, but I was alone all that time. I got to where I was used to it, and now I'm at the point where I don't *have* to be alone, but I enjoy it occasionally. I don't want to be *left* alone; I like to *be* alone. There's a difference there. And I don't have it here. I'm never alone here. And I miss that. And that may cause problems with me mentally before the end of the season comes. And the lack of sanitary facilities is atrocious. I mean, I don't think there's any reason why there couldn't be portable johns, at least. I can see why the show wouldn't have showers *every day*, seeing as how it does one-night stands. But they should have them occasionally. Some of these people here are quite willing to let themselves go for a full season, probably, without taking a shower.

"Those are the only two things so far that I really dislike. The people who are here, I expected to find basically that kind of people. And I adjusted myself to that. But I *didn't* expect to find no sanitary facilities."

Did Joe expect to stay the whole season?

"I like to finish things I start," he said.

What Joe meant when he referred to the sort of people he had found in winter quarters was winos, bums, and drifters. Which is not to say that all winos, bums, and drifters are bad. They are not necessarily criminals; they do not necessarily hurt other people. Some of them are as decent and moral as the rest of us. But they are not always the steadiest of workers. Al-

ready several who had come to winter quarters in response to
the classifieds promising travel had blown the show. Some of
them left even before their names were known by the others, or
before they were able to acquire nicknames. Nicknames in the
circus are more important, in a way, than real names, for they
identify someone by the job he does or the way he looks. It is
unlikely that many of the workmen or performers or even the
musicians would remember that Jeff's last name was Woosnam.
They would remember him as Tuba Jeff, despite the fact that
he played a sousaphone.

They used to be called roustabouts in the circus business,
but now they were known as workmen, or sometimes as workingmen, or, for those who put the Big Top up when the season
got going, as canvasmen. Hoxie and his agents got some of the
workmen through newspaper ads, but they also got them by
going down to missions and bus stations and bars and Salvation
Army offices and luring them to the show.

It was a never-ending process; the recruiting would go on
almost every day of the season, for men were always blowing
the show. For most of the workmen, the pay in winter quarters
amounted to a few dollars a week and an occasional sack of
Bugler cigarette tobacco, along with a right to sleep in the
sleeper and eat in the cooktent. The pay was just high enough
to allow the men to get good and drunk once or twice a week,
and just low enough to prevent them from leaving the show by
any means other than their own feet. It was understood by most
of the men that the pay would rise to twenty-five or thirty dollars a week once the show got on the road and started making
money. I honestly believe that, for many of them, the amount
of the pay was not terribly important. It was important only
that one receive enough money to allow one to walk or hitch in
to Sweetwater and purchase a bottle of Mad Dog (the name
came from the brand, M. D., which actually stood for Mogen
David) or Thunderbird. The wine was not parceled out over
the week; it was drunk immediately, in active and enthusiastic
anticipation of the drunkenness and, later, the hangover that it
would bring. The pay was once a week, on Saturday night. The
men were entitled, too, to a draw against their wages, and

Wednesday was the draw day. So a wise workingman could get falling-down, knee-walking drunk twice a week on the circus.

Bob Brown was in charge of what was laughingly called "personnel procurement." Bob had slicked-down hair and a skinny little moustache from the twenties. He and his wife followed the show in their camper, and behind the camper he towed a little blue Volkswagen. He would get to a new town, unhitch the beetle, and take off in search of talent. His beat was the skid row of any city; he knew all the missions and the Salvation Army offices, which he called "the Sally." Bob had had a complicated heart operation that had left a long and prominent scar on his chest. He liked to wear open-necked shirts that showed the scar, and part of his technique with new men, when he needed to get their attention, was to tell them about his "new heart" and his "new life." It was as if he were promising *them* a new life if they went with the show.

"Well, we've got the bear with us now," said Billy Joe. Billy Joe was young, and he had been in winter quarters for most of the winter. He seemed displeased, but not surprised—maybe just irritated.

"What kind of bear?" someone asked. They were in the cooktent, drinking coffee after the evening meal.

"No, you don't understand circus talk," said Billy Joe. "The bear is somebody who steals things."

"Oh," said the other man. This was his first day on a circus.

At night, a strange rhythmic jingling, like a flock of Hare Krishna people walking down the street. I got out of my tent to see what it was. The sky was pitch-black, and the only light came from a 747 that was landing. A small furry animal ran past me, brushing my leg. I did not know what it was. A pig? But they were not furry. Later I would learn that the jingling was the elephants. They were smart enough to know that if they shook their shackles enough there was a possibility that the clasp would work loose. It was perhaps a one-in-ten-thousand possibility, but elephants have plenty of time to gamble.

♦

Johnny, a young man who had returned from Vietnam four months before: he worked with the animals. We sat outside on folding chairs one evening, drinking Busch Bavarian and watching the sun go down.

"Some things happened that I didn't cope with in my mind," he said.

What kind of things?

"Just people getting killed. I was seventeen when I got drafted."

A long silence. This life must be very difficult.

"It's more or less for people that can't settle down. There's a lot of people who know it isn't time to put in their roots. They can't stay in one place. They're always seeking. And it's for people who seek."

Are you seeking?

"Yes, I'm seeking."

Are you getting enough money to get by on?

"I barely get by."

Could you make more money elsewhere and still be able to seek?

"Oh, yes."

Then why are you here?

"Well, it's more or less for the time being. To be honest with you, I don't expect to be here the whole season. I wouldn't tell Hoxie that."

Are you looking for a particular part of the country?

"I was thinking about Virginia. West Virginia. I heard there's mountains, and it's pretty, and a lot of small towns."

You like small towns?

"Yeah. People there, more or less everybody knows everybody in a small town. It's not like a big city. It's someplace where I can put my roots down."

He was like a little boy. He was twenty now.

How had the killings in Nam affected you?

"I'm a different person now than I would have been if I hadn't been there. It disturbed my mind a little bit. It's a shock, you know. People get shocks and it changes them."

Did you see people killed?

"People next to me, people in front of me."

Did you kill somebody?

Very softly he answered. "Yeah." The sun was almost gone now, and a gentle breeze had started. It was a little cooler.

Do you feel bad about that?

He waited a long time. "I really don't know. I can't really condemn myself, you know. Because they stuck me out in that field, and it was either me or him. And when it comes to that, even an animal, you know, will kill. When they drop you off in the middle of the field, they're the enemy, you know."

Are you a gentle person?

"Yes. I think that I am. I mean, violence doesn't suit me any more. Before, it did. I just can't cope with it now. Before I went to Nam, I got in fights all the time, and I busted a couple of heads and things like that. But you get a little bit too much violence, you know, and all of a sudden you reject it, and any time you see someone else is in pain, you feel the pain with him. Or at least I do."

He pulled at the beer in silence for a few moments. The elephants were swaying in silhouette. "There were two machine-gun nests," he said, spontaneously, "and the next thing we knew we heard bursts, and we all dropped, and we were pinned down bad. We didn't have no cover at all. And we were just laying there. And we couldn't really shoot, because if we did, we'd get shot. And they had a beautiful shot at us. And guys getting shot all the time because they didn't have no cover or nothing. And we even laid behind bodies for cover. And we had to get to the men.

"I was scared. I was just laying there and I wasn't going to move. All the other brave guys, they tried. There were about forty-two of us. One of the guys got over there and put a grenade into them, and he got killed.

"And by the time it was over, there were only eight of us left out of forty-two people. And I was one of the eight. Us eight, we went back. I dream about the killing a lot."

How often?

He got up, crushed the beer can in one hand. "About three

times a week. Sometimes more. I guess I'll dream about it tonight." He walked off toward the sleeper.

And then there are those whose home is the circus, like the elephants. Art Duvall, Dirty Art, who ran the water truck and operated the back door. Leo, the elephant groom, been here for years and always would be here, angry at the food and angry at the bosses and angry at everything except the elephants. Inarticulate, they were sometimes impossible to understand. No long, formal, tape-recorded interviews with Leo and Art; just watching them through the season, trying to understand them. You do not ask them if they plan to stay until the season is over and the show starts the home run for Florida again; you know they will.

And others, like Gypsy Red, people who liked their drinking but who didn't let it overcome them, and who stayed on shows because they had found some sort of home there. Intelligent, somewhat articulate people—Gypsy Red knew all about canvas, and he played a trombone in the band, too—who moved from show to show, season to season, almost like the performers.

And the performers. They would come in Sweetwater. Ringling rehearses for weeks, but this mud show has one run-through before hitting the road. We move to Sweetwater tomorrow, Saturday, and there will be a rehearsal on Sunday. The season opens Monday night, March 25.

And the bosses. Hoxie appeared on the lot once, briefly, on Saturday, and then he sped away. His hatbrim was down. Since his heart attacks and his nervous breakdown Hoxie had been trying to stay out of things that he knew would make him nervous and angry, and the opening of a season was one of those things. John Hall, the general manager, had been in and out. Bill Hill, the manager, pulled his house trailer on the lot late in the week. The bossing seemed to be done mostly by Junior and by the young blond-haired man, whose name was Stash.

On Friday night there was a feeling of anticipation, but not as much as you would expect for the nation's third- or fourth-largest tented circus on the night before it was to start another season. Paul, the mechanic, went around making sure the trucks would run. As often as not, on season openings, a truck or two would refuse to run at all and would have to be towed to the first lot. Plans were made for gassing up the vehicles the following day (these plans were intricate, because the fuel crisis of the winter of 1973–74 was still with us). After the evening meal, the cook struck the cooktent and stored it in the truck.

Wahoo seemed to sense the change in routine, and she demanded friendship from everyone who passed her. One of the workmen, a man who wore a navy watch cap all the time, even in the heat, said he had heard a rumor that Wahoo was not going to Sweetwater. Another workman said he knew for a fact that she would go; he knew which truck she would ride in and everything.

A telephone had been installed on the lot, and its bell was up on a pole nearby, and it rang for a long time Friday night. John Lewis finally answered it. He was part owner of Lewis Brothers Circus, a small show that Hoxie was putting on the road this year in addition to his main show. The main show could play cities and towns of almost any size; Lewis Brothers was designed for tiny towns that ordinarily would be passed by. Lewis Brothers had been sharing the winter quarters with the Hoxie show.

John Lewis was a tall, skinny man with black hair, who sounded, when he talked, like a real shitkicker from east Tennessee. He had been in premed at the University of Alabama, and when one summer vacation came he and a friend had gone into the tourist-trap business on a temporary basis. That was three years ago. They bought lions and bears and other animals, and while they were waiting to sell them they displayed them for the tourists on a highway between Knoxville and Chattanooga. Since that time he had been in show business.

John adored Hoxie like a father, and he said so. He was talking about his love for Hoxie on Friday night, while drinking beer with his shirt off, when the phone rang. It was Phil

Chandler, the ringmaster. He was at the Miami airport. He had just flown in from Dayton, and he wanted to know how to get to winter quarters. John Lewis said forget it, look around in fifteen minutes for the only man in the airport with no shirt and a baseball cap on; and then he finished his beer and went to pick up the ringmaster. It took him a long time to get back, and in the meantime the winter quarters fell silent, except for the elephants' jingling and Wahoo's occasional rattling of her chain.

The stars were out, and it was amazing how many you could see from here, so close to a city. Occasionally a flashlight beam cut through the darkness as somebody went someplace on some business or other. The dew gradually settled, and the talking stopped in the sleeper. The elephants gave up their attempts at freedom, for tonight at least. And during the night Junior quietly moved his trailer off the lot and blew the show.

SWEETWATER

The move to Sweetwater was uneventful. Most people woke up before the sunrise (for even the winos there was something exciting about the start of a season), but the purple trucks did not start moving out until around eight-thirty on Saturday morning. Most people found out about Junior's departure quickly, but once the basic fact of his leaving was known nobody seemed to say very much about it. There was amazingly little speculation about why he had done it. None of the trucks broke down, and none of them lost their way.

It was only a four-mile hop, but circus trucks have been known to get lost in less than that. King Charles arrowed the way thoroughly; his first arrow was on the gatepost at winter quarters.

King Charles had been Hoxie's bandleader since 1967. He was as well known around the show as Junior had been; he was a permanent fixture. His real name was King Charles Weathersby, and he was from Ville Platte, Louisiana, about one hundred and twenty-nine miles west of New Orleans. New Orleans jazz had influenced his style greatly. He played the American Selma trumpet, and with it, using subtle changes in his tone or a sudden flip of the instrument, he led the five other band members through dozens of musical changes in the course of a performance.

Hardly anybody on a circus does just one job. King

The arrows out of winter quarters

Charles's other job was being the arrow man. Each night after a performance, except on those infrequent occasions when the show had a two-day stand, King Charles would put his trumpet in its red velvet case, get into his Ford station wagon (Hoxie bought a new one, or, rather, a new used one, each year), and travel to the next lot, leaving paper arrows all along the way. The pieces of paper were eight and one-half by five and one-half inches in size. Printed on them, in purple ink, was the letter H. The top of the Ĥ had been turned into an arrow point. King Charles put the arrows on telephone poles, trees, highway signs, bridge abutments, and anything else he needed to in order to route the trucks and trailers from one town to the next.

Occasionally, a policeman or a sadistic towner would tear some arrows down; Charles seemed to know when such incidents might happen, and he would come back later in the night to make sure the arrows were still there. An arrow pointing straight up meant go straight ahead; arrows pointing down meant slow down and get ready for a change; arrows pointing to the side meant turn. The final turn on any jump was always a bouquet of purple arrows that led you right onto the lot. When King Charles had finished arrowing the show, he pulled the station wagon into a corner of the empty lot and lay down on the front seat and slept. He referred to his automobile as the "Ford Hotel."

Now the arrows led out of the dairy farm, through the back roads of Sweetwater and Miami, around some construction sites where condominiums were being built, onto the main road, and into the lot at Sweetwater. From a distance, the lot looked large and flat and suitable. But up close you could see it was a mass of coral.

The coral tore chunks out of automobile tires and pieces of rubber and leather out of people's shoes, and it was hard for the people and animals to walk without staggering. If you cut yourself on it, you were doomed to a painful infection. There was much griping about the coral. The fork-lift, an important vehicle in the circus's fleet, immediately suffered a flat tire.

Sweetwater had been a one-horse, two-bar town only a few years ago, but now it was suburbia. Its population was about eighty-seven hundred people, half of them Cubans. The community seemed to range from middle to lower middle in economic status, and in many ways it was a model of the perfect town in which to present Hoxie Brothers Circus. There were a lot of children in such places, and most of the families had enough money for the show (prices were a dollar twenty-five for children and two dollars for adults in advance; on circus day they were a little higher). More than anything, there was in such communities a feeling that children *deserved* to see the circus; there was an absence of the feeling that it is somehow unsophisticated to go inside a big tent and sit on planks and encourage your childhood fantasies to try to repeat themselves.

The Cristianis were on the lot when the first trucks pulled in. They had loaded their horses and leopards and the trampoline into the red-and-white trailer the day before in Sarasota. Gilda had put sheets over the furniture, Lucio had put bug poison along the window sills, and they had closed the house for another season and driven to Sweetwater. They were entirely professional. They got where they were supposed to be on time, and they did the work they said they were going to do.

To say the Cristianis were professional performers was to make an understatement. They were consummate in their work. The Cristianis had started as a show-business family more than a century ago, when Emilio Cristiani, a blacksmith in Pisa, got bitten by the circus bug. He went into gymnastics and tumbling with his son and became a star. His son, Pilade, produced a large number of children who went into the business. In about 1925 Ernesto Cristiani, one of the children, started his own show, featuring himself and his children.

An agent from Ringling Brothers saw the family in Europe in 1933, and in the following year the Cristianis were imported to the United States, playing in a number of circuses owned by Ringling and in the Big Show itself. John Ringling North gave them their own railroad car. "The Cristiani Family," it said on the sides. The Cristianis were fantastic with horses. Circus posters, which often exaggerate a bit, showed five of the performing brothers hurling themselves from the ground to the back of a galloping horse, and that was exactly what they did, day after day, performance after performance, in city after city, on circus after circus. The greatest feat, though, was Lucio's. He was the only person in the world consistently to execute a somersault from the back of one moving horse, over a second horse, to the back of a third horse.

In 1956 the brothers took out a circus under their own name. The show closed in 1961, the victim of financial problems and family dissension, two difficulties that traditionally affect the circus world. As the brothers got along in age, some of them gravitated toward less strenuous portions of show business, but Lucio and his second wife, Gilda, remained on the mud shows, pulling a red-and-white trailer full of horses, leopards, and props all over the country. On the side of the trailer it said "Cristiani Family Mobile Home."

Their two sons, Armando, who was eleven this year, and Tino, who was fourteen, traveled with them and shared in the performing. Back at home in Sarasota they left volumes of scrapbooks and piles of photographs, all of them tributes to a fascinating life in show business.

Now Lucio and Gilda and Armando and Tino were in Sweetwater, ahead of most of the other performers, waiting to start a new season—in Lucio's case, his fifty-ninth year on the road. They waited for Bill Hill and Johnny Walker to lay out the lot so they could see where to park their rig. Bill Hill, the manager, was in charge of all the physical work that went into the show, except for the performers, and Johnny Walker was the concessions superintendent, the boss of the butchers. Ordinarily Johnny would be concerned only with pushing as many hot dogs and Cokes and cones of cotton candy on the towners as he could, but since Junior had blown he had been given the additional duties of boss canvasman.

Lucio looked out at the clumps of coral that covered the lot and mumbled something about what a hell of a way it was to start a new season. He hated what the coral would do to his horses' hoofs. Ordinarily he would refuse to work on such a lot, but this was to be the opening night. He was reassured a little when he learned that Hoxie had ordered a truckload of dirt to be placed in Ring Two, where the horses would perform.

Someone asked him how it felt to be starting a new season.

"It's a mixed feeling," he said. He was a short man, with blond hair and a blond moustache, quick, easy, intelligent eyes, a voice that always bordered on hoarse. "You hate to leave your home, but it's the call of the wild, you know. I don't know any other explanation than that. You feel like going, you know. And besides"—he made a shrugging gesture—"I have to make a living.

"It's a mixed feeling. On a day like this, on a lot like this, you complain about it, but then, in the last days of the season, it's a sad feeling. You get all upset, and you don't know what it is, but then you find out it was because of the split-up of the company. And you go back home and then you've got to get resettled again at home. And then you like it, for a while, anyway."

What do you do in the winter?

"This year I had to have a hernia operation, and I spent about ten weeks on that. And then I went back to practice, to put together the act again. Ordinarily I work dates in the winter. We go out and play a few dates for the winter and then come back home. They call it *indoor*." He said he himself preferred the outdoor, under canvas.

"They're both good, and you get tired of one when you're in it, and when you're in the other one you get tired of that," he said.

Lucio sighed and looked down again at the coral. It was a beginning-of-the-season sigh; not one of tiredness, because he was not yet tired. Perhaps it was a sigh of anticipation of the tiredness he knew would come later. Armando, a handsome little boy with light blond hair, came out of the trailer and stood next to him.

"I have had my career already," said Lucio. He patted Armando on the back. "I was with every big show in the world."

Last year, when the Big Top crew had been properly broken in, it took four hours to put the big tent up and two to take it down. Today, with raw men doing the work, it took more than six hours.

American circus tents are usually oblong; viewed from the air, they take on the shape of eggs. Several tall poles, called centerpoles, are lined up, and the tent hangs down from them to the quarterpoles and then out to the sidepoles. In 1972, John Hall, the general manager, started designing a round circus tent for Hoxie. John had taken some courses in architecture, and he laid out the Big Top on paper first. Then he made a model of it. Hoxie thought John was crazy at first, but he eventually went along with the scheme.

The advantage of a round tent, as John saw it, was that everyone would have a good seat. In the traditional tents, some of them hundreds of feet long, the three rings ran in a straight line, and if you were sitting down at one end you couldn't see what was going on at the other. John arranged the rings within an imaginary triangle under the round top; in the spaces between the rings he added sheets of canvas, called stages. In the circus, some performances take place in the rings and some take place on the stages. The result was a Big Top that was much more efficient in its use of space, and one that provided a better view for anyone sitting in the seats.

The single centerpole, a fifty-five-foot-long tube of aluminum, went up first. At its tip was attached the American flag, and then an elephant or the fork-lift pulled a cable attached to the top, and the tall pole was raised to the vertical. There were eight cables fixed to the top of the centerpole and staked to the ground at eight points around the perimeter, and when the pole was up they served to hold it straight.

While the centerpole was being raised, men and machines went around the outside of the circle, which measured one hundred and sixty feet in diameter, driving stakes into the ground. Usually, when it wasn't broken down, they used the stakedriver, a truck with devices on its back that looked like pile drivers. When the machine was broken, men drove the stakes with sledges.

The spool truck was a funny-looking truck with, literally, spools on its back. The heavy cylinders were driven by engine, and they slowly rolled the Big Top canvas onto the spool and off again. When the centerpole was up, the spool truck made two passes along the ground below it, excreting huge sheets of canvas. These were spread and laced together by the workmen. In the center there was a bail ring that slipped up and down the centerpole; the center of the canvas was laced to this ring.

Forty-eight sidepoles were inserted into sockets along the outer perimeter of the canvas. Fixed to the sockets were the ends of heavy ropes, and gradually the sidepoles were raised and the ropes tied off to the outer circle of stakes. At this point the Big Top resembled some outlandish plastic back-yard swimming pool in the process of being set up; the canvas was raised along the edges, but it still lay on the ground everywhere else. Once the sidepoles were in place and the ropes tied off, an elephant in harness was attached to the main line that raised the bail ring up the centerpole. Slowly the canvas lifted off the ground and rose toward the top of the centerpole.

Now the quarterpoles were inserted. Men and elephants went under the sagging canvas and fit the quarters, six of them in an inner circle and twelve of them in an outer ring, into their sockets. Ropes hung down from the sockets; these were pulled snug and tied to the poles to keep the pole-points from jumping out of their sockets in the event wind tried to lift the canvas. They were called "jumper ropes."

Then came the final touches. John Hall, because he had designed the tent, supervised the tightening of the canvas. An elephant in harness dragged each quarterpole toward the vertical until John gave the signal to stop. Then the side ropes were tied off tightly (this was called "guying out"), and the tent was up. Then the sidewall, a ribbon of canvas that hung from the top of the sidepoles to the ground, was added. The men now could start filling the inside with seats and props. At the time all this was going on, another crew of men had been erecting the sideshow tent, a much smaller one, which was traditional in shape. Two trailer trucks were placed nearly back to back in front of the sideshow tent, a platform and ticket boxes were installed in the space between them, and that became the entrance to the sideshow. A porch of canvas was added to form the main entrance to the Big Top; it was called the marquee. The show people called it and the area around

Putting up the Big Top

it the "front door," because that was the way the audience came in. Halfway around the Big Top from the front door there were two other openings in the sidewall, doorways with sliding curtains for the performers and animals to come in and out. They were called the "back door." Between the two openings was the bandstand.

This Saturday, as the Big Top went up for the first time of the season, a small elderly man patrolled beneath it, cracking his eye at every rip and tear. There were plenty of rips and tears. Circus tents generally have a life expectancy of about two years, and the one John Hall had designed was now in its second year. Leaf, the canvas maker in Sarasota, had sewn it together from alternating sections of blue and white canvas, but the white was brown with dirt, and the blue was deeply faded and dirty, too. There were dozens of small holes, where the canvas had torn on rocks or brush while it was being put up or taken down. "I think it'll last the season," said John Hall that day. "It better," he added with a little smile.

The elderly man wore a hat that had, where its hatband would be, several lengths of coarse waxed cord. The cord was threaded through heavy needles. The man carried a worn canvas bag full of more cord and more needles and a block of wax. In his belt he carried a long knife. His name was Superchicken. He was seventy-seven years old, and he introduced himself by saying, "I am the sailmaker."

There were many problems that day, as there are on any first day on the road. It was a hot day, and Art Duvall had not arrived with the water truck, so there was no drinking water for the workmen. The lot fronted on the busy roadway, and all around its other sides there were narrow stretches of thick, jungle vegetation. Just beyond the vegetation were the homes of the people of Sweetwater. There were few places where a workman could relieve himself without either being seen by the general public or exposing himself to the mysteries of the thick weeds and bushes. Jeff Woosnam and Joe Hamilton were particularly displeased by the lack of donnikers; Joe wandered down the road and found a luncheonette and went inside and ordered a cup of coffee, and that gave him temporary title to the facilities there.

And there were no elephants, for a while at least. Someone had decided to leave the elephants and their trainer, Bert Pettus, behind at winter quarters for the first half day. Meanwhile, the workmen had to put up the tent without elephants and without the elephants' major substitute, the fork-lift, which was waiting for a new tire. "Where the hell the goddam bulls?" yelled one of the old-timers. But the bulls didn't come until the tent was halfway up. Nine of the circus's elephants, and all the adult ones, were females. But circus people call all elephants bulls, regardless of their sex.

Bert Pettus was in charge of the bulls, and Leo was his assistant. Bert was a tall, erect, strong-looking man with something of a potbelly. He wore western clothes. He chewed to-

bacco a good deal and finished many of his sentences and all of
his paragraphs with spurts of brown juice. He had a pleasant
face, but one that could cloud over and become angry in a
moment, like a sudden summer thunderstorm. Bert, like most
boss elephant men, was constantly decrying the management's
and everyone else's lack of proper attention to and care for the
elephants. He thought they weren't getting enough to eat, and
he thought they were working too hard. It made him angry
when some half-crocked workman called for the bulls to do a
job the men could have done.

Bert was born in Forrest City, Arkansas; he would reach
the age of sixty while this season was under way. His
father had been a veterinarian and a farmer, and his mother
had been a housewife. Bert went only to the second grade.
When he was thirteen, he said, "I joined the circus. I didn't
run away to join it. I think that's just a phrase, anyway. Nobody runs away to join a circus. If they want to join it, they
join it. I just liked to roam around. You know—riding freight
trains. You didn't do much hitchhiking in those days; you rode
freights.

"And I come into a town where the circus was showing.
I had no idea of staying with it, but hell, I was broke. I was
not quite thirteen then. I was broke and hungry, so I went to
work for them. Still had no intention of staying. I went to work
as a ring stock groom, on horses, because I was raised up around
horses.

"That was on the old Floto show in '27. Sells-Floto. And
I worked there a while. And they closed. It was the fall of the
year. So then the next year I just beat around with the Barnett
show, and a few others, as ring stock hand. And in the thirties
it was the only time in my life I was ever fired. Me and the
assistant boss horseman got into a fight and he fired me. I went
to leave the lot and the boss prop man hired me. Which in them
days was very hard, to get from one department to the other.
I worked for him, helped set up the show, and we was in the
prop wagon playing poker, and the owner of the show came
back."

Bert spat and interrupted himself. "See, I used to go watch the elephants. Like everybody else, I was amazed at them. You know, big farmer boy and all. And the owner came and called me out of the wagon. I thought he was going to run me off the show. But he told me to go work on the elephants. I told him, 'I don't know about these things.' He says, 'That's all right. You go over there; the boss'll learn you.' Well, I went over. And I learnt to be a trainer. And that's all I want to do now, is just train. See, there's a difference between being a trainer and being a worker. After they're trained, almost anybody can work them, if he's got any voice or any savvy at all. But it's damn few trainers."

Bert said he was in sort of semiretirement when he was asked to go on the road this season. He was sitting under the live-oak trees at his home in Malakoff, Texas, he said, thinking about going simultaneously into the animal training and laundry businesses, when Hoxie called. "See, at Corsicana—our place is between Corsicana and Athens. And Westinghouse was building a new Laundromat there. So we were dealing with them to run the Laundromat, Marie and me. We had went to the bank and the deal was through, you know. The Laundromat wasn't finished, though. When *this* deal come up, we just went down and told them we didn't think we'd take the Laundromat. So if I hadn't told Hoxie I'd come with him, we'd probably be sitting there watching washing machines now.

"I wasn't going to quit the *business*, though. I was just going to stay home and train animals for people who wanted them trained. I'm not a young man. I get tired, you know. Things aggravate me that didn't use to. What I was going to do was I wasn't going to handle elephants any more. I've handled a lot of elephants. I mean, I've been everything from a three-dollar-and-a-half-a-week workingman to the half owner of a circus. I've handled elephants long enough. What I was going to do was this. Say, for instance, Hoxie wanted some ponies broken for him. He'd send them to my place, I'd break the act, and if he wanted somebody to come in there and work it, okay, good, they'd come in and work it. I'd break them to work it. When they were broke and trained, then he'd take them. That'd be the last I'd touch them unless I had to come in at some later time and straighten them out for him.

"But instead of all that I'm here with a mud show, getting ready to go out for another season." Bert spat on the ground.

As the men struggled with the tent for the first time, it was apparent that Junior would have been helpful. He knew every trick there was to putting up the Big Top, and now that he was gone there were Bill Hill and Johnny Walker to get it up, and both of them were competent old-timers, but they were a little rusty. Stash helped a great deal. He had joined the show late in the previous season, and he had gone out with Hoxie on a nine-day December tour of Florida cities, and he knew the round tent. Stash had also made most of the new seats, which were called "lumber," for the show.

As the seats were going into the Big Top, a small truck and trailer with Ohio plates approached the lot. It rolled cautiously across the coral and came to a halt. A young woman got out. She wore a grey athletic shirt that said "Libby Girls Staff" on it. She had ash-blonde hair and a pretty face. She was Linda Chandler, the wife of the ringmaster. She asked where her husband was, and she got several conflicting answers. Linda was tired, because she had driven from Dayton, so she went to the trailer and rested until Phil showed up.

Towners came around to watch the process. The Jaycees, who were the committee in Sweetwater, set up a trailer on the corner of the lot and sold hot dogs and soft drinks and advance tickets. There was a vegetable stand nearby, and its owner was doing a good business selling bananas and onions and real vine-ripened tomatoes to the circus people. The Jaycees and their wives wore straw hats that identified them as Jaycees. They sold quite a few tickets this way until the sun started to go down. Then they closed their trailer and the vegetable stand closed and it became Saturday night. The big tent stood there like a sail growing out of the coral. The elephants had arrived and Bert had staked them out along the highway, and every once in a while a motorist would come batting along and then slow down suddenly to look at the grey monsters. Myrtle, the leader of the herd, shook steadily at her shackle. Bert went to his trailer, which was parked not far from the bulls, and snapped open a can of beer. He sat beside the trailer, his bull-hook not far away, and drank it slowly.

At Bill Hill's trailer, which was parked on the midway, the workmen lined up. Bill came out the door, sat down on a folding lawn chair, and removed a big roll of money from his pocket. Someone produced a clipboard, and Bill took the rubber band off the roll of money and started asking the men their names. As each man filed past Bill gave him a sum of money. For some it was ten dollars; for others it was twenty-five; and some got fifty. The men seemed excited. Most of them took their money and turned toward the highway and started walking down toward the Seven-Eleven and Sweetwater.

The men soon returned with bottles of Mad Dog and large paper bags filled with six- and twelve-packs of beer, and they went to the sleeper and consumed the alcohol quickly. By nine o'clock a good portion of them were solid drunk, and they sounded like it. There was a television set in one section of the sleeper, and it was turned up loud, and there were at least three radios in the section and they were on, too. There were occasional shouts and screams and obscenities, and there were periods during which nobody spoke. Men volunteered their life stories to each other; men talked about what really bothered them.

It was Saturday night, the traditional night for a lot of Americans to get drunk and raise hell. The men in the sleeper, many of them, were highly representative of that sort of American. If you asked one of them to describe himself, he would probably tell you he was just a good old boy who liked to have a little fun on Saturday night. Liked to listen to country-and-western and drink a few beers. No plans for the future; just travel around and see what life brings.

The drinking and shouting and occasional fighting went

on well into the night. And from inside the sleeper the television told you about the extra-strength pain reliever and the stuff that turns the water in your toilet blue.

On the other side of the Big Top, a small group of bosses was gathered beneath the light outside Bill Hill's trailer door. Some sat in lawn chairs, some sat on coils of heavy rope, some sat on the ground. They, too, were drinking beer, but they were drinking it slowly, and they apparently were not trying to see how fast they could get drunk. The alcohol made the workmen violent and suicidal; it made the bosses, most of them, mellow and relaxed.

Johnny Walker talked about the World's Fair, and how his kid had been arrested for trying to sell raincoats whenever it rained. The people who ran the fair ran it like a coal-mining outfit runs a company town; they controlled everything. When someone like Johnny came in from outside and didn't want to pay the owners their percentage, the owners made life pretty hard. Johnny said he had had to go to considerable trouble to grease the cops so he could keep on selling things.

Bert Pettus talked about the old days on Sells-Floto, when there was always a certain group in a town that looked upon circus day as an invitation for hell-raising. "In the old days," he said, "you used to have to force your way into town and force your way out. There was many a time on a lot where there'd be a café across the street, but you didn't dare go over there, because you'd get your head beat off you. At that time, when the circus came to town, for a certain element of the people it was just a field day for them to fight. They'd come out looking for it. You take the hard-coal region of Pennsylvania, places like Mount Carmel, Shena'doah, around there, you had them Polacks in there. Well, that was a field day for them when the circus came in. Upstate New York, the Eye-talians. Get down in North Carolina around Laurinburg and down in there and you had to fight *those* characters. You get into the hills of North Carolina and you had to fight *them*."

"Damn right, buddy," said Johnny Walker. He was from Morganton, in the hills.

A workman lurched past the bosses, carrying a paper bag of beer. It was his second run of the night. He stumbled over a stake.

Bill Hill, a fifty-one-year-old man with a face ravaged by wrinkles and sunshine, laughed at the sight. "You know," he said, "the government ought to send Hoxie a check every month for the people he carries on this show. If it weren't for this show, and shows like it, these people would cost the government millions of dollars in welfare, and state hospitals, and prisons and things like that.

"You take like Leo. He maybe finally hit a circus when he was forty years old. He come like a bum, with nothing, and then he turns around and finds a circus and he's been in the business twenty-some years, and he still doesn't make any money, but he just likes this show. He's going to *die* on the circus, because he loves it, summer and winter.

"And there are a lot of other people who're still looking for their home, and they think they'd found it on the circus, but they haven't."

Johnny Walker had been partly listening to Bill and partly trading stories of the old days with Bert Pettus. "Jackpotting," it is called in show business. He threw a cigarette on the ground. "This thing has got to get out of quarters before it can work right," he said. "Because everybody's first of May, you know." The term was used to designate people who were with the circus for the first time.

"We don't get the same type of people working here as we used to, because they aren't as desperate as they used to be. When they see how much work there is to do, they usually stay one day or two days and then pack it in.

"You can get a beautiful green lot, the grass is mowed low, and the next day you're in a sand pit or in the garbage dump, and you've got to set it up because, you know, you're here today and gone tomorrow. And then it'll start raining and everything will change. That's the only thing that changes in this business—the weather. And when it rains, these first of Mays you hire, first time it rains they take a mope. That's when you see who the real showmen are.

"A real showman is somebody that, if everybody else left the show, he could do it himself. Any department. When you hit that rain and mud, and you get your feet wet real good, you're in that mud for about two weeks continuous. It separates the men from the boys. All the boys screw. They leave. Electrical department, prop department, animal department, everything else—Hoxie can do all of them. He's a showman. He don't know it *fluently*, probably, but he can get by until he gets somebody else to do it.

"My advice is, whatever comes up, let it pass over. It's not like working in a factory or something like that. You just hit it rough at times. But you're *free;* if you really like the business, it seems like you're *free*. Because when you hit the sunshine and fresh air it's all forgotten. Whatever happened in the mud and windstorms and wickedness of nature, and the tornadoes you hit in the Middle West, and all of that, and out west you get sandstorms—but you get used to it.

"From the beginning of time there's been the circus, almost."

HOXIE

Sunday morning: The sun rose fast and hot and clear. I expected things to be very quiet at that hour, but a few of the workmen had stayed up all night drinking and arguing, and they were still at it. Crushed beer cans and empty Mad Dog bottles were all around the sleeper. One man walked over from the direction of the sideshow, stretching and yawning, and he said he had slept in the cab of the truck that contained the sideshow animals. "As bad as they smelled," he said, "they didn't smell as bad as that toe-jam in the sleeper."

Gradually the rest of the men woke up, and they woke each other up, and they stood in the doorways of the sleeper and urinated on the ground. And then they started to work. It was amazing how they were able to work with such obviously terrible hangovers.

Hoxie drove onto the midway in his carryall, took everything in with a few glances, and consulted with John Hall and Bill Hill and Johnny Walker. His hatbrim was down. He climbed back into the vehicle and asked me if I wanted to go over to winter quarters.

"Well," he said, after we had bumped across the coral and were on the paved road, "at least we got the thing up once more, ready to go. Got to go out and try to make a little money. Been here all winter spending it, nothing coming in, so it's time to make some more."

Hoxie Tucker

I asked him why he hadn't been around the show.

"The last few days, I've intentionally stayed away from it. I've done a lot of correspondence. Been on the phone about ninety per cent of the time. Been talking to a woman in Tampa, see if I can hire her to work her act. She has her own cats, her own act. If I can make a deal with her, I'm going to."

Were you angry when you found out Junior had blown?

"No. My old expression is this: if the man *died,* I'd have to get along without him. So in my mind, I just play like he's dead."

If Junior came back would you welcome him, no questions asked?

"No, I would not. Not with open arms. Not when he walks on a man who's been with him as long as I have. Junior has worked hard for me, yes. But I have paid Junior a good salary for working hard, and I have financed his obligations for the last six or seven years. Every trailer, everything he's had, I have either stood good for it or advanced some money for him to get it with. And he didn't have to walk off. All he had to do was tell me, 'I've got a better deal. I think I ought to take it.' I'd of told him the thing to do was to take it. Because any man who won't *better* himself, there ain't much to him."

The rumor was that Junior had gone to Circus Vargas, a big show out of California that specialized in multiple-day stands, as boss canvasman, and that he had been promised a great deal of money. Hoxie laughed at this; he said a lot of people *thought* they were going to get big salaries at Vargas, but that he had heard they didn't always get them.

"I don't think there's ever been a man on any of these shows that worked for me that needed something that I could help him in any way that I didn't do it," said Hoxie. "I'll admit the last few years I've slowed down an awful lot because of three heart attacks and a nervous breakdown. But up until that time I was always helping other people. I could do it all."

We got to the winter quarters, and Hoxie started checking everything out. The Lewis Brothers rolling stock was still there; they would go on the road a little later. The steel arena was still up, but it enclosed only weeds; the lions and tigers lay in their cages, where Junior had left them. Wahoo was very glad to see us. Hoxie was evasive when I asked about the baboon's future. Hoxie showed me how to water the lions. On the ground there were enormous piles of Bavarian cans and other debris: empty whiskey bottles, a Pepto-Bismol bottle, pants, shirts, socks, plastic bags, scraps of canvas, objects that were unidentifiable, pages from a copy of *Rolling Stone*, scraps of dirty toilet paper, piles of elephant, zebra, camel, donkey, pony, horse, and pig excreta. Off to one side there was a pair of crutches, still in usable condition. I wondered how they got there.

Hoxie picked up a hoe and stuck it through the feeding slot into the cats' cages and started pulling a thick brown mixture out. "Now I suppose you can say you've seen me do everything, including shoveling shit," he said. His hatbrim was up, and he was happy.

Leonard Basil Tucker *had* done just about everything. He

knew everything about his circus: where every rope went, where every piece of wood should go, how to set up the Big Top, the sideshow tent, and the cooktent properly, how to move props, how to talk a crowd into the sideshow, how to read the clouds for rain, how to drive any of the seventeen trucks, how to avoid highway weight stations, how to talk to elephants, how to run the light plant. For years he had run around doing a lot of these things himself, for he was short on patience and it bothered him to see a green or lazy man *fool* at doing something when Hoxie knew how to do it twice as fast. "He'd last longer if he'd just use his finger and point, rather than doing it himself," his wife, Betty, once said. "He never gives up, never. Always going." But Hoxie rarely pointed, at least, not until after his third heart attack and his nervous breakdown; after those, he tried, some of the time, to stay out of the way and let other people do it. He gave John Hall a lot of the responsibility for the show. But he continued worrying; a few years ago Hoxie chewed his lip so much that it looked like a big chopped-up wart. The doctors finally had to cut him a new one.

Hoxie was a pleasant-looking man of medium height. He was slightly overweight, with light pink skin. He had greying hair, and it was tonsured like a Trappist monk's, but you hardly ever saw it because Hoxie almost always wore a hat, usually a size-seven Stetson, Open Road model, or a straw that looked a lot like it. He was born on August 7, 1910, in Somerset, Kentucky, and he still talked like a Kentuckian. His father had been nicknamed Big Hox, for some reason, and Leonard Tucker added the *ie*, partly because there was a cowboy star named Jack Hoxie at the time. Hoxie went into show business when he was fifteen.

"I was just like a lot of other kids, many years ago," Hoxie once said. "When I was fifteen years old I ran off from home. There was no reason for me to run away; I had a wonderful home. My father was in the wholesale grocery business. We had an automobile. I had no problems. My father was wonderful to all us kids. But I had, I guess, the lust for travel, and I just had to go. I went and joined the show. The people who owned it I knew pretty well because they had played my home town every year. So I went over there and asked them for a job." The show was the Red Path Chautauqua, and Hoxie wanted to join as a prop boy. A prop person is responsible for getting the performers' props to the right place and at the right time.

"So the man said, 'I will talk to you in a few minutes about the job.' I figured what he was going to do was call my father, which he did, and my father told him, 'Yeah, give him a job. He'll be back home in two or three days.' Well, it took me twelve years to get back home. I stayed with the show for twelve years."

Hoxie went from Red Path to the Heffner Venson Stock Company, a touring dramatic troupe, and eventually he became boss canvasman. Betty, who was to become his wife, had been a professional dancer since she was thirteen, and joined Heffner Venson when she was fifteen. Four years later they were married, and after a while Betty gave birth to a daughter, Irene.

Later Hoxie started his own show, a Hawaiian presentation, and then he managed another touring company. Then he took several of the stars of the Grand Ole Opry out under canvas; they would tour with Hoxie during the week, then fly back to Nashville to appear in the Opry on Saturday nights.

That was real trouping in those days, said Hoxie. "I'm what they call a kerosene-circuit man," he said one time. "I like the crossroads and the backwoods. I'm an old Kentucky hillbilly, and they used to call it the kerosene circuit or the coal-oil circuit back then. When they didn't have electric lights, we used to play through there with the old pan light. At night in the tent we used to hang up lanterns to have some light with, because sometimes there wasn't any electricity. *Sometimes* there *was* electricity, but we didn't have the money to have the lights turned on. I've never been on a wagon show, where they walked the elephants all over the country and used horses to pull the wagons, but I've been mighty close to them."

In 1943, Hoxie went to Georgia to visit a friend who had

a circus. The show wasn't doing too well, and the way Hoxie remembered it, the friend "talked me into hiring the people and putting out the circus." He changed the name to Hoxie Brothers, and the show opened on November 17, 1943, in Greenville, Florida. There were no brothers involved, but it had been fashionable ever since Ringling to make a circus sound like a family operation.

It was a one-ring show with no elephants and a sixty-foot tent. "I advertised it as the world's largest one-ring circus," said Hoxie. He added, with a smile, "It *was*, at that time, the world's largest one-ring circus. *At that time*. For one thing, there were very few of them." American audiences did not exactly take to the one-ring idea, which would have been standard in Europe, and Hoxie had a tough first year. "We was so damn poor that after we got the damn thing out, we stayed out seventy-two weeks without closing. Couldn't *afford* to close it. I had too many people around there who had to eat all winter, and I couldn't take 'em *home* and feed them! So I just played that old circus all winter. Didn't own nothing but the top and the seats and the light plant. But I kept the thing going so everybody could keep eating; those were pretty rough times then. I kept it to where everybody could have some food all winter, and we'd get a little bit of money every once in a while."

Whenever Hoxie used the words "food" or "eating," he seemed to be equating the terms with "life" and "living." Hoxie was not a big and lavish spender, on himself or on his shows; he provided the essentials—clothing and shelter and food—and when you listened to him you had the feeling that this was really what life was all about. The whole procedure of running a circus was designed to give some people something to eat, something to wear, and something to protect them from the rain. If they borrowed money from Hoxie and bought flashy new trailers, they were not purchasing elegance at all, but simply a slightly more comfortable means of sheltering themselves from the harsh weather that surely would come as the show progressed north in the springtime. If they bought new television sets, well, those were not a luxury, either, because even show people had to get information and entertainment. It was food that counted most, that kept you alive, and Hoxie almost always provided enough of that.

Gradually Hoxie added trucks and elephants and rings to his circus, but every once in a while he would have a bad season and slip backwards. He was up to two rings and down to no elephants in the early fifties when he played the small Virginia town of Halifax, where an eighth-grade farm boy named John Hall, who had an insatiable interest in circuses, saw the show.

Hoxie was careful all the time to protect the show's reputation. There was a time, and it was not too long ago, when circuses provided crooked gambling, prostitution, and other means of quickly fleecing the public. You would walk into the freak show and get a look at the exotic people there, with their strange, silent dignity, and if you wanted a little extra they would ding you for a quarter or a half dollar more and open the curtain to yet another cubicle, where the "morphodite" sat patiently waiting. And there would be men in darkened corners of the midway with folding tables and they would play the shell game and three-card monte with you. All this was called the "grift," and Hoxie wanted none of that. He ran a Sunday-school show. "We don't allow things around here like a lot of shows do," he once said. "We allow no gambling around here; we carry no freaks of any kind. More or less it's a case of our families entertaining your family. There's nothing ever said, seen, or done around this show to offend anyone. We never have any trouble booking this show. We just call up last year's sponsor and say, 'Do you want us back?' We go to a town, and the people are glad to see us come back, because we carry the strongest show for our size of any show there is. We try to keep the best of equipment, we try to hire the best performers we can get, and we try to operate it as a business to entertain the public, and that's exactly what we do."

Hoxie also prided himself on his business dealings with other people in the circus world. He said he had never beat anyone out of a nickel unfairly, but he was quick to add that he always demanded everything that was his fair share. In the circus business, he said, it was frequently necessary to act mean. If you weren't mean, some people would try to walk all over you.

"You have to be experienced," he said, "and you have to be mean where nobody likes you to start with. If anybody likes you, you'll never own one of these things." I told him that he didn't seem mean to me. "Well," he replied, "I'm not too mean now. You should have known me years ago, in the days when you slugged it out and *then* talked about it. There'd be *no* conversation. They either did what you told them or they didn't stay here, and you'd *never* tell a man twice to do something. When you told him to do it and he didn't do it, you'd call him out in the back yard and say you wanted to see him about something. Then work him over pretty good and just leave him out there. He'd come back and he'd be a good boy.

"But I'm too old to do that foolishness now."

Hoxie was not quite right about that. He had said all this about being mean about three years ago, and a week before he said it I had seen him approach a strapping young canvasman who had made the mistake of walking into the Big Top during a performance with his shirt off. Hoxie had lectured the young man on this, because it was possible that he didn't know he had violated the rules. But the young man had said something snotty back at Hoxie. Hoxie had literally picked the man up by the neck and carried him out of the tent and run him off. Only a year or so before, Hoxie had retired his motorcycle chain. He used to carry it around his waist, like a belt, and when someone gave him trouble he unwound it and cast it, in the manner of a fisherman, toward the offender's neck. The chain would wrap itself around the neck like a bullwhip, and Hoxie's assailant would immediately become Hoxie's victim.

"He's rough," said Betty once. "Believe me, he'll bite a buzz saw. I've seen him go in and pick them up, and their feet just dangle. He's strong. If somebody doesn't behave around here, Hoxie sees to it."

It was relatively easy to tell whether Hoxie thought every-

Hoxie's hatbrim

body was behaving. You had only to look at his hatbrim. "Everybody in show business, around this show especially, knows this pretty well," said Hoxie. "I come on the lot, my hatbrim is turned up, they have no worries. I come on here and that brim is turned down, everybody moves out of my way because they know I've got something on my mind, and whoever I meet I'm likely to take it out on them."

Hoxie believed that if you acted mean enough, and if you worked hard enough, you could go anywhere you wanted to in the circus business. Certainly his own life was proof of this. One time he told me, "If you want to learn something in the circus business, you can be whatever you want to be if you put your mind to it, whether it's a clown or a trapeze artist or an elephant trainer or whatever you want to be. First of all, you can't be afraid. If you gamble your life to do what you want to do, I think anybody in the circus business can achieve what they want, regardless of what it is."

In Hoxie's case, that phrase about gambling one's life had special importance. He had suffered, in the past few years, three seizures that had been diagnosed as heart attacks. Some of the circus folks doubted that they were true heart attacks, since Hoxie was invariably back on the midway a few days after each collapse. But Hoxie said his doctors had called them heart attacks. And he had come down with what he called a nervous breakdown.

I once asked him what the breakdown consisted of.

"Well," he said, "it consisted of the fact that you just go out of your mind. You don't know what you're doing. You make too many mistakes. I could walk into that tent, and if things didn't look just right, I'd just fall down and start crying. I still have a problem. I was riding down the road in Miami the other day"—he pronounced it *mi-AM-uh*—"and I didn't know where I was at, where I was going, or nothing about it. I had to pull over and stop. When I come to, I was in Hialeah, a long ways from where I wanted to go. It's bad for me to be out by myself like that."

What does the doctor say?

"The doctor tells me not to never go anywhere by myself.

"You see, I stayed in the hospital six weeks, out there in St. Louis. That Barnes Hospital." Barnes, a modern teaching hospital, had a psychiatric section. "I was in the hospital four times that year."

I asked him why he was so willing to talk about it.

"Well, I think it's better to. I'm not ashamed of it. It's *happened* to me. And I think when you've got a problem, you've got to talk about it to get it off your chest, and then you're better off."

I said I had been to a headshrinker myself. I was trying to make Hoxie feel as if he had some company.

"Well, there ain't nothing wrong with that," he said. "All he did was take your money. And if you go to these hospitals, they do things for you and they do a lot of good for you, and I'm not ashamed of it. I can't help it. There's no insanity whatsoever in my family, so I know I'm not *crazy*. But I'd just be walking along and something would happen to me, and I'd get scared.

"After I came out of the hospital, that was the worst part of it. I wanted to come back to the show, and Betty wouldn't want me to come back, but she'd bring me. And I'd go to the front end, and as soon as I'd see it I would get afraid. I wouldn't go around it. I'd make her leave me on the street, and she'd go in and talk to John Hall and see if everything was all right, and he'd come out and talk to me.

"I don't know what I was afraid of; I just wouldn't want to come around the show. I stayed away from it. I'd get Betty to drive me by and let me look at it.

"But I don't think it's anything to be ashamed of. I think it could happen to me, you, or anybody else. And when it does, the best thing to do's try to talk about it and get it off your mind. And I think that doing it the way I did is the greatest thing that ever happened. Because that doctor in St. Louis, he said, 'I just can't figure you out at all. Anybody that can recover like you do!'"

It was absurd, of course, that someone in Hoxie's position should add to his worries and troubles by buying another circus. But the purchase of Lewis Brothers seemed to delight him. "That's what makes it *good*," he said. "That's something *new*. That's what's *interesting*. We've got a hell of a show over there. It's a real high-class show." Then: "You've got to do something that nobody else will attempt to do."

I asked Hoxie about the workmen. Surely a lot of his tension and grief came from the fact that the workmen, working at the wages he paid them and in the conditions he provided for them, could not be counted on exactly to transcend themselves.

"A lot of them are misplaced persons," said Hoxie. "They don't really know what they *do* want. They just drift. They come by, they get a few dollars in their pockets, and they're gone. And don't kid yourself. We get all types—winos, paregorics, dope fiends. You get everything there is. Because we're on the move, and everybody's hiding from something, I don't care what it is.

"This is the way I figure it. If a man is any good to *begin* with, and was capable of going out and making a decent living, he wouldn't be doing what he is doing when he comes over here."

I asked if there weren't some exceptions to that rule. What about Joe Hamilton and Jeff Woosnam?

Hoxie thought a moment, recalled who they were, and said, "Well, they've got a weakness of some kind. Or else they wouldn't be here.

"Everybody's got some kind of weakness. There's some reason for that man not doing something to better himself. I can go out in the back yard and make the rounds with these men, every one of them, and I can bull with them for a few minutes and come up with what's wrong. Some of them it's women, some of them it's whiskey, some it's dope, some it's something else. There's some *reason* why a guy gets into the position that he's gone to that mission or someplace like that, where we find him."

I asked Hoxie what his own weakness was.

"You mean why am I with the circus?"

"Yes, why?

"Because I got a weakness, too. A circus."

REHEARSAL

The top was up, rolling in the breeze; it was a quiet, lazy Sunday, with little traffic on the road. The Jaycees came and opened their food wagon, and some of them had on clown costumes and makeup. After church let out, the clowns tried to stop passing cars and sell tickets to the occupants. Before the props and lumber went into the Big Top, the tent looked strange and naked inside. Bill Hill showed the workmen how to tie down the jumper ropes on the quarterpoles, how to lay out the ring curbs so that when the last segment was placed it formed a perfect circle. Joe Hamilton had been more or less arbitrarily chosen as a prop man, and he learned quickly. Stanley Winter, a short man with a disproportionately large head and very curly hair, worked with Joe. His hair was blond and of the sort that aunts and sisters refer to as "ringlets."

Stanley had been born on a houseboat on the Green River in Kentucky. In 1961, the houseboat caught fire and Stanley's mother burned to death.

"I guess there might be some other people who've had it rougher than me," he said, with a little half-smile, "but I don't know who they are. My face is half silver." It was true that only half of his face really moved properly when he talked. "I was raised up on a farm, and we was poor people, you know, and my daddy, he was a wino. I worked on another farm for four dollars a day and that's how I got all messed up. I fell into some machinery and I got my jaws all messed up. I probably could have got some money out of it, but I didn't try to. Went to the hospital and stayed there about three months, and they kept my jaws wired up for about four more months, and I had to eat soup and water, no food. One whole side of my face is nothing but silver. And the other side, they patched it up."

Stanley tied off the jumper ropes in the manner of a country boy used to work, slowly but well. "And after my mother got burnt up I've been on the road ever since. I've done carnival work, mostly. This is my first year to be with a circus. I like this better than the carnival. It's harder work, but I just like the people I work with, you know. Lots friendlier. Just lots nicer people. And if I still like it when we get to Kentucky, I think I'll stay the whole season. I think I'm going to like it."

I asked him how he felt about his work. "I'm working here to please the public," he said. "Everybody that wants to come in and see the show." Did Stanley get a kick out of seeing the show himself? "To tell you the truth about it, I haven't never seen too many of the performances because I haven't never went to the circus in my life."

Stash wheeled around on the fork-lift, carrying great pawsful of seat lumber from the flat-bed truck to the inner periphery of the Big Top. Unlike some of the workmen, he seemed to know exactly what he was doing and almost to enjoy his work.

Stash was about thirty years old, a tanned man of medium height and weight, piercing eyes; obviously bright. He was born in a Rocky Mountains town. Like many of the people with the circus, he had left home when he was young. He quit school when he was fifteen. Stash had been a competition roller skater, a truck driver, and a steeplejack. He had worked in plant maintenance for an airline, and he had been a painter in a shipyard, a welder, a carpenter, an employee in a service station. He got married, had two children, got a divorce. He was a cowboy on a ranch in Nevada.

"I took a lot of hard knocks," he said. "I've been in jail. For checks. I got messed up with a couple of guys, and got drunk, and I was the fall guy. I took the weight. I did a nine-month sentence back east. Got out after seven months."

How did you get from all that to here?

"One day on the ranch I got mad and said to hell with it. So I left. I said, 'I'm going back up north where I have friends.' I went over to Newark. This was last summer. I had heard this truck come by, saying, 'Circus here today,' and I went out to the lot. Had a pint of vodka in my back pocket. Very rarely do I drink liquor; mostly it's beer. I see this guy leaning against a station wagon with a Stetson hat on. I walked over to him and said, 'Hey! Who the hell do you see about getting a job around here?' It was Hoxie! They got a guy to run me in and get my clothes, and I came back.

"A few days later, I had been on one of those Sunday-night-and-Monday-morning deals, and it came time to work, and I ain't had no sleep, and I still had a few beers left, so I poured them into this canteen. I'm out there setting the rigging for the centerpole. Hoxie and John Lewis came around and says, 'What you got in that canteen?' I said, 'Beer.' Well, that blew them apart right there, because they expected me to lie about it.

"They said, 'Well, if you want to work here, you better pour it out.' I handed him the canteen, and I said, 'I don't have the heart. You want it out, *you* pour it out.'"

Stash was making twenty-five dollars a week at the end of the season, and he stayed with the show in winter quarters. The pay there was ten dollars a week. On Christmas Eve, Stash got to thinking about his children, and about how there was no way for him to see or talk to them, and he started drinking a lot of beer. "I tied one on, and I tied on a pretty good one, too. And I blew the show.

"It took Hoxie two weeks to find me. He said, 'You ready to come home?' I thought he'd be pretty well mad at me. 'Naw, we're not mad,' he said. 'Everybody goes out every once in a while.'"

Stash thought for a moment and then continued. "There's no excuse in the world to drink and get loaded. If a man wants to drink, he's going to drink no matter what. I was president of the steering committee of AA for about a year, when I quit drinking. That's how deeply I got into it. I don't need an excuse for drinking. I drink because I like to drink. It's satisfying. Anyway, I came back to the show because I liked it. I knew what work had to be done. I knew that all these seats had to be made, and I knew who was going to make them. Because I'm the one that laid out the plan and everything, and made the samples.

"I don't consider myself part of show business. I consider myself part of seeing to it that the top is up and everything."

Well, that's part of show business, isn't it?

"Well, yeah. And you have to like it to be out there in the mud, and the sweat, and the blood, and the rain and the sand, and places like this lot."

The blood?

"Yeah. Sometimes the blood."

The layout of the lot: Imagine a rectangular field. In pretty much the center of it was the Big Top, with its front

The layout of the lot

door facing the most obvious way for the crowd to come in. Extending in two parallel lines from the front door forward was the midway. Everything on this side of the Big Top was called the "front end."

On the far side of the midway, at the end of one of the parallel lines, was the pit show, an alleged apelike man's corpse lying in a glassed-in box inside a small trailer. The trailer's doors opened to frame the show. On the doors it said, "Himalayan Monster. Neither Man Nor Beast. Homopongodies (Meaning Ape Like Man). As Seen on CBS Television and Discussed on the Johnny Carson Show and Canada's Perry's Probe. The Creature That Has Baffled Thousands (as Read About in) Life, Look, and Argosy Magazines and All the Major Newspapers." Hoxie had bought the show from a man on the side of the road, and he was dinging people a quarter to see it. The hairy creature, which appeared to be made of papier-mâché, was complete in most details, including his penis, and when towner girls went in to look at him they invariably were giggling on their way out. Hoxie thought the monster was ter-

rific. "I don't have to feed him, or pay him, he doesn't get drunk on Saturday night, and he don't cause no trouble whatsoever, and he's always there when I need him. He's a gold mine," he said.

Across the midway from the pit show was the place where Bill Hill usually parked his trailer. Between the two, in the area where the crowd walked, was the souvenir stand, which sold flags and balloons and other trinkets. A little farther on, also in the middle of the midway, was the cotton-candy stand.

Next to the pit show, between it and the Big Top, was the sideshow—the two tractor-trailers parked with stage and ticket boxes in between. Past Bill Hill's trailer, on the other side, was the office trailer, where the tickets were sold and where John Hall maintained his records. In the middle of the midway, between the office wagon and the sideshow, was Johnny Walker's concession wagon. They cooked hot dogs in there, made popcorn, dipped candy apples, and mixed flukum. Flukum is any soft drink that you mix up yourself. Johnny mixed two kinds of flukum, orange and purple.

The layout was varied sometimes, to make the most of a tight lot, but always the midway led directly to the marquee and the front door.

Usually the light plant was parked about halfway around the side of the Big Top. This was a huge tractor-trailer, with two large generators inside it, that supplied electrical power for the show. It hummed from the time it was started, in the morning, until it was shut off at eleven-thirty or midnight. Thick black electrical cords led from the light plant to the various vehicles on the midway, and other cords snaked into the Big Top and into the back yard.

In the back yard there was the cooktent and truck, and the pole wagon and seat truck were parked there, too. The performers parked their rigs in the back, as close to the back door as they could get, just as the bosses parked theirs close to the front. It was seldom that you saw a performer in the front end or one of the bosses in the back yard.

Harry was hurrying around the sideshow tent, making sure

things got put together properly. Harry was the fire-eater. He was a little man with light blue eyes and white hair. His face was covered with creases. He said he was with shows off and on, and that, "actually, in civilian life I've been a very good electrician, a lousy plumber, a terrible carpenter, and a good commercial fisherman." He had developed several nicknames, each attached to one of his jobs, so that when people addressed him he could know which of his several lives they were talking about. He said he had had two heart attacks, and he stopped frequently in his work to catch his breath.

"This first week," he said, "is a sorting-out basis. We have to ascertain in the first few weeks which, and who, and what, and why, can work and can't work together. A lot of the people are only efficient under pressure, and a certain number of people are efficient only if they're drinking. And the show has to sort out those who are going to drink too much and those who're just going down the road."

I asked Harry if there was not another category, a group of people like himself, who had done it before and who knew what they were doing. Harry had been helping some of the green men, teaching them the correct and efficient way to tie off ropes and put up poles.

"Well," he said, "sometimes you try to help out and do the right thing, even though it's not your department. You feel that, after you get to a certain age, you should teach the young ones, because you don't want to see show business drop down to nothing. And if it keeps the way it's going, it's going to be nothing. Nothing but people who don't want any responsibility and think it's a quick way to make a few bucks.

"This business is a closed community of people who live together for seven to nine months a year, tightly together. It's their own little city, and you have to treat it like your own little city. Otherwise forget it."

You haven't exactly reached a certain age, have you?

"I'll be sixty-one in a while."

And you think part of your job is to teach the younger people?

"I hope I can, yes. Because I'd sure as heck hate to see the circus disappear, and if they keep on hiring help who know nothing about their particular jobs, then it *will* disappear. It'll be like TV. And the circus shouldn't be TV."

I asked him about specific people. There was a man called George, who had stayed up all night drinking and fighting. "Never make it," said Harry. "Matter of days. He's an alcoholic, and he has achieved the ideal, where he thinks he can work just a little bit and drink a lot, and it's not possible." Another workman "might make it."

"See," said Harry, "he's a little different. There's a certain amount of ingrained decency to some circus people—to *real* circus people. They go for children, and they go for dogs, and they go for animals. They're the ones who'll stay. The people who stay are really easy marks, because for them the show comes first—the idea that the people who pay their money are satisfied. The next thing that matters to them is that nobody gets hurt in any way, shape, or manner, if they can help it. And a lot of these other guys, those things don't come first with them. Drinking comes first, or chasing women, or the fact that they've never had any responsibility and they can't accept it.

"Most people run away from home and take a job in the circus, figuring, 'I can't handle the jobs at home because they know I drink and I can't get.to work at the right time,' and so forth and so on. And you have to weed out these people, and you have to look for the ones who have a little bit of innate decency, where they will hang on and help take care of the small things. They call it a tradition, but really it's an actuality."

How do you describe your attitude toward life?

Harry patted himself on the heart and said, "It's like I've got one more day. Day by day, just like an alcoholic. Nothing to worry about on the day after that. Why should I?"

Phil Chandler, the ringmaster, and Linda walked over, and Harry introduced himself to them. Phil would also be the side-show manager, at least in the beginning weeks. He would do the grind from the platform that would get the customers into the sideshow. Linda was going to help out with the sideshow and be on the platform during the bally, displaying a large boa constrictor. Harry seemed intent on explaining everything about the operation to Phil and Linda, and when he was through I asked him why.

"Because I might not be here someday, and they ought to know about it themselves," he said.

The rehearsal would start soon. A full hour beforehand, Bert Pettus showed up in clean, neatly pressed khaki pants, a white western shirt, a neat black tie, and a hat with gold braid. His belt buckle was a representation of an elephant's head. He was the first one ready. He had gotten a look at the program that the circus would use on opening night, and he had discovered that it called him "Captain Bert Pettus," and he wanted to make sure that he was not introduced that way. "I can't explain *why* I hate that word," he said. "I just do. I got all the way up to buck private when I was in the army."

Bert was also angry about the coral and what it would do to his elephants' feet, "especially the poor little babies." He talked to John Hall about this, and John said, well, the babies had performed on coral a year ago. Bert stalked off, scowling. "I'm going to give these folks a lot of trouble," he said.

Some of the acts had spread out their trampolines, and they were practicing somersaults inside the tent. Superchicken, the sailmaker, stood on his elderly, wobbly legs at the front door and watched them. A few townspeople who had stopped to buy tickets walked up the midway and stood beside him, watching the performers. Superchicken edged away.

"I wonder what these people would do if I went to *their* house and walked in and started watching their television," he said. "This is *my* house, you know."

A handsome woman with high-piled blonde hair parked a Cadillac in the midway and got out. Immediately a Jaycee clown tried to sell her a ticket. She declined, politely. The clown insisted. "*No*," she finally said. "You see, I own the circus." Betty Tucker walked on up to the Big Top and looked inside. She was upset because the costumes had come and she didn't like most of them. Betty used to make all the costumes herself, on her sewing machine in South Miami, where she and

Hoxie lived. But recently she had started having them made, and there was no pleasing her. She wanted the women's costumes as brief as possible, and the designer had done that, but she didn't like some of the details. She did like the brightly colored coveralls she had ordered for the prop men and elephant handlers to wear during the performances.

Joe Hamilton said the bear had gotten his contact lenses. Impossible, I said; nobody would steal contact lenses. "But they did," he said. "They were in a little box down on the bottom of my pack, and when I went to the sleeper the pack was turned inside out and the little box was missing."

The rehearsal started about twenty minutes late. Phil Chandler stood near the centerpole and told the audience, in his deep, professional voice, that the theme of this year's show was "Happiness Is a Circus Parade." Then King Charles and the band struck up the music for Spec, "Happy Days Are Here Again," and the performers and animals started the walkaround. Stanley Winter led the camel around the track, and Joe Hamilton towed several ponies. Except for Bert Pettus, the performers were not in costume.

Each of the musical instruments, except perhaps King Charles's trumpet and Jeff Woosnam's sousaphone, was playing in its own special key, and the rehearsal was quite ragged, but the audience applauded Spec and each act that followed it. The audience was made up of the bosses, the butchers from the concession wagon, a few members of the local committee, and some visiting circus people and relatives.

When Phil Chandler introduced Bert Pettus, he called him "Mister Bert Pettus." And the baby elephants did not walk over the coral in the rehearsal.

Four or five acts were left out entirely, either because the rigging for them was not yet up or because the performers had not yet arrived. Junior's absence was apparent. Ordinarily, he would not have worked the cats during the rehearsal; the arena would have been there, a reminder that he would work them on the following night. But the arena and the cats were back among the weeds at winter quarters.

After the rehearsal was over, Hoxie asked everybody to sit down in front of Ring Two. "Yawl come on now, I want to get through here," he said. The performers, bosses, musicians, canvasmen, prop men, and butchers all gathered in the seats. There was an air of happiness that the season was about to start. Some of them tried to act offhand about the whole thing, but the air was there nevertheless.

"Everybody give me your attention just a minute, please," said Hoxie. Then he shouted, "Now *evvabody* look at *me*, not at the centerpole, not at nothing." The people quieted down.

"I don't do this but once a year, and I kind of expect that everybody will listen to me. *I'm* not running the show. John Hall is. But I furnish the money for it. The same show you're going to do tomorrow night is the same show I'm going to pay you for the last day you're here. And the last day you're here, I want the same type show I got the first night."

Jeff laughed, because he thought the first show, if you could call the rehearsal the first show, had not been of very high quality. Hoxie zeroed in on Jeff, pointing his finger.

"I don't want a lot of conversation out of musicians or nobody else," he shouted, and everybody looked at Jeff. Jeff's face immediately went serious.

"I mean it. Now, I don't mean to be mean. This is a business with you. This is a business with me. Now, if you can respect me when I'm talking, I can respect you. I'm sorry, folks, I had to do that, but I wanted to straighten it out one time and that's the end of it.

"We're glad to have you with us. We're glad to have everybody with us. I need everybody who's here with this circus tonight. And I hope that on the last day of the season everybody's here who is here tonight. Now, if every person does what he's supposed to, you won't hear one word out of me.

"I'm not here all the time. Mr. Hall, he is the general manager of this show. This man here is the manager of this show, Bill Hill, who most of you in the show business know. Mr. Hill has nothing to do with the performers on the show at all. John Hall handles that. Mr. Hill is to handle everything else. If he has a problem, and he can't handle it, between him and who has it, he'll go to Mr. Hall. I'll always be here within a day or so any time anything happens.

"Now, I'll explain to all of you why I'm not here all the time. The last few years I've had a little trouble. I've had three heart attacks and a nervous breakdown in the last three years. I don't have any business with this thing at all. And if I listened to the doctors I wouldn't even be out here tonight. This is my *life*. I love it. I hope to *die* under this tent. That's part of me. Just the same as these performers inside of this tent, that is *their* life." Everyone applauded.

Hoxie asked everyone to conserve gasoline as much as they could. Then he asked John Hall to stand in front of the gathering. "John is the general manager of this show," Hoxie said. "If you've got a problem, don't bring it to me. That's what I pay him for. I'm talking about performers. . . .

"I've never had any serious problems in the back yard. I think people will tell you that last year—did you ever see me in the back yard over one time? I had no reason to be in the back yard because people did their job. And I won't be back there this year if you do your job.

"Now, there's only one more thing I want to say, and then I'm going to get out. In case of a storm, or something happens around here like that, I need everybody on this show—performers, everybody, musicians, everybody—if John Hall or Mr. Hill come and ask you to help, I expect you all to come out in an emergency and help. It's a tradition in this business that in case of a storm you don't go call people; they're out there. Everybody will be out there—men, women, kids, everybody who can help do something will be here. And I know everybody will do that, because that's where they make their living. If this rag blows away, you're out of business.

"I never beat anybody in my life out of a nickel, and I don't intend to do it now if I can help it. You all co-operate with me, and I'll try to give you as long a season's work as you want. And treat every one of you just like I want you to treat me. I ain't no different.

"I come up the hard way—" The crowd applauded again.

"I come up the hard way. I started just like these men do sitting around here. Slept under trucks, did everything in the world, the only difference is I had more guts than a lot of other people did to extend my credit as far as the creditors would go to get in this business. I want to help everybody, and I know everybody's going to help me."

Hoxie introduced some of the other bosses, and then he named some of the show people. Bert Pettus, he said, had been in show business "over three days." He announced that Johnny Walker would be the boss canvasman, and that he would be assisted by Gypsy Red. "Most of you who have been in the business know Gypsy Red," said Hoxie. "He's here today and gone tomorrow, but while he's here he's *with it*. But he's liable to be gone tomorrow."

There was laughter after this last remark, and Hoxie added, smiling, "Don't laugh, boys. Hell, I'm the same way."

"Well," said Hoxie, "I think I blowed off here long enough. I don't know much else to say except to keep my mouth shut, and, everybody, tomorrow night let's have a good show. Do the best you can, and I tell you, this is the truth. This is the worst lot of the lots we've ever been on. We were here last year. The only reason we're not on that nice lot across the street is that the man wants twelve hundred dollars for it, and I ain't going for that. So that's why we have to put up with these rocks. Thank you, ladies and gentlemen."

Afterwards, Jeff approached Hoxie and apologized for laughing. Hoxie accepted the apology. Then Hoxie called Stash over and told him he was raising his wages seventy-five dollars a week. Hoxie told Stash, "See here, you sumbitch, the seats look good, don't they?" Stash said, "Yes, they do." Then Hoxie offered him the raise. Stash said afterwards that he was full of "self-satisfaction. And he really gave me some incentive," he said.

Hoxie left the lot. Some of the performers were still practicing inside the Big Top, and the lights were still on. You were aware of the sound the light plant made, and you knew that in a few days you would be completely oblivious of it and that it would sound strange only when it was *not* running.

The American flag waved from the top of the centerpole. The elephants shook their shackles. The Jaycees and the towners were all gone. The sleeper was relatively quiet, because the winos were broke again, and would be until Wednesday. Some of the old-timers gathered again outside Bill Hill's trailer, and some of the first of Mays, Jeff and Joe among them, hung on the fringes of the conversation and listened.

OPENING DAY

It was a wide-open sky, deep blue with a few scattered clouds that would do no harm; a nice breeze that moved through the Big Top and made the translucent green fingers of the palm trees vibrate. People woke lazily. There had been talk yesterday about how much work was still needed, but now that opening day was here there was no sign that anyone was panicked.

Myrtle, the oldest and wisest of the elephants, had shaken her shackles successfully during the night, and she had wandered off and eaten a good percentage of a palmetto tree on a woman's lawn. She had done precisely the same thing one year before. More of the acts came in, in trucks and trailers that gave no sign that these were show people, that strange, brightly chromed props were inside. A family of clowns arrived; they were named Fornasari, and they were cousins of the Cristianis, and there was much hugging and kissing when they pulled onto the lot. The aerial act came: two men in a painted-over Ryder rental truck with bunk beds built inside. For the first time I saw the McGuire sisters, although they had been there at winter quarters all along because Margaret McGuire was married to Mike McGuire, who worked in the office. They were absolutely strikingly lovely women. They put their doves out in the sun for a while. Maureen's young daughter, Margaret Ann, wandered around the lot, looking for somebody to play with.

The men in the Ryder truck started setting up a cable that stretched from the ground outside the Big Top through the sidewall and up inside the tent to the very top of the centerpole. After a while they discovered that a vital part of their motorcycle was missing, and they took the rigging down. They did two acts: they rode the motorcycle up the wire, and they did a tight-wire-walking act. They started setting up the rigging for the wire act.

Hoxie came on the lot. I asked him if he had anything approximating opening-night jitters.

"It don't bother me a bit in the world," he said. "Whatever's going to be is going to be. If something goes wrong, it's going to go wrong. If everything is right and wonderful, then that, too. But if after all these years you can't take a little hardship with you, you ain't got no business in it."

Hoxie had said, years ago, that he was always glad to end a season, but that after a few days at home in Miami he got to itching to get back on the road again. I asked him when the itching had started this year. He said it hadn't.

"I'm not itching now," he said. "Not a bit in this world. Not one day since the show closed have I wanted to go back on the road. I've got sense enough to know that my health comes first now, which I didn't know for years, and I know that I can't do what I used to do. It's just a regular old opening day for me."

Hoxie was wearing a pair of light blue seersucker pants and a short-sleeved shirt with blue stripes. He had a straw hat on, and its brim was turned up. He wore no tie, but he did wear his tie clip, which was made out of two lion claws. His shirt was open at the collar, and his white chest hairs stuck out. In his shirt pocket there was a pair of glasses that I had never seen him wear.

Are you ready for another year?

"I *stay* ready. I don't want to go, but I go. I'd lot ruther stay home for about another week, and *then* I wouldn't mind going and staying a few days." He laughed.

A lot of the workmen had been asking about Wahoo.

"Don't worry. We'll take care of Wahoo."

Bill Hill sat outside his trailer, in the shade under an awn-

ing. The biggest part of his work was over for the morning; all
the canvas was up, all the props and lumber were in. Some of
the circus people were genuinely frightened whenever Hoxie
was on the lot, and when they saw him coming they invented
work to do, as privates will when they see the sergeant coming.
Bill Hill had enough job security so he didn't have to do this.

I asked him what sort of thing he thought about at the
beginning of a season.

"Getting back home safe, for one thing. You hope for not
too much bad weather. But we're going to get our share of it,
I imagine, going up in the spring."

Are you excited?

"Well, I don't know. When you've done this all your life,
that's all you know. Getting too old to try something else." Bill
had been doing this for thirty-seven years, thirty-three of them
with circuses. The other four were with carnivals.

"It's been good to me. When I first started in show business I got five dollars and eighty-five cents a week, and my
room and board. And by the time Sunday come—see, we got
paid on Sunday. And they had a commissary outside the cookhouse, like you used to have in the coal mines, a company store,
and you were lucky if you even had a dollar coming after you
paid off the commissary."

Bill was from Harrisburg, Pennsylvania. He ran away from
home when he was almost fifteen. "I didn't want to go to
school," he said. "I went to Indianapolis, and had no place to
sleep, and I went into a mission. Wheeler's Mission—I'll never
forget it. Was riding a freight. And the boys said, 'At least we
can stop and get a meal and a place to sleep in Indianapolis.'
So I got off at Indianapolis. Those guys were older than me
and they knew. So I went to the mission—it's still there—and
they took all your clothes and fumigated them. You had to take
a shower, and they gave you a big sack that looked like a cot-
ton-picking sack, and you put that on. And the next morning,
if you went out and chopped wood—because they sold the
wood—you could stay another day, and you'd get another three
meals. First we had to go to chapel.

"Those days, nobody much worried about a fifteen-year-old runaway. The biggest percentage of the people in the country were hungry anyway. I went with a show that year, in 1938, and everything in the country was in bad shape. The show went broke, and I worked eighteen weeks on the show and didn't even get a penny. Had good food and a nice place to sleep, but some people weren't even getting enough to eat. I was thankful that I had something to eat and a place to sleep.

"And I worked my way up. You keep your nose clean. I worked my way up to where I was a boss and I did a little bit of everything—run concessions, superintendent, that kind of stuff."

So you can do any of the jobs that need doing around a circus?

"Oh, yeah, that's why I'm here now. Anything that turns up I can do. Get by with it, anyway. Some things I naturally can't do as well as the guy who's the head of the department, but I've got enough knowledge of show business that I can do enough until they get somebody else to replace him."

I asked if that was how you got status in a circus: by mastering a lot of different fields.

"Right. It ain't who you know. There ain't a college in the United States will teach you this business. You've got to learn it right on these muddy lots and up and down the highway."

Bill had a gigantic ring on one of his fingers, and it had a large stone in it. I asked if it was a diamond.

"It damn well better be, or me and the man who sold it to me's going to have some problems."

A young man walked up to Bill. He was in his twenties or thirties, and he needed a shave. "Are you Bill Hill?" he said.

"Yes, I'm Bill Hill. Somebody send you to see me?"

"Yes. I need a job. I'm a welder, and I can drive. I can do almost anything. I'm a good rider."

"Good *rider!* We don't have no openings for horse riders here. All I can tell you, if you want to go to work—you have a car? You drive?"

"Yes, I got a car."

"Then get some clothes. We don't have the best place in the world to sleep, if you know what I mean, and we'll feed you and give you a place to sleep. When we start, it's a small salary. We've got some guys here who make twenty-five a week and some guys who make like two hundred and fifty dollars a week. If you can show us you can do a good job—"

"Oh, I can work real hard."

"Well, we've got to find that out."

"Well, where do you go from here?"

"Sunrise."

"How long before you come back to Miami? Seven months?"

"Seven months."

"And that's all the pay is, twenty-five a week?"

"No, I didn't say that. We start them off at that for the first week. Some people like it, some people don't."

"Where'll I come to? Right here?"

"Yeah. I'll find a department to put you in. If you don't like that department, we'll look around for another department. But you can't have no cars on the show, because we've got to have guys to drive these trucks. These trucks move every day."

"What does the truck-driving pay?"

"Oh, that goes with it."

"Five speeds?"

"Some five, some ten speeds. And you might not like it there, and you like animals, and we get an opening in animals, we'll put you over there, you know what I mean?"

"Honestly, Mr. Hill, I'm worried about that pay."

"Well, I'm not going to say we're going to pay you a hundred and fifty a week, and then payday comes around and you're going to get mad at me. Some people love to travel, and be around the atmosphere—"

"Well, I like to travel, but I like to make money, too."

"Sure, I like to make money, too." Bill's diamond flashed in the afternoon sunlight. "My advice is fine, if you want to come back, do."

"Well, I'll think about it."

"Okay."

The man walked away and he did not return.

Bill Hill

In midafternoon of the last Monday of March, it was ninety degrees in the shade of the Big Top. Some of the clumps of coral seemed to be worn down, as if a lot of heavy traffic had passed over them. But the coral was still painful to walk on. The workmen no longer worried about snakes; the lot had become civilized, after a fashion. The weeds were flattened out on the ground now.

Some of the workmen cleaned themselves for the first time in weeks. They shaved, using cold water from Art Duvall's truck and the mirrors of trucks, and they changed clothes, and some of them washed their hair. Two of them came back from a shopping center with T-shirts that said "Hoxie Brothers Circus." They had paid someone to heat-transfer the letters onto the shirts.

The opening show was scheduled for six o'clock, and the second and last show at Sweetwater would be at eight. In the late afternoon a few people arrived on the lot, and it looked as if they had come for the performance, and performers and bosses started remembering to do last-minute things. Harry appeared in black pants, a white shirt with a big collar, and a cummerbund, and he pushed and shoved the sideshow ticket boxes until they were in a straight line. "Got to be straight," he said. "It's flash. You're selling looks here. Even an old bum like me gets dressed up and cleaned up for the show. You have to present a front like a salesman who has nothing in his pocket or his suitcase, and he has to sell himself by what he's dressed like. All show business starts with the front, the flash, and it goes from there on in. But first you must dress yourself neatly. There's no other way."

Phil and Linda Chandler appeared, and together with Harry they outlined the sideshow. Harry produced a suitcase similar to one that is used to transport cats and told Linda that the boa constrictor was inside. He showed her how to wrap it around her neck without hurting it. "Then there's the Electric Girl," he said.

He pointed to an old and scarred wooden box, which had an electrical cord leading from it. "It's just a simple diathermy machine," he said. "You stand on it, and you hold my hand, and in your other hand you hold this fluorescent bulb, and it lights up. You won't feel a thing, if it's working right."

The opening performance started about twenty minutes late. A half hour before, Linda and Phil and Harry had guided a good portion of the ticket holders into the sideshow tent, where they had paid fifty cents each to see Linda hold a snake, Harry eat fire, Linda turn into the Electric Girl, and Phil do a series of magic tricks. The sideshow crowd had looked at the animals who were housed in the tent, and then they had gone into the Big Top. The house was about half full—about fifteen hundred people.

At about quarter past six Phil left the sideshow and put on his ringmaster's costume, a red morning coat and trousers, and he appeared near the back door. He blew loudly on his whistle and shouted, "Five minutes!" The performers and animals, and the workmen who were to lead the animals, all gathered at the

back door well ahead of time. Bert Pettus was there first with
the elephants, although they would go in last. The elephants
had been brushed and dusted. They were lining up for Spec.
Myrtle, at the last minute, urinated copiously on the ground.
She had been taught, years before on some forgotten circus, to
do that just before a performance.

Shortly before Spec started, an elderly woman slipped and
fell off her seat inside the Big Top. Representatives of all sorts
of public agencies ran to her side and carried her to a place
right in the middle of the front door, where they laid her on
the ground and started feeling for broken bones, and where,
coincidentally, the late arrivals could get horrified glimpses of
her. Each public agency seemed to have its own set of walkie-
talkies, and information went back to at least three different
headquarters. It was an amazing show of Sweetwater's strength.
The police were there, and the fire department, and the rescue
squad people. They put a plastic splint on her leg. Hoxie came
over and consoled the woman. She was the sister of the show's
purchasing agent, Jim Hodges. Later, it turned out that she had
a twisted ankle.

Spec started. Phil Chandler told a live audience for the
first time that Happiness Is a Circus Parade, and the people
and animals started around the track. John Hall led the first
horse around. The horse carried Linda Chandler, and Linda
carried the American flag. She had a lot of makeup on, and she
didn't at all look like the young woman in the sweat shirt that
said "Libby Girls Staff."

Behind Linda came performers, carrying banners and full
of smiles, and the animals, and last the elephants, including the
babies. The workmen led the animals, and some of the beasts
obviously were not used to walking in front of an audience. Joe
Hamilton, looking a little sheepish and wearing international-
orange coveralls that were not quite long enough for his six-
foot-three-inch body, led three of the white ponies. Behind him,
Stanley Winter, half of his face smiling brightly, led the camel.
Behind them some of the winos struggled with other horses,
and the zebra (the one who was not too mean), and the llamas,
and I thought to myself, *You know, they really are all God's*

children. Some of them are slightly misshapen, and some of them are somewhat retarded, and many of them are still hung over, but they're still God's children, and maybe they're the right people to be putting on a circus.

Stanley Winter was halfway around the track, almost in front of the front door, when he tripped on a chunk of coral. The camel shook its head mightily and snatched the reins from Stanley's hand. The camel took off toward the crowd.

Joe Hamilton saw what had happened behind him. He dropped the line that held his ponies and he grabbed for the camel. He caught the camel's harness. The camel, who was amazingly strong, dragged Joe through the coral for ten or fifteen feet. Joe managed to stop the camel just as it approached the front row of seats; there were children there, and they were screaming. Someone took the camel from Joe and dragged it on around the track and out the back door. The ponies broke into a trot, went around to the back door, then decided to go around again. Some of the spectators apparently thought this was just part of the show. The ponies caused no real trouble. Someone finally caught them and took them out, and the show went on.

Hoxie walked out to the centerpole and took the microphone from Phil Chandler. He welcomed the crowd to the Big Top, and then he went into a little impromptu speech. The circus and Sweetwater, he said, had been good neighbors while the show was in winter quarters. "We stay out here in winter quarters at the old dairy," he said, "and nobody bothers us, and we don't bother nobody except once a year, and that's when that same old elephant gets loose. This year she did four hundred and fifty dollars' worth of damage, instead of last year, when she did nine hundred worth. . . ."

Hoxie apologized for the condition of the lot. "You know this is the worst lot anyone could put a human on," he said. And then he outlined the season. "We will travel twenty or twenty-five thousand miles before it's over if we can borrow the money to buy the gas. What you're seeing tonight is our opening performance, the opening of the season. I hope you have a good time."

Phil introduced the first act, "the bounding troubadors of the trampoline." Ordinarily this is where Junior would have spent his eleven minutes with the cats. The Cristiani family rushed through the back door and into Ring One, and the Fornasari family went into Ring Three. The prop crews had set up chromed trampolines in each ring. Each of the families had a gag routine, and each of them ended the performance with a three-high stack of tumblers.

Then came the Spanish web, with Linda Chandler and Margaret and Maureen McGuire. Spanish web is traditional with circuses; in the routine, pretty girls climb heavy ropes and execute turns and spins and graceful poses while someone, another performer or a prop man, holds the rope at the bottom.

The baby elephants were next, presented by Mister Bert Pettus. The babies were named Irene (after Hoxie's daughter), Janet, Kelly and Stacy (after his granddaughters), Betty, and Hoxie. Hoxie was a baby African male, something of an oddity on a show because African bulls were believed to be unpredictable.

Next came the foot juggling. Two members of the Fornasari family occupied two of the rings. When they finished, Phil Chandler introduced himself as "the Amazing Chandler" and went into Ring Two to perform his magic tricks, which were quite spectacular. He stuffed Linda into a small basket, ran swords through its sides, and ended up by removing the swords and kneeling inside the basket himself, with Linda still inside. Then he did a levitation trick with Linda, and he ended up by locking her in a trunk and raising a curtain around it while he stood on top. Within four seconds Linda had appeared on the outside. She unlocked the trunk and Phil was inside.

The hand-juggling acts were next. Two members of the Fornasari family juggled in two of the rings, and eleven-year-old Armando Cristiani, whom Phil introduced as being nine years old and the world's youngest juggler, went to work in the third. The display ended with all three of the jugglers handling flaming wands.

The Murillos, the two men who had driven on the lot in the ex-rental truck, performed their high-wire act. It was disappointing; they just walked across the wire a few times and came down. There was no net. Then Bert Pettus put the "military ponies" through a routine. The women who had done the Spanish web came back and swung from the aerial ladders.

The Fornasaris came on and did their musical-clown-family routine. They were followed by Gilda Cristiani's uncaged-leopard act, in which Gilda performed with two large leopards in Ring Two. They were on leashes.

The McGuire sisters came out with what Phil called their "feathered fantasy." Margaret stood by the ring curb and released doves, which flew through the air to Maureen. On opening night, some of the birds got their directions mixed up, and two of them roosted for several hours on the top of the tent.

The big elephants followed—Myrtle, Bonnie, Sue, and Hazel—and they performed just as they have performed for dozens of years, waltzing in time to the music, spinning when they were told to, ending up in a big elephant pileup that made them seem twice as big as they really were, which was pretty big indeed. Then came the Cristiani riding act. Lucio and Gilda and Tino took their horse around the ring just as in the old days. Gilda looked like a lovely teenager as she pirouetted daintly on the back of the flying horse. Lucio pulled his drunk routine; he entered from the audience in a raggy jacket, announced that he wanted to ride the horse, and of course he did, very well.

The Astros, who were also the Murillos, would have been next. Luis Murillo was to have ridden his motorcycle up the wire, and Jorge Del Moral would have sat on a trapeze that was cradled beneath the motorcycle. But the important part was still missing, and the Astros did not perform on opening night.

Then the show was over. Phil reminded the audience that those who had missed the sideshow and wild-animal menagerie would have another chance to see it now, and he hurried from the tent and changed into his other costume for the sideshow bally.

Between the end of the first performance and the beginning of the second, Jorge Del Moral explained why he and Luis Murillo had done so little on the tight-wire. A wire walker's

The McGuire sisters and their birds

wire must be really tight, and for that reason guy wires are attached to it at intervals. The guys run out at angles to the ground, where they are tightened, and this causes the main wire to stay taut. The guys were not properly tightened tonight, said Jorge, and so the men didn't do anything that was too risky.

Hoxie drove onto the lot. It developed that he had decided to leave after the first show opened and be by himself for a while. He looked in good shape when he got back. A man walked over to the cotton-candy booth and looked around for someone to wait on him, and Hoxie saw what was happening and he sold the man a stick of floss. "That'll be forty cents," said Hoxie. The man dumped some nickels, dimes, and pennies into Hoxie's hand. Hoxie looked at the money for an instant and said, "You're a nickel short."

A friend of Junior's, who was a lion-trainer on another circus, had watched the show, and now he stood in the front door saying hello to people. He said he thought Junior had left because he was afraid the cats would attack him again. "It happened to me, and I know how he felt," said the man. "It happened to me at a five-thirty show. The next show, I went back and worked, and then I wasn't able to work for nearly eight days. But I knew if I didn't get back in there right away, I might not *ever* go back in there. It's like somebody has a car accident. Unless they go back to driving a car right away, a lot of times they get scared. If you lose your nerve, you'll never do it.

"Junior hadn't been in the arena for nearly a year. Both times he was in he got hurt. And, you know, it's a terrifying experience, even for somebody like myself, who's been doing this for twenty years. It seems like you get the butterflies just as much after twenty years as you did the first time you went in. I sympathize with him, and I know how he felt.

"I was here when it happened. In fact, I helped run the lions out. He got a pretty bad gash through his right hand. He was hung by a claw. They took him to the hospital, and they stitched him up, which they never should have done. And then he got an infection and his whole arm swole up. A lot of times you can't get that across to a doctor. Claw marks, see, they have to drain. You have to keep them open. Teeth marks are even worse, because a cat's teeth aren't sharp, and when they bite you they bruise the entire area. It's pretty painful."

The second show started. There was a lost child, and the camel did not make Spec. After the show was half over, Bill Hill and Johnny Walker showed the canvasmen how to take down the marquee. Already the circus was coming down, getting ready for tomorrow's move. Betty Tucker was on the midway, and she asked how things had gone, and I recounted the camel incident. I told her it looked as if Joe Hamilton had done a pretty courageous thing. He had been taken to the hospital in an ambulance, along with the woman who had fallen from the seats.

"Was he the tall boy with the orange coveralls?" asked Betty. I said he was.

"Well, I sure hope he didn't tear those coveralls. They were brand new."

The season had started. It would not end for two hundred and two days, and before it ended Hoxie Brothers Circus would have played in one hundred and seventy-eight towns, villages, cities, and hamlets, in all sorts of weather, on all kinds of lots. The hundred or so people who called themselves the circus would have traveled up the East Coast, through the mountains, and into the Midwest in the spring, when the rains would come, back to the Northeast and into Jersey, and then back down the coast to home, and by the time they made it back all their lives would have been changed a little. Some of them would not make it back. Along the line, there were others waiting to take their places.

And along the line there were children waiting to see the circus. And adults, too, perhaps less outwardly excited about the prospect, but still carrying within themselves some childhood memory of the Big Top and the animals, and the performers and the food, of the sounds and the smells, a memory that was also a wish, a wish that could be satisfied only by going to the circus again. Phil Chandler made his announcement at the end of the second show about how the circus needed young men to stay and take down the seats, and a dozen of them stayed to make their three bucks. A young woman stayed, too, and she wrestled the heavy boards up on the fork-lift just like everybody else.

I asked her why she had stayed. Partly it was because of the money, she said. "And partly it's because it's something I haven't done yet."

2 ON THE ROAD

SUNRISE

The trucks left well before dawn. After the last performance, the men had taken all the props and lumber and rigging out of the Big Top, and they had loosened the quarterpoles and the cable that held the bail ring up, and the big tent had fallen to the ground with a *whoosh* at about midnight.

Then they had unlaced the canvas and folded it, and the spool truck had gone around eating it up, and the poles and stakes had been collected. Leo had walked Bonnie around the stakeline; she had a harness on and a chain attached to the harness, and Leo had snatched the chain a few turns around each stake and had given the signal, and Bonnie had lifted the stake from the ground as if it had been a toothpick in a mound of cream cheese. Everything had been packed on the trucks, and the men had slept for four hours or so. Then Bill Hill waked them, and they moved to Sunrise.

The performers and some of the bosses slept a little later, and then they, too, moved. By the time the sun cleared the condominiums to the east, the lot in Sweetwater was well on its way to being a vacant lot again, one with a few mobile homes parked on one side of it. The weeds had received some nourishment from the nightime dew, and they were starting to recover, to lift their heads again toward the sky. Even the clumps of coral seemed to be regenerating themselves, although you knew that was not possible.

It was a relatively short hop. We went around Miami on the Palmetto Expressway, then north on Highway 441, through contiguous bedroom communities, running against the morning rush-hour traffic, until we hit the suburb of Sunrise. The lot was a small field next to a Jewish temple; the committee here was the Men's Club of Temple Beth Israel. The community around the lot was obviously upper middle income, and it was new. It was a tight lot, but there was plenty of water. The temple building had three or four outside faucets, and the show people filled their water tanks and some of the workmen put on bathing suits and took long, soapy baths.

The lot was surrounded by the temple and its school and by housing. It was difficult to see where the workmen would

relieve themselves, but every once in a while you saw one walking off the lot. Johnny Walker told Alice, his wife, and Debbie Caldarea, who worked in the concession trailer, that there would be no hot dogs in Sunrise, because the ones the show had weren't kosher.

The Big Top was up in front in about five hours, an improvement over Sweetwater, and already things seemed to be falling into place, into a routine. The performers pulled in one by one, and they seemed to remain aloof from the rest of the circus people. Perhaps aloof was the wrong word. Just apart, maybe, because the performers' whole lives were built around what they would do later in the day, and this was the only time for them to relax in their trailers. An exception was the Cristiani family. Gilda walked the baby leopard almost every morning; she wanted to get the animal used to people and to commands, so it could be used in the cat act later.

Lucio got out and inspected the lot. He did not like this lot at all. It was coral, too—not as bad as Sweetwater, but still bad enough to pose a threat to his horses. And he knew the show would not haul in dirt for the horse ring today; that was something that was done only on special occasions, such as opening night. Lucio joked and talked with the prop men. Tino and Armando were outdoors almost all day, exploring and playing. Armando practiced his juggling so much that his parents warned him about becoming exhausted.

The Murillos spent a large part of the day looking unsuccessfully for their motorcycle part, so late in the afternoon they started putting up their wire-walking rigging.

Several workmen left the show, complaining that they needed something more substantial than "tomato and rice soup" in order to stay alive. The cook had fixed what he called Spanish rice for them for the noon meal. One of the workmen who stayed, the tall, skinny man who always wore a watch cap, and who had become known as Slim, said he didn't like the short rations, either, and that if they kept up he was going to leave, too. Stash, who had no love for Slim, told him that it would probably be to the show's benefit if Slim left.

♦

Two of the workmen were discussing Wahoo's fate. One of them said he had learned from an unimpeachable source that Hoxie had given Wahoo to the man who owned the dairy farm. "If that's true," he said, "I'm going to feel mighty bad."

Joe Hamilton came limping out of the sleeper. He had returned during the night from the hospital. "The ambulance man said I rode three-point-eight miles for a Camel," said Joe, smiling. He said he had gotten five stitches in his leg from the cuts. Then he started recounting the events of the night before.

"I could have gotten out of the camel's way," he said. "But I *do* work for the organization, and it was better for me to try to catch him than it would be for him to run into the crowd. And I knew the ponies wouldn't do that. I figured they'd probably do what they did, which was run around the track. And I was under the impression that a camel was like a beast of burden, and that they were rather tame animals. And suddenly I found out that that was one strong camel."

Somebody said that Joe seemed to feel pretty good about his first day on the road with a circus.

"Sure," he replied. "What better way to do it? That's kind of what it's all about, you know. *That's* what the audience is here to see. I think a lot of these people are really sadistic. They *want* to see people make mistakes. They'd *like* to see that guy fall off the high wire. They *like* to see that camel running around. That's what it's all about, for some of them."

A moment later, Joe confessed that the real high point of his evening had been finding the donniker at the hospital. "They had a beautiful set of bathrooms right in the emergency room," he said. "A women's and a men's. The men's room was spotless. I saw it and I couldn't resist. I went right in!"

At quarter past five, the band and Phil and Linda and Harry gathered outside the entrance to the sideshow. The band tuned up a little. Jeff Woosnam knocked off a little Brandenburg Concerto on his sousaphone. Then King Charles gave the signal, and the band did a few Dixieland pieces. When they played "Sweet Georgia Brown," that was the sign for the sideshow grind to start. Phil mounted the platform.

The crowd was all gathered at the Big Top entrance, not around the sideshow. Phil's first job was to get them to reassemble in front of his platform.

"Now, ladies and gentlemen, girls and boys," he said, "a very special announcement. First of all, I don't know who it was who started the line down there. *This* is the way you get into the circus. So if you'll all gather around here, we have a very important announcement before the show starts. There seems to be a little bit of confusion regarding the tickets and this sort of thing. Come on in close, so you can hear everything that I'm about to tell you."

The crowd on the midway dutifully came over to the platform.

"Now, first of all, we would like to welcome each and every one of you to the midway of the Hoxie Brothers Three-Ring Circus. . . .

"Now, ladies and gentlemen, a lot of times, when people come onto the show grounds, they miss the biggest portion of the circus. Now, this is where it all starts. The same man who owns that tent over there owns all this in back of me. And he is not going to let you miss one thing.

"Now, first of all, the animals that are displayed in there —most of the animals that are displayed in there—are *not* seen in our Big Top. And I'm sure that you people, when you come to the circus, you want to see everything. Now let me explain to you a little bit about what you're going to see on the inside here. First of all, we have Hoxie Brothers' performing elephants. . . . Also we have the humpbacked camel, zebras, llamas, the baseball-playing monkeys, the black-maned Nubian lion. They're all inside right here, plus a little midget horse from the lost canyons of Arizona. He's right inside here; the boys and girls can see him and pet him.

"Now, not only do we have wild animals, but we have a few domesticated animals, just like a big petting zoo and wild-animal sideshow combined."

The crowd was not yet convinced. The psychological moment that Phil and other sideshow talkers always waited for had not yet arrived. So Phil continued.

"Now wait a minute. Listen to me carefully. You just don't come in here and look at animals. In just a few minutes we are going to bring out a few performers who are *not* seen in the big show. A few select performers that are quite unique and a little bit different. We'll bring them all out here."

The band started a low, rambling number that is usually associated with a striptease dancer. Harry and Linda climbed up the ladder to the stage.

"Now, as I mentioned before, you do not go in here and just see animals. We have a few select acts. A few select acts. The gentleman standing on my far right, from Paris, France, is the world's champion fire-eater. This man swallows fire, eats fire, and he blows a ball of fire as big around as a bale of cotton.

"The young lady on my immediate right over here, she is our Electric Girl. A strange phenomenon that I'm sure will amaze and mystify you. She defies all laws of electricity, and I'm sure that you'll enjoy seeing her work. Plus we have the funny old magician in there; he'll keep you laughing by the hour. All in all, it's a great big show.

"Now. I told you about all the big things that we have on the inside here. There's only one small thing about this, and that's the price. Now, people worry about two things— time and money. Well, you've got the time, because you've got, oh, I would say, possibly a good twenty, twenty-five minutes before the main show starts. And as I said before, the man who owns this show is not going to let you miss a thing. He *wants* you to see everything. Don't be disappointed. So this is where it all starts.

"Do you have the money? Well, that you only know. But the price is less than a jumbo hamburger. Everybody goes on a child's ticket, and that price is just fifty cents." (There was no such thing as an adult ticket for the sideshow.)

Phil had turned the tip, in midway language. He had turned the crowd—the "tip"—around and was now about to turn some of them into the sideshow.

"Now, right over here is a man who'll be happy to wait

on you, to sell you a ticket to get in. Over here we have another gentleman who will be only too happy to wait on you and send you right on in to see the Hoxie Brothers big sideshow and menagerie and petting zoo. All the features that we told you about. . . . Bring the kiddies. A lot of fun for everyone. Hurry right along now. . . . Everybody goes on a child's ticket, just fifty cents. . . ." Phil also reminded the crowd that there was on view inside, at no extra charge, the mummified body of an Egyptian princess, some forty-seven hundred years old.

The mummy was real, although there was no certainty that she was a princess. Hoxie had rented her from a man in the East, and he insisted that the University of Chicago had authenticated the body, which was mostly bones and which was encased in a plywood coffin covered by glass. Each day four workmen carried the mummy, pallbearer style, from its storage space in the office wagon to the sideshow. It was also a fact that the baseball-playing monkeys seemed always to be between innings. The black-maned Nubian lion was old Clarence, who was spending his declining years largely in sleep. The leopards were one jaguar. The midget horse was a baby pony. The wild animals were housed in dark, dank cages on the back of a truck that had been pulled into the sideshow tent. But, through the season, hardly anybody complained of being clipped out of his fifty cents. The elephants really *were* there, up close, and kids in town after town squealed with delight when they touched their trunks.

Johnny Canole walked through the back yard, waving at old friends and thrusting his ball-point pens on newcomers. Johnny was sort of a visiting archbishop in the circus world. He sold cars, trucks, and mobile homes to show people from two locations, Altoona, Pennsylvania, and Miami. Almost everybody in show business had one of Johnny's ball-points. "Save Money with Johnny," they said on the side. Often Johnny took ads in *AB,* or *Amusement Business* (old-timers still called it *The Billboard*), the weekly newspaper of the outdoor entertainment industry, thanking someone for buying a trailer. Johnny visited shows whenever he could, and a season's opening was somehow incomplete without him.

Now he was on the lot in Sunrise, smiling and looking prosperous. He conferred with performers who were in the market for new rigs; he slipped a little folding money to Art Duvall, who was waiting to open the back door; he conferred with the curious on the rumors about Junior. He was "virtually certain," he said, that Vargas had offered Junior seven hundred and fifty a week. Johnny moved from performer to performer, boss to boss, workman to workman, chatting and offering ball-points. In the old days a priest used to come out to the railroad shows on opening day, blessing the train and distributing wishes for a good season. Johnny Canole was the mud-show equivalent of this.

The six o'clock show started more or less on time, and everything seemed to be going according to schedule. The crowd was small; about two hundred and fifty people turned up for the first show. Phil Chandler finished his magic routine and walked back to the microphone to introduce the next act, the Murillos. "Fantastically Fearless Feats by a Dauntless Duo of High-Wire Daredevils," said the program. Tonight the wire seemed to be guyed out much better than in Sweetwater. The two men walked it forwards and backwards with great agility, and you could see that the previous night's performance had been just a skeleton of what they could really do.

At one point, Jorge Del Moral walked to the center of the wire and he squatted down. Luis Murillo walked up behind him, hesitated a moment, and jumped over Jorge. He landed on the wire on the other side, but as he touched it the wire moved slightly and Luis fell. Luis grabbed the wire in his hand momentarily; then he fell through the air. A prop man, Paul Jordan, ran to get under Luis, and Luis's body struck Paul's with a glancing blow, but most of the shock came when Luis hit the ground. He lay there motionless. For a moment everything was quiet, except for a few screams from people in the audience who had seen the fall. Then King

Charles went into the music for the next act. Bert Pettus went right into Ring Two with the ponies as if nothing had happened.

They called for an ambulance on a police radio, and after several minutes the men got a stretcher under Luis's body and took him away. One of the canvasmen who had been around shows a long time said that these things went in threes, and that this was number three. Paul Jordan was very distressed. "I got his arm," he said, "but I couldn't get enough of him." Someone asked if Paul had been underneath the performers just in case something happened. "That's what I was there for," he said.

Bert Pettus stood at the back door, ready to take the big elephants in. He seemed to have taken something of a liking to me, and one way he was expressing it was by trying to educate me in the traditions and sayings of the old days.

"Punk can mean two things," he said. "It can mean a kid, a child. People would refer to a young boy or even a young girl: 'Get the punk out of the way.' It also means the baby elephants.

"In the cookhouse, in the old days around a circus, punk was also bread. And you'd sit down at the table, and when you wanted the sugar, you'd say, 'Pass the sand.' And butter was referred to as axle grease." Bert spat a copious brown stream on the ground.

"There are so many things that these people don't know today," he said. "Listen, when I broke into this business, you had to be there and ready at least two acts before your act. Just like when that guy fell. If I hadn't of been here when he fell, the act wouldn't have been ready. They *taught* you this, you know? And another thing they taught you was you didn't walk around in the show. If you weren't working in there, you didn't go in there. You didn't smoke a cigarette in there, and when another act was working you stayed the hell out of there. Hell, today they'll walk clear through the ring when you're working."

I mentioned that the night before, in Sweetwater, I had noticed that he had walked the babies halfway around the track toward Ring Two before his act was announced.

"I was doing that for the simple reason that the poor little guys were walking on that coral, and I wanted to walk them slowly to as close to the ring as I could without hurting their feet, rather than running them.

"I'm the boss elephant man here." Spit. "And if I figure I'm hurting the animals, I think I ought to have a say. Just like Cristiani and his horses. He won't take his horses in there and work them on bad lots. But most of these circus people, or so-called circus people, which is damn few today, they don't respect the elephant at all. All they want is for him to be there when he can work. The management has no feelings for the elephant. I'm not talking about this management alone; I'm talking about *all* of them. The elephant has no feelings, as far as they're concerned, you know. He's just an animal that can do what they want done, and the hell with him after he's done.

"They cut his rations. They come into winter quarters cutting his food, say, 'It's all right, he ain't working. Cut it down.' But not me. If he eats a hundred pounds of hay a day out here on the road, give him a hundred and twenty-five in winter quarters, because he's got more time to eat it there.

"So this is where me and a lot of managements get into a lot of trouble with elephants. Course, I've never been fired off a job in my life. I usually explain to them what the score is, though. Course, I've had one or two of them that didn't like it. They didn't want to come up with the money to feed them. But as long as I was in charge of them, they did.

"Like those poor little old babies. Their feet get so sore. *Mine* are sore from walking on these rocks. Just imagine what those poor devils were going through."

The Cristianis did not ride their horse in Sunrise because of the coral.

We sat in the back yard, talking about the fall. Mike McGuire came back from the hospital with the word that Luis had suffered a "severe muscle strain of the back." Nothing was broken, but it would be a while before Luis was back with the show.

Jorge Del Moral and Paul Jordan had a drink or two and discussed the fall. "This is the first time I've ever gotten paid for working the high wire," said Jorge. "Now, I haven't gotten paid yet, and I doubt if I'll *get* paid. This is the second time, actually, counting Sweetwater. And now here Sun—What is it? Sunshine? Sunrise."

Jorge was twenty-two years old, and many of his relatives were in the circus business, mostly in Mexico. Someone asked him if it had been a traumatic experience.

"That's hard to answer," he said. "I was shocked, of course, just like any other human being would have been who was in my position. It's just a thing that happens on the spur of the moment. You really lose your head a little bit. Obviously I would be lying to you if I said I knew exactly what I was doing and all that bullshit. It's not true. It sure was a big shock. It happened so quickly. It's like he is my brother. He's been taking care of me."

Luis was from Chile. He had been in the United States for fourteen years, and before that he had been a high-wire walker in his homeland. He was an extraordinarily friendly man, full of fun despite the conditions of his life: he lived in the truck, without running water or privacy; it took hours for him and Jorge to erect the rigging for their two acts, which lasted only a few minutes each.

Paul Jordan said, "He didn't jump far enough, and he was off balance when he hit the cable. He didn't jump far enough. He came down on his right foot and—"

Jorge interrupted. "No, it wasn't the jumping, sir. If you would have realized—the rigging, for one thing. You have a guy line in the center. The reason why it's there is because it's not tight enough without it. The wire was a little tighter than it was in Sweetwater, but it still wasn't tight enough." Jorge was assuming that Paul knew nothing about high-wire rigging. "We had to set most of the rigging by ourselves. And we were tired. We didn't have five minutes between the time we got it up and the time we had to run out there for Spec."

Paul Jordan was a little tipsy now. "I've only been forty-three years in show business," he said. "I was born on a circus." And then his life spilled out. He had been married to a Wallenda. They had split up. Paul had been a prop man with the Wallendas, a job that is very important, since so many lives depend on the proper setting of the rigging.

He talked about accidents that had happened with the Wallendas. There have been many of them. He said he was a fifth-generation circus person on his mother's side. Then Paul drifted back to what was really bothering him. He said he thought he should have caught Luis.

"The minute he hit the cable, I knew he was going to come down. And he didn't tell me he was going to do this, or I would have been prepared. I would have been over there. But he didn't tell me he was going to do it. By the time he got into position, I knew what he was going to do, but then it was too late. If he had told me he was going to do that ahead of time, he never would have hit the ground."

Might he have broken your back?

"No. No. I've got too strong of a back for that. He would have been maybe bruised a little bit, but that's all."

As we talked, the Cristianis' baby leopard got out of its cage nearby. For several minutes it silently stalked the Cristianis' poodle, which was minding its business by the side of the trailer. The Cristianis were inside, eating their dinner. Then the leopard pounced. The dog put up a terrible barking, and Lucio and Gilda came out and separated them. Lucio unleashed a torrent of profanity in Italian, but he said later he knew the leopard was only doing what its instincts told it to do.

DAVIE
AND THE DRAW

The lot was called the Davie Show Grounds, but it was a wholly inadequate site for the circus. Last year the show had played Davie, but since then some of the land had been sold off for condominiums, and the lot was not large enough for the Big Top. Johnny Walker got to the lot before daylight and tried every way he knew to squeeze the tent on, but none of them worked. He planted a slender metal stake in the middle of the field and stretched a chain out from it. The chain represented the radius of the Big Top, and it extended halfway across a paved road next to the lot.

"You know," said Stash, "if we hadn't had bad luck in the past few days, we wouldn't of had any luck at all."

I asked John Hall what he did in a situation like this. He replied, with his usual reserve and a small, brief twinkle in his eye, "Solve the problem."

John called the fire department and asked for permission to erect one portion of the Big Top out over the road, leaving one lane open for possible use by emergency vehicles. The fire department said okay. A workman walked along the road with the chain, putting dots of fluorescent paint from a spray can down where the stakes should be. Other workmen followed him, hammering thin metal stakes through the asphalt. Elsewhere, on the ground, they used thick wooden stakes.

The lot was dark sand, like those of Sweetwater and Sunrise, but it was blacker and more powdery, and it got into your shoes, and before long your whole lower leg was black. There was no coral, though. Davie used to be an upper-middle-income community, the locals said, and rather horsy, but in more recent years it had fallen into the condominium craze, like everyplace else in this part of Florida, and it looked junky. They were building a set of condominiums just a hundred yards away, on land that used to be part of the show grounds.

After a few hours the Big Top was up, looking strange because it was partly on the street and because it was so obviously bigger than the land beneath it. John Hall thought he had the problem all solved, but then the police chief and an assistant came and said the stake line would have to be moved off the roadway. There was no way to do that without moving the tent. John politely explained that "you need the stakes to keep the tent up." For about forty-five minutes, the authorities and John talked, and in the end there was a compromise. All show vehicles would be moved off the road; the ends of the street (which was just a block long, anyway) would be barricaded to traffic and parking; and the tent would stay where it was. There would be rescue apparatus standing by in the event of some catastrophe.

The police went away, and I asked John how he handled a problem like that. "You've got to stay polite and patient," he said. "If you lose your temper, then he'll lose his, and he's got the authority behind him, and he'll tell you to take the whole thing and get out of town. You have just got to be quiet and patient with him, and reason with him, and show him some alternative answers in hopes that he'll pick one of them."

John Hall was an extremely cool person, and it was tempting to speculate on how worked up Hoxie would have gotten in a similar situation, but Hoxie was not with the show this day. To many of the show people, John was something of an enigma. He was the general manager, and yet he was not a rough or rambunctious person at all. He hardly ever got angry. He was thirty-nine years old, with straight black hair. He was six feet, three and one-half inches tall, and he weighed two hundred and fifteen pounds, and he was a great presence when he appeared in the front end or the back yard, or when he was helping the elephants tighten the quarterpoles. But, like many big people, he hardly ever *used* his size or his weight. John never fought, never cursed, didn't drink, and didn't smoke. He did not gossip about other people. Everything he did, he did with the utmost in coolness. And yet you always had the feeling that things were churning inside of him, that all of the tensions that seemed to roll off his back and shoulders were somehow ending up in his stomach.

Some of the circus people coped with their inability to understand John Hall by referring to him as a "circus fan" who happened to work with the show.

A circus fan is a towner who is in love with the circus. Some of them belong to organizations of fans, and many of them turn up on the show grounds on circus day, walking through the back yard and greeting the performers and bosses and sometimes handing out photographs they took a year before. Some of them are quite bothersome, but most of them aren't. They genuinely love the circus, and they do what they can to keep it alive and healthy. When a circus person refers to someone as a circus fan, the term can be used with approval or it can be a put-down. It can mean the same thing as calling somebody a "fire-engine fanatic" or a "police buff." When one of the people who worked with the Hoxie show referred to John Hall as "just a circus fan," it was a derogatory comment. Some of the detractors even resented the fact that John's and Lisa's car, a bright yellow Volkswagen, had a Florida license plate that spelled CIRCUS.

John knew all this, but he seemed not to be bothered by it. He moved smoothly through the seasons with the show, knowing that the circus would get its share of hard times and that he would get his share of criticism, and knowing that the proper way to deal with such trouble was with forbearance and patience. The show went on in Davie that day, despite the quality of the lot and the objections of the police chief. Luis Murillo was still in the hospital, and Jorge Del Moral had stayed behind with him, and that left a big hole in the program, but John calmly started rearranging the schedule so the customers would still get a first-class show.

Johnny Walker

⬤

Johnny Walker was philosophical about the whole thing.
When the word came to go ahead with the Big Top, Johnny let
a smile run across his big, cherubic face, and he said, "Regardless of what the lot's like, you're here today and gone tomorrow.
You've got to get it up and get it down, regardless. Carry it in,
carry it out. And when it stops being like that, there won't be
no more mud shows. That's what they call this show. Anything
on trucks they call it a mud show. And when you hit them *nice*
lots, that's when you feel good."

Gypsy Red sat in the cooktent, eating soup with his own
spoon. His hair was faded red, and his features were those of a
black man, but his skin was light. I asked him how he got his
name.

"When I was a little kid, growing up in show business," he

said, "I'd always go from one show to another, trying to make them all in one season, me and a friend of mine. And the name got attached that way—'Gypsy,' for going from one show to another, always traveling, here today and gone tomorrow. There was two of us running together, and one of us they called 'Yellow' and the other they called 'Red.' Everybody thought we was brothers.

"I was born in show business. I go back as far as 1931, my first circus, Al G. Barnes. I was born on the Reuben and Cherry; it was one of the largest carnivals. My mother was a chorus girl and my father was a musician."

They say you shot somebody in the stomach last year, when you worked on the Beatty show.

"Oh, that was an accident. That was in Commack, Long Island. That was last year. I didn't shoot him. He pulled a pistol, and I grabbed his hand, and it went off. And they couldn't prove that I did it, so they reduced the charge to attempt assault. He had the pistol. I would have been out a long time ago if they could have found him. They couldn't find him. It happened on a Wednesday morning about one o'clock, and on Saturday morning he came out of the hospital and left town. But I admitted that I hit him with my fist, so they charged me with assault. Attempt assault.

"A pistol's a bad thing to have around a show. I been in many a fight, and I never cut nobody. I never shot no one. I was working on the canvas then."

Is that what you mostly do?

"Well, mostly around shows I do anything, you know. Like here, I'm playing in the band. That's my job. But if they need an experienced man to set seats and rig a pole or guy out or something—you know, push the men, teach men how to work—well, this is an extra job for me. It pays extra. And I drive a truck, too."

Can you make a decent living doing that?

"Oh, yeah, I can make a decent living. I don't have a mother or father, sister or brother, wife, or nothing like that. I'm by myself now. So I make a decent living on the salary I get on the trombone. This is something extrey here, working canvas. Something that if you're a *showman,* you like to do it anyway.

"Some people say they're in it for all the money they can get. Well, everywhere you go it's like that nowadays. People are in it for all the money they can get out of it. *Real* show people are different. Like when Hoxie gave his little speech the other night. He says he's going to stick with it as long as he can, and he hoped to die under this canvas. Well, that's a real showman that says something like that.

"A lot of people, when it rains you won't see them. They disappear. A real trouper, a real showman, the first thing he thinks about when it rains is his boots. And his raincoat. He don't care where he walks, he knows he's got his boots on. A lot of people, they run and hide when it rains. They in it for the bread. The fair-weather people, we call them."

Do you like the outdoors?

"Oh, yeah, I like the tent circus and the carnival. I travel a lot with carnivals sometimes. That's another reason they call me Gypsy. I'm here one season and then I'm gone to a carnival another season. I like the environment. I go around a circus maybe a year or two and then I get a yen for a carnival. I want to stay a week at the time, the way a carnival does, instead of moving every night or every morning. And the pay is just about the same."

Do you think you'll be here all season?

"I *got* to be here all season this year, because I blew the season last year. I got no clothes, you see. The things I left over on the Beatty show there when I got in jail, well, that stuff just disappeared. I didn't even go to the winter quarters and ask about it. I said there ain't no use worrying about that. I'll stay here, and I'll make enough to close the season with a good bank account that'll last me the winter, and I can draw unemployment this winter."

Harry, like Bert Pettus, had taken it upon himself to educate me on the subject of the circus. Maybe he was so despairing of having any younger people on the show to whom he could pass on his knowledge that he decided to pass it on to a towner.

"The circus is built as a family," he said, "as a small city. For seven to nine months the people live together, as a big family, or a small city. That's why you won't hear much cursing, because they wouldn't allow it in their own families.

"Same way with chasing. A man who works here can chase outside the show, but the actors have their own class. It's a feudal class system. There are three classes here—the actors, the bosses, and the workers. And they don't fraternize." I thought about Jeff Woosnam, who at that moment was tossing a Frisbee with Armando Cristiani. What about musicians?

"They're in the class of the actors. They have a function that is necessary, absolutely necessary, and if they don't work the actors can't work, because they get the cues from the music."

What's the punishment for people who break the class rules?

"Gone. There's a warning and then you're gone. And that's a lot nicer than it used to be, in the old days." Harry led me to believe that in the old days the punishment, in extreme cases, was death. "Falling" from a moving train at night; being knocked out and then having the Big Top rolled up around you.

What about sex? It seemed to me that the circus was a large group of men, with relatively few women around.

"Not necessarily," he said. "It's the other way around. You know, a young man goes to the next town, and he finds there's more sex in the next town than there is in his own home town. In the next town, they know he's going to go back to his town and nobody's going to say a word. So as you move with the circus from day to day, every single day, changing towns, many of the town people who wouldn't indulge in extracurricular fantasies, or whatever you want to call it, will, because they know the circus will be gone in a matter of hours.

"If a canvasman wants a little bit, he goes down to the nearest bar and he can get more than he can handle, every single day, seven days a week. No problem. Because the women in town who are married and who want to run around will come down and beg for it.

"Sometimes they come down here to the lot and walk around and beg here, too. They let you know about it. There have been three makeouts so far on this lot that I know about. Without paying attention I know of three, already."

It was Wednesday, and between the shows the workmen lined up at the office wagon and got five-dollar draws on their salaries. They walked straight off the lot and over to the main road and into a liquor store and came back with bottles of Mad Dog and six-packs of beer. Stash got a dozen Busch Bavarians and sat on the pole truck, drinking most of them. Leo drank half of his six-pack while he was walking back from the road, and he went straight to the cooktent and started raising hell.

When some men get drunk, they think of nothing but sex. For others, it is the oppression of their wives or the conditions of their work. For Leo, it was almost always the food. Leo and the cook had a running battle over the quality of the food served on the show, although it was difficult to understand Leo's side of the argument because of the way he talked. "He could have been reciting the Declaration of Independence and you wouldn't know it," said someone once.

It was clear on this occasion, however, that Leo was very much down on the peanut-butter-and-jelly sandwiches and vegetable soup that the cook had fixed for lunch. The cook was having his own troubles getting enough money out of the show so that he could buy decent food for the men, and he raised hell back at Leo. He suggested that Leo butcher one of the elephants and he would turn out lots of steaks.

That was the wrong thing to say to Leo, for Leo was a true elephant man, and a true elephant man loves elephants. He thinks of them as his babies. He spends almost all of his time, waking and sleeping, in the company of elephants; he is, more than anything else, in thrall to the animals. The suggestion that violence be done to one of Leo's elephants was the worst thing the cook could have said. Leo stormed out of the tent, knocking over bottles of catsup and peanut butter with his bullhook, and vowing never to return.

The cook laughed and announced to the other workmen that the evening meal would consist of macaroni and cheese.

Leo and one of his elephants

"I'm terribly sorry," he said, "but the ham isn't ready yet. And they failed to deliver the wine for the punch." By that time the majority of the workmen were half-drunk, and they missed the humor completely.

Not only had the committee steered the circus wrong about the quality of the lot; it also had failed to sell very many tickets. Davie was an all-round bad lot.

There was a show of municipal responsibility that rivaled Sweetwater's. Police cars blocked off both ends of the street, and there were a couple of uniformed policemen on the lot, and an ambulance was parked on the road in case it was needed. Nobody fell or otherwise hurt himself in the show, though, and by the time the second performance started the ambulance attendant was reading a paperback book.

I walked around the Big Top to see what was going on in the back yard. Halfway around I met Slim, the workman who always wore a watch cap. His face was covered with blood; it was starting to collect in his eyebrow and his eye. He was carrying a suitcase.

"Stash did it," he said. "Stash did it." He was crying. "I want a policeman."

I called the ambulance driver, and we got Slim on a folding stretcher outside the ambulance. The attendant turned on a spotlight on the rear of the ambulance and started looking at the cut. It was over the right eye, and there was a lot of blood.

"Tell Hoxie he can't keep any men on this lot. This is why. The same thing happened last year. Stash got drunk and did the same thing last year. Him and another guy tried to kill me last year. At the main lot. Winter quarters. He slammed me into a sharp truck-gate. Started kicking me into it."

The ambulance man was trying to see if Slim's eye was cut. He was treating Slim with professional respect, as if he had been a member of the audience, a respectable citizen of Davie. Slim was dirty and he smelled bad and of Mad Dog.

"It happens *every* week to *somebody*. And these people, they don't do anything about it. They don't get rid of the people like that. I'm going to go right downtown and I'm going to press charges against the whole Hoxie Brothers

Circus. Because I hold them reliable for something like this."

John Lewis came hurrying over. Lewis Brothers had not gone on the road yet, and he was still helping out with the Hoxie show. He looked at Slim and surveyed the situation for a moment, and then he said, "When you mess with shit you get shit on you."

Slim asked John to go to the office and get the money he had coming. "Get my money from the office, John, will you, please?" He was crying again.

"Now, you know that we pay off on Saturdays," said John.

"Well, I won't be here to get it. And I'll never get it if I don't get it now."

The ambulance man said, "Don't worry about your eye. There's nothing wrong with your eye."

"If I don't get it now, I'll never get it, and I know it."

Where did it happen, Slim?

"Right back there. You know where those stringers were on the trucks? He was on me ever since I was out there working. Like yesterday the girls, the sisters, they wanted me to carry the pigeons into the front door, and I helped them. And he was mad about that."

"It's going to take some stitching, quite a few. He's opened outside of his eye, to the bone above the eye. It's opened down to the bone. And he has about a two-inch cut across the eyebrow that's going to take stitches." The ambulance driver's voice was dry and clinical, but it was not without compassion.

Two policemen arrived, and then two plainclothesmen came. Slim saw them out of his left eye. "He says, 'If you talk to the po-lice about me, I've got somebody who'll come to the jail and kill you.'"

"The police are right here, sir," said the ambulance man.

"That's what he said. He said they'd come right into the jail."

One of the uniformed policemen spoke. "How old are you, Mister . . . ?" Slim shook uncontrollably.

"Are you cold, sir?" The ambulance man was watching for shock.

"No. I'm just nervous." They covered him with the blanket.

Slim gave me his billfold. I looked through the cards, but his age was nowhere.

"Just get my money out of the office for me. Because I know I'll never get it if I don't get it now." Harry appeared, and Slim repeated the request.

"Okay, don't worry about it," said Harry. "You've known me for a good many years, so don't worry about it."

The policeman asked Slim's age again. Slim said he did not know his age. Someone gave him a cigarette. Another policeman, one of those who had been on the lot all evening, came up and said he believed Slim had just staggered into a wagon. He said he didn't see anybody hit Slim. The policeman was grinning sadistically.

"I did not," said Slim. "Stash did this. Stash is the one that done this."

"William"—the policeman now knew Slim's real name—"have you got a permanent address?"

"No, unh-unh. Right now just with the show."

"What's your age?"

"I don't know. He's got it there. Get my money from the office, please. If I don't get it now I'll never get it. I'll never get it." He started crying again. The circus music was throbbing in the background.

"Take a big breath and hold it for me, okay? Take a big breath and hold it, Bill." The ambulance man no longer called him "sir." Slim was sobbing and shaking now and asking everybody who came up to get his money for him. Harry said, "Harry's here now. Quit that, now. Stop that baloney."

"Somebody, please."

Harry: "You had bad luck. You've had bad luck before, you know. that. Hold yourself down. I'll have a bottle of wine for you when you get back."

"I hurt. I hurt. I hurt. I hurt."

"There's nothing wrong with your eye, Bill. I checked it. There's nothing permanently wrong with your eye. It's just the only way I could bandage it. The cut is above your eye. The only way I could bandage it to stop it from bleeding was to cover your eye. There's nothing wrong with your eye,

I promise you. You believe me? There's nothing wrong with your eye now. The only reason your eye is covered is that I had to stop the bleeding just above it."

The cop who had been in the back yard said to Slim, "I don't know how you got that."

"*I* know how I got it."

The ambulance man: "Believe me, Bill, believe me. I've been in this business a long time. . . ." There was no indication that Slim was really worried about his eye.

"I ain't never bothered nobody."

The ambulance man: "People get drinking, Bill, there's no telling what they're going to do. No telling what's going to happen." From his voice you could tell that he had changed his opinion of Slim. Slim was a wino now, rather than a respectable citizen.

"I've never bothered anybody like that. I used to go off by myself and drink, because I don't fool with such people." Slim said that this was the way it happened: Stash had hit him; he had decided to leave the show; he had gone back to get his suitcase; another man, whom he did not know, had then attacked him. "I'm not a fighter. I don't fight with nobody. I don't care to."

"Where are you from, Bill?"

"Virginia."

"Where in Virginia?"

"Staunton." From the other side of the canvas came the words "A double somersault."

The plainclothesmen, a sergeant and a lieutenant, had been listening to all of this. Now the sergeant started asking questions.

"What's your date of birth?"

"January—February fourteenth, 1932."

"What's your home address, William?"

"My mail in Florida is Miami general delivery. That's where I get my mail."

"You have any address?"

"Not really. Just the show, and wherever I decide to live. Hotel or something."

"What happened, William?"

"Same thing that happened last year. He got half loaded and he started the same fucking shit last year."

"Fist fight?"

"No, I didn't even try to hit him."

"What'd he hit you with?"

"He started banging on me and knocked me into the trailer and stomping me and—"

"What's his name?"

"I don't know. They call him Stash."

"Does he work for the circus also?"

"Yes." Slim looked toward the sergeant. "Please get my money from that office. Because if you don't I'll never get it." The sergeant ignored the request. The uniformed policeman told the sergeant that he had seen Slim run into the side of a trailer.

"I did not. I honest to God did not run into the side of that trailer. I'm not lying. My mother is a bitch if I did. I *swear* I didn't. I swear to God that I did not. I was *beaten* into that trailer. Stomped into it."

The sergeant: "You know the guy?"

"I know him when I see him. The guy who done this job on me, I know him I see him."

The sergeant: "What's his name?"

"They call him Stash."

The sergeant: "Who's in charge of the circus here?" Someone told him that John Hall had been summoned.

"You can't believe anything these people tell you. They'll tell a lie just to get out of trouble. And I know this."

The sergeant: "Did he hit you with anything?"

"No, he hit me and knocked me into the trailer and kept stomping me into the trailer."

The sergeant: "What'd he hit you in the head with?"

"He hit me with his fists. Knocked me into the trailer and then started stomping me into the sharp part of the trailer. And after I fell off the trailer he started stomping me into the ground. Kicking me in the back."

The ambulance man: "He's ready to go, as far as we're concerned."

Slim raised his head toward the lieutenant, who had been silent. "Will you listen to me just a minute, please?"

"Yes."

"Anything that you ask these circus people, they going to tell you a lie just to get out of it. I know. I've been around them too long. I know this. They all stick together like glue."

The lieutenant: "How long you worked for them?"

"I worked for them the last part of the season last year, and I just started back this year."

The sergeant, who was shorter than the lieutenant, took stock of the situation, and said, "I want this man Stash. If he doesn't show up in fifteen minutes, I'm closing this place down." It sounded a little dramatic. From the background came Phil Chandler's voice: ". . . jungleland fantasy. Presenting at this time Miss Gilda and her uncaged leopards."

John Hall walked up. "Both of these men, officer, are employees of ours. And they both got draws today. Wednesdays the men get a five-dollar draw. And, like a lot of people, they take this money and they go straight to a beer joint and drink. And both of these men were drunk, and they got to fighting. That's what happened. And a lot of people, in circuses, downtown, everywhere in the world, get to fighting when they get drunk."

John had been talking to the lieutenant, who so far had remained sort of neutral. The sergeant interrupted him. "They're not going to do it in Davie, I guarantee you that, mister, right now. I want to talk to this Stash right now. I don't need any excuses. I want to talk to him."

"All right," said John. "But I wanted to explain what happened. They were drunk." John towered over the cop.

The sergeant came down a little. "I can understand that, because I can smell this one." He gestured toward Slim on the stretcher.

"Okay," said John. "It was just two drunks fighting each other."

The sergeant calmed down a little more. "Okay," he said. "We want his whole name and all that."

"All right," said John. "We've gone to get him."

While they were waiting, the lieutenant introduced himself. His name was Jim Andres. Andres explained to John that "if he wants to file charges, the fellow who was assaulted, he can come to the police department and file charges. I doubt if he will. But if he should want to—I imagine they'll settle it among themselves."

"I think so," said John. "I think when they sober up they'll be friends again."

Andres: "I know how show people are. I used to work with—"

Hall interrupted. "Both of them have been here quite a while, and I don't think it's a real problem."

Andres: "Yeah, I used to be a catcher years ago."

Hall: "Oh, yeah?" He sounded as if he were not taking it all in.

Andres: "Yeah. With Lamar. Long time ago."

Mike McGuire walked up. He had heard the last exchange.

"Yeah?" he asked. "What's your name?"

Andres introduced himself. Mike said he didn't recall the name. Andres said that had been a long time ago. Mike said that, well, he had caught a trapeze act himself one time, and he had worked with the Wallendas. Before long the two men were jackpotting. The sergeant looked perplexed about the whole thing.

"You know ———?" Mike said.

"Sure."

"———'s a floor cleaner out in Hollywood now. The last I heard he tried to make book in a beer parlor out there and they got him."

The ambulance pulled off. The siren was not on.

"You know ———?"

"Sure I did."

"What's he doing?"

"He's dead," Mike said.

"You kidding?"

"No. He died of too many pills four years ago."

"That's hard to believe."

"Yeah. You know, he kind of lived life to the hilt."

"What do you do here?"

"Oh, I just work in the office. You know, I only caught for one season. I get seasick, you know, hanging upside down." Mike was always belittling himself. In addition to having been a trapeze catcher, he had been a member of the most famous wire-walking troupe in the world.

"Yeah, I got a torn shoulder."

A man walked up. "This is Stash."

The sergeant took over. "What's your name?" Stash told him. He furnished his date of birth, and he explained that he had no address other than the show.

"What happened?"

"Well," said Stash, "as you probably heard, this is about our third day out on the road. This man was with us last year, and he's a habitual drunkard. And I saw that we had work to do this evening before the last show was over, and he was a little bit woozy, and, you know, it was 'Mother-eff you,' and he swung at me. And the next thing I know he was running, and it was someone else chasing him."

"Did he run into a trailer?"

"I didn't see him. He took off running and he lost my vision, and I told him, 'I'm not going to put up with you being drunk. Don't raise your hand at me, because whether you're drunk or you're sober, talk to me tomorrow. Go to bed.'"

The sergeant: "Okay." Stash walked away.

When he was gone, I asked Lieutenant Andres if his position was that nothing would happen unless Slim pressed charges.

"Right," he said. "Which in most cases they don't. Show people usually work things out. But we still have to make a report."

Are show people different from other people?

"No. But they take care of their own, though. They might be different that way. Because they do take care of their own people."

A little later, I talked with Stash.

Did you beat Slim up in winter quarters?

"Yeah. I beat his ass in winter quarters."

Did you beat him up tonight?

"I didn't beat him up. I smacked the shit out of him, though." Stash smiled.

He said you told him that if he filed charges you'd hurt him. Is that true?

"I don't see why it should be. Why should he be hurt? The only way he would be hurt is if he would be put in the same cell with me. There's no way that he can prove that I hit him. The protocol on the show is that you catch a thief, he's in a lot of trouble."

You mean that was what it was all about? That he was the bear?

"Right. Like I said, protocol. You catch a thief, and you make him pay."

The next morning, as the trucks and trailers were moving off the lot at Davie, Slim appeared in the company of John Lewis. Slim's face was all puffy and black-and-blue and bandaged, and he wore his watch cap. He said he had gone to the police station and sworn out a warrant for Stash, and that the police were looking for Stash. He said he had decided to work with Lewis Brothers, to keep away from Stash. He said he had twenty-seven stitches over his eye, although it looked like fewer.

Slim went off with John Lewis in John's car that morning, headed back to winter quarters and the Lewis show. On the way, while he was sitting in the back seat, Slim involuntarily moved his bowels on himself and the car, and John Lewis ordered him out of the car and drove off.

JOHN HALL

Coral Springs was a big, beautiful lot, level and wide and covered with short, thick grass. It was in the middle of sort of a mini New Town that the Westinghouse people had built. There were apartments, houses, and condominiums all strategically scattered around the grounds, with pleasant little shopping centers and an air of sterility and conformity. There was deep green grass everywhere.

Underneath the grass, said the men who were driving the stakes, there was tough coral, because there was coral under almost all of this part of Florida. But Westinghouse had covered the coral with soil and planted grass. It was a fine lot; the finest one so far.

And it was big, and a circus needs a big lot to show itself off properly. The day before, in Davie, everything had been jammed into a tiny space, and the show had looked junky and tattered. Here there was room to maneuver; to lay out the Big Top in the central place, to complement it with the sideshow tent and the midway, to give the circus the sensation of enormity that it deserved and required if it was to live in any children's memories. The trucks and trailers in the back yard fanned out from the back door the way they should have. The lot made a difference in people's tempers and temperaments. Even some of the workmen seemed contrite about the previous night's orgy, and they, too, seemed to be *celebrating* the new lot a little in the way they talked and worked.

Superchicken and the canvas

There was a feeling in the air that the bad luck was over for a while and that the house would be full tonight. Overhead, there were lots of thick, fat clouds, but they were not the sort that meant rain.

Superchicken eased himself out of the sleeper and adjusted his eyes to the new lot. He said, when I asked him how he was, that he was in great pain. "You see," he said, "I had this meeting last night with Mr. James Beam." He produced an empty bottle with Mr. Beam's name on it and threw it under the sleeper. Then he got his cánvas bag together and went off in the direction of the Big Top. Before long he was patching the little holes and tears that had occurred the day before.

Harry blew the show this morning. He gave no reason, or

at least no reason that I could detect; he simply packed up his belongings and left. He spoke to few people on his way out.

Bill Hill said he liked the lot. He had not been surprised about the fighting in Davie. "It's just like downtown in a bar," he said. "Two guys fighting. It's like two guys working for Reynolds Metals or Standard Oil. They don't like each other, never have, so they fight. I worked for Westinghouse Electric right after the war, and two guys got in a fight and one guy bit the other guy's ear off. They fight all over the world, don't they? The circus ain't no different."

What was the chance that some of the trouble had to do with the condition of the lot in Davie? It was a rotten lot, and maybe it had depressed people.

"No," said Bill. "Just the fact that they got an advance in their pay, that's the only thing. And the beer joint was too close. We should play closer to churches and further away from beer joints."

What percentage of the workmen would you categorize as alcoholics?

"Oh, Christ, I'd say about eighty per cent of them. I've worked guys that had college diplomas. And some of 'em're preachers, too. But somewhere in life something happened. You know what I mean? Because I've talked to a lot of them. You get a good guy, he's good and intelligent, stays clean, washes his face, wants to live like a gentleman, and as soon as he gets money he gets on a drunk. And goes haywire.

"I had a guy tell me one time, I asked him, I says, 'What the hell makes you do that? You're a perfect gentleman, you stay clean, and everything.' And finally he told me, he says, 'Bill, I spent four years in the Second World War. I had a family, four kids. And when it was over my wife didn't want me.' He said he had a beautiful job in the post office before he went. And when he came back, he couldn't throw it off. Some guys can and some can't. And he became a drunk.

"Another guy one time, same deal. Well dressed, stayed clean and everything. Payday—blip, he went out. And I talked to him and I asked him what happened. I said, 'Something must have happened.' He says, 'I had one child. Twelve years old. She was riding a bicycle and she got run over. Killed her. From then on I couldn't get it out of my head.' Some people can get it out, some people can't get it out, right? And that got him on booze and there he is. That's his life now. There's a lot of other things that'll do it. If you could analyze them all, something would come out. Something in their life."

But something bad apparently didn't happen in *your* life?

"No, because I was small. I was only fifteen years old. I had a good home. But I just didn't want to go to school. And then when I finally got on a show, I liked it, and I stayed with it. And I'm just lucky that in the fifteen years that I *did* stay at home, I had a beautiful family. I was raised as a Catholic, and it stuck with me, what I had during the little time that I had."

Bert Pettus was angry about what had happened the night before, partly because the workmen's drunkenness had caused the elephants to work harder than they needed.

"They stood right in the *back door* drinking," said Bert. "This just don't happen around a show. I mean, if that's the kind of men they are, you don't need 'em. The show's still gonna move; there's enough of us sober and reliable to move it if we have to. So my idea would be to take a club and go back there and knock them goddamn in line, if nothing else."

Was that a problem that might straighten out as the season wore on?

"No, it probably won't." Bert spat on the grass. "We're gonna keep on getting these mission bums. Ain't worth a damn. I guess they figure they got to have them. I *don't* figure that. I figure that if a man can't do his job, I don't need him. If I gotta come in here and do his work, I'm sure as hell not going to pay him to watch me do it. That's *my* motto on it. I'm supposed to be the boss. If I gotta do his work, I'll take his salary."

Bert acknowledged that he had put up the sideshow tent largely by himself that morning, because he had wanted to show some of the new men how to do it efficiently and without breaking their backs. He was angry because so few of the bosses seemed interested in teaching people how to do the work.

"We've got one or two others, but they ain't interested in showing anybody. When Mr. Tucker gets here, he can do a lot of straightening out.

"One thing he can straighten out is feed to the elephants. That hay out there ain't worth a damn. They won't even eat it. It's no good. It's rotten. It ain't even hay. If elephants eat that stuff, they'll get sick. It's just some kinda old grass that some bastard rolled up and baled up and is charging a buck thirty a bale for it under false pretenses. I'd like to stick his goddamn head through one of them bales and smother him to death. It's just not right to take a man's money for shit like that."

When the crowd came for the first show in Coral Springs, they turned out to be as neat and conformist as the homes they lived in. Those who had not yet bought their tickets formed a neat line in front of the office wagon, and when the line got long they formed a neat curve in it. Nobody tried to break in line. When they had the tickets they formed two more neat lines in front of the entrances. Phil Chandler had a devil of a time getting them to come over to the sideshow. Those who did go in had a lot of ten- and twenty-dollar bills, and they were dressed nicely, and their children were dressed nicely. A lot of kids rode around the lot on new ten-speed bicycles, and this bothered some of the old-timers, because a bicycle on the midway is a sure sign of bad luck.

Inside, when the Spec started, the audience applauded voluntarily. They applauded again when it was over, and they applauded without urging throughout the show. It was a well-mannered, orderly, upper-middle-class crowd. There were two full houses that night. During the first one, there was a small problem. Margaret, the more amply endowed of the two McGuire sisters, was climbing the Spanish web and about to go into her routine when one of her bra straps broke. She descended gracefully. A policeman who was watching said, "Whatever happened to 'the show must go on'?"

John Hall watched the beginning of the first show, saw that all was well, and started toward his trailer, where Lisa was cooking dinner. A member of the committee walked up to him and said, "I hear you've had some problems." John asked him which problems he was talking about; there had been so many in the past few days.

John Hall was eight years old when he saw his first circus. It was the Dailey show, and it had elephants, and one of them was Myrtle. She was full-grown then. John saw the show at Halifax, Virginia, where he had been born on May 16, 1935. "I fell in love with the business instantly," he once said. "When I first saw the circus, I knew this was what I wanted. I was only eight, but I wanted to own a circus from that very time until the present day, and someday in the future I plan *to* own one."

Few circuses came to Halifax, because there were so few people there, but once or twice a year a show played South Boston, which was five miles away and which was larger, and John always went. Then he would go home to the Halls' tobacco farm and literally dream about the circus.

"One of my jobs, when I was small, was to cut down the tobacco stalks at the end of the season," said John. "I used a long knife. And I made a game of this. We had maybe twenty acres of tobacco stalks that I would cut down. And I would lay out a circus in these fields. I would cut the stalks in such a way that, if you had a bird's-eye view, you would see the Big Top there, the sideshow tent, the horse tents, the dressing tents, the midway tents. And, of course, my family, and anybody driving down the highway, thought it looked a little bit odd. They couldn't figure out what it was. But I knew *exactly* what it was. And then, of course, eventually I would go back and cut down all the stalks."

When John was in the eighth grade, Hoxie brought his circus to Halifax, because Halifax was not too small for Hoxie. "It was on the school grounds," said John. "His Big Top was smaller than our sideshow tent is now. He had two rings, but they weren't too big, and he had no elephants. He had about four or five trucks, and that was twenty years ago. They had nine acts. I can remember very clearly almost everything about the show."

John had an older brother, but he was fourteen years

John Hall

older, and so John was essentially an only child. He became
a loner, and loners are people who cherish their memories of
loneliness. John remembered walking two and one-half miles
to school in the morning in the winter, and hands so cold when
he got there that he had to wait a while before he could un-
button his coat.

When he was eleven, he still was gripped by the circus
fascination, and he heard that Ringling Brothers, which was
under canvas in those days, would play at Lynchburg. It
was the fall of the year; Lynchburg was sixty miles away, and
John's father was busy getting the tobacco crop ready for the
market. "He wouldn't take me," said John. "I was very determined that I was going to go. And I had in the bank, in my
own name, four hundred and thirty-five dollars which I had
made on my own tobacco crops since I was eight years old.

"And my schoolteacher in the sixth grade kept me after
school one day, and that made me mad, so I decided that I
was going to leave home right then. This was about ten days
before the circus was due in Lynchburg. So I asked my mother
the next morning to let me see my bankbook. And when she

went into another room, I went out the front door. Instead of going to school, I went down to South Boston, waited for the bank to open, went to the bank, and took out the four hundred and thirty-five dollars. And I went to a bus station and took the first bus out of town.

"It just happened to be going to Lynchburg. So I went there and I spent two days around there, killing time. I was going to kill time for ten days, see the circus, and then go home.

"In Lynchburg there were four movie theaters, and I went to all four of them, and then at nighttime—I was a little afraid to go to a motel or hotel, because I thought they'd call the police for an eleven-year-old boy coming in there. So the first night I got on a bus that went to Washington, D.C., which was about two hundred miles from Lynchburg. This gave me a chance to sleep, and I had never been to Washington. My parents had gone there on their honeymoon, so it was a town I had heard them mention."

John got to Washington at two in the morning, hung around the bus station until eight, and caught another bus back to Lynchburg. He saw all the same movies again, and then returned to the bus station. He saw a map of the United States on the wall. "Out by Oklahoma City it had a little Indian tepee on it," said John, "and it said 'Indian Reservation.' I had never seen any Indians. So I thought I would go out to Oklahoma, see the Indians, come back to Lynchburg in time to see the circus, and go home."

Were you worried about what your parents might be feeling?

"I wouldn't let myself think about this, because that would probably make me homesick."

John went to the train station and bought a ticket to Oklahoma City, with changes in Cincinnati and St. Louis. All day the following day he was on the train; at eight o'clock in the evening he arrived in Cincinnati. He stepped off the train, and a man walked up and said, "Hello, John."

"This surprised me," said John, "because I didn't think I knew anybody in Cincinnati. This man was a plainclothes detective. When I didn't come home from school, my father went looking for me. He found out I hadn't been in school. He checked with the bank, found out that I had taken the money out, checked with the bus station and found that I had gone to Lynchburg, and he went to Lynchburg. They announced it on the radio stations, and the railway ticket agent who had sold me the ticket heard the announcement and told them I was on the train to Cincinnati. So they wired ahead and had the detective come down and pick me up."

The authorities in Cincinnati called John's parents, and while they were waiting for the parents to come they lodged John in a jail cell, and then took him to a reform school to spend the night.

"The next night, my father came on the same train and picked me up and took me back home," said John. "He didn't punish me at all. We missed the circus in Lynchburg, but about two weeks later he took me to see it in Durham, North Carolina. He felt perhaps a little guilty, but he realized that I was so determined, that I wanted so much to see the circus, that he probably felt it was safer to take me than it was to take a chance again on my running away."

In John's fantasies he insisted, from the very beginning, that he wanted to be a circus *owner*. "I didn't associate with the lion-tamer or the wire walker or a clown or anything. I think most young boys would do that. But I always wanted to own a big circus, and I wanted it from that very early time.

"I made a model circus out of cardboard and toothpicks. Later on, after I finished college, I made a model circus that looked real. I used toy trucks, and I made my own tents and little figures and so forth. I made a lot of my own games, because I had very few toys as I was growing up.

"One thing I did because I was a loner was read a lot. I was very fortunate that on the grounds of the school I went to was the county library. So I read many books from the library. When I was very young, I found two children's books on the circus. And these I stole from the library and kept.

"All my life I've read a great deal. I love knowledge, and I love to pass on knowledge to people who're interested. But

I never give it to them unless they more or less show an interest."

John spent seven years in college, because he could not make up his mind about a career. He studied architecture at the University of Virginia, but he didn't like the idea of five years of study and then three years as a draftsman, so he changed to education. He became active in the Baptist church in college, and further changed his plans: he would become a foreign missionary.

One of the requirements for missionaries was two years of teaching experience, so John moved to Florida and taught at a fancy finishing school in Palm Beach. "But I decided," he said, "after I came to Florida, that the mission field wasn't what I really wanted. I wanted the circus more than anything else. So I decided to get into the circus business."

John entered the business by an indirect route: through carnivals. Although to many people the two fields are not all that different, they are. A carnival almost always sells *things* to people—rides, food, novelties. Often there are sideshows, but what they offer is passive entertainment of a slightly perverse nature—a glimpse at the freaks, a look at the girl in the iron lung, an opportunity to study a human embryo in a glass bottle. Sometimes there are girlie shows, offering the towners something they cannot get in town. A circus is show business, as different from a carnival as the legitimate stage is from a movie house. A circus offers active entertainment—people displaying their prowess and sometimes challenging death and injury, almost always in a manner that is considered in good taste. A carnival usually stays in one place for several days. A circus is here today, gone tomorrow. Circus people consider themselves more a part of show business than carnival people do. Circus people believe they have more of a tradition. The feeling of superiority extends even to the workingmen, whose jobs in a circus and a carnival often might be interchangeable.

At any rate, John bought a kiddie ride and put it on the James E. Strates midway, and he ran a funhouse and a couple of sideshows and a spin-painting stand, and he lost money. "And I decided," he said, "that the circus was what I really wanted, and that the carnival was just a substitute for it, so I joined with Hoxie." That was in 1965. John was trying to sell some of his rolling stock and buy a truck, and he was in Johnny Canole's office in Altoona, and Hoxie was there. They had lunch together. Six months later, John looked up Hoxie in Florida and said he wanted a job. "I was broke and I needed a job, and I didn't want to go back to teaching," said John. "I had quit teaching twice, and I was kind of determined that the last time *was* the last time." Hoxie hired John to work in the office.

"The show was small then," said John, "and Hoxie had always done everything himself. He had some office help, but I started working in the office and making it more efficient. I started doing things that I saw needed to be done. I was always finding work for myself to do, and I was always assuming more and more responsibility, and just working like the devil to try to improve the show."

Hoxie remembered that John also spent a lot of time trying to dodge his creditors. "My phone was ringing all the time, people wanting to know where John Hall was," said Hoxie once. "Finally he got it all paid off." At first, Hoxie thought that John was like everybody else; that is, that he was weak in one or more ways. It confused Hoxie when he saw that John was not interested in dope, alcohol, or paregoric, and that the women John was seen with were always high-class. So Hoxie concluded that it must be money.

"When John came here," said Hoxie, "I hid money everywhere around him to *make* him steal, and I ain't never made him steal to this day. I put money *all around* him. And he'd tell me, he'd say, 'Go get that money.' It'd been laying up there in that closet or wherever I hid it, three or four weeks, or months, waiting for him to pick it up. John would say, 'Get the money. I ain't going to take it.' John just ain't made that way. You know, I don't have a son. If I had a son, I'd want one like John Hall."

♦

Why was it the circus? If John wanted office work, couldn't he have worked anywhere?

"Each person has his own answer about why it is the circus," said John. "I think basically that circus people just love the circus. That is their thing. And for a lot of circus people, there's a certain amount of freedom involved. Circuses allow people to be themselves. They get to travel and see the country. They're not hung up on some of the restrictions that they might have.

"It's hard to explain. The best way to explain it, I guess, is to say that some people seem to be born in life to do certain things, and since the time I saw my first circus, I've always wanted to join the circus. It was just a very clear-cut, strong desire from the very first time I saw the circus. And this is why I say it's almost like being born to this particular idea—like I came into this life to do that."

John said that last with something like a strange light emanating from his eyes, and it was clear that he was talking very seriously. It was not as if he were saying he was born to be in the circus business, as some people might describe themselves as "born to fly" or "born to raise hell." It sounded as if John meant there was some Force which ordained that he be doing what he was doing. I asked him if that was what he meant, and he said yes, it was.

He was starting to tell me about his belief in reincarnation, and in the occult, and in alpha-waves and the lost continent of Atlantis, when Hoxie knocked on his trailer door. Hoxie's hat-brim was way down; he had heard all about the troubles in Davie, and he was very angry. For the rest of the day, anyone who crossed his path got himself handsomely straightened out.

HEADING NORTH

Okeechobee was the season's first jump of any real distance, a hundred miles in all: up the coast and into the center of Florida, around Lake Okeechobee, which meant "big water" to the Indians, and on to the town on the lake's northern side. Below the lake lay the Everglades and the coral and black sand and condominiums; north of it the palms disappeared and the real citrus country started, and beyond that, eventually, there was the rest of the United States.

We left behind the suburbs with names chosen by committees and bankers, names like Sandalfoot Cove and Boca Madera, plastic places, whose names bore no relation to reality, and the plastic institutions that served them, places called Dunkin' Donuts and Burger King and Chicken Unlimited. It is easy, fashionable, now, to call these places plastic, but there is no more descriptive word. They are creatures born of television's triple spots and the conglomerates' lusting after growth at the expense of craftsmanship and individuality. The people's houses all look alike, and the cars and palm trees in front of them all look alike, and the water in their toilets is a uniform blue, and they all eat the same bad food, most of it coated with and soaked in strange-sounding compounds, the rest of it bought "fresh" at the supermarket chains, wrapped in clear plastic so you cannot smell the clean, cold air in an apple, cannot touch an onion's covering of thin tissue.

Their luncheonettes, those places that used to serve an

occasional slice of real apple pie and a palatable cheeseburger, now have disappeared, and in their places people in suburbia drop by Seven-Elevens, which open before seven and close after eleven. They have machines that drop a premeasured dose of Taster's Choice into a disposable cup with some hot water, and that is what they call coffee. They give you a characterless plastic paddle to stir it with. You accompany the coffee with a plastic-wrapped sandwich that was made in some other city and that is heated in a little oven.

Every store is a World. Shopper's World, Rug World, Pet World, Wig World, Cheese World, Tire World, any kind of World you can name and then some. And inside these Worlds there is more prewrapped garbage, the garbage tiny in comparison to the size of its blister packaging, all of it guaranteed forever if you send it back in the original carton and packaging, along with two dollars to cover handling. It is, of course, not worth two dollars to begin with. But the people in suburbia have been trained better than most to buy things, and not to complain when those things fall apart.

People actually live in these places. In fact, *most* people in the United States live in these places, and they turn their lives into plastic out of choice, to be sure. Or maybe out of fear of niggers or hippies or "urban unrest," and maybe out of some belief that life Out There will be good for their children. The schools are always high on the list.

Who can really blame them for being there? It would be unfair to call the people in Sweetwater and Sunrise and Davie and Coral Springs plastic; they are real people, underneath their blister packaging. They are just trying to make ends meet, just trying to provide better things for their children than they themselves had, and they are the sort of people who go to circuses and smell the lions and occasionally step in the elephant shit and manage to take it all in their stride, and maybe even cherish it a little. At least once a night I was approached by an anxious father or mother, towing a child in an obvious piss-tight, inquiring where the bathrooms were. At first I was embarrassed when I had to reply that there were none (at some of the towns the committee rented plastic donnikers, and I was pleased to direct them there), but later on I began to lose that embarrassment, and I suggested that the parent take the child around by the side of the Big Top. Every child should have the experience of urinating on the ground at least once before he or she is absorbed into the mainstream of American life. Every child should be able, at least once, to share something with a circus workman.

The farther we got from Coral Springs and the other suburbs of Miami, the less plastic it all got. We were paralleling the beaches that, for many Americans, *were* Florida—Fort Lauderdale, Pompano, Delray, Palm Beach—and the circus world would never get to see those beaches. Jeff had wanted to swim in the ocean, but he had not yet had an opportunity. He had not even seen salt water. The Dunkin' Donuts petered out, and there were more places with rustic signs offering Bar-B-Q. There were fields that advertised you could pick your own tomatoes. Then long stretches smelling of fertilizer; longer stretches where the road ran alongside canals; oranges and onions and grapefruit and celery by the mile. A huge farm, with signs warning against trespassing, broken only by a migrant-labor camp, and then the store that sold things to the migrants. On the road, the splattered carcasses of little animals that had tried in the night to make it across the macadam to the canal for water. Giant fields of sugar cane and, with them, even more no-trespassing signs. A crop-duster, an old-fashioned biplane, strafed a field maybe fifty feet off the ground, and then it turned around some imaginary pylon and came back, and I stopped and watched until it was done, and I wondered if the pilot was having as much fun as he seemed to be having. Maybe it was just a job for him.

In Okeechobee, John Lewis immediately found a hole-in-the-wall restaurant that had the best catfish in Florida, and when they brought you the menu they asked you which three of six fresh vegetables you wanted. And there were hush puppies and iced tea. Several of Okeechobee's streets were unpaved, and people rode around in pickup trucks, and when we took the sound truck out to advertise the show a lot of people waved.

The lot was right in the middle of town, a sandy field where towners came and stared un-self-consciously as the Big Top was going up. It was a country town, as much a country town as Coral Springs had been suburbia. It wasn't *too* country, though; the committee had installed a half-dozen portable donnikers, and the workmen welcomed that.

The circus people seemed cheerful, more so than usual, and one reason for this was that they were really on the road now, out of Miami at last, and another reason was that the next two days would be spent in Melbourne, on a two-day Shrine stand in a shopping center, and that meant almost the same thing as a day off for many of the workmen. For everyone it meant that they could wake up more or less at their leisure on the second day and not worry about traveling. Bert Pettus was not happy about the two-day stand, though. "You get out of the rhythm of the thing when you stop," he said. "And if you stop moving you get lazy. I'd just as soon work seven days a week, straight through."

Somebody told Gypsy Red that the show would almost certainly play Valdosta during the season.

"If we play Valdosta," said Gypsy Red, "you're going to have to get someone else to play in the band."

"Why?" someone asked. "Are you hot in Valdosta?"

"Hotter'n I was in Indiantown," replied Gypsy Red with a smile.

"That's some hot."

"It sho is."

Phil and Linda Chandler always parked their rig in pretty much the same place, slightly to the right of the back door, where Phil could see what was going on in the back yard. As the ringmaster, it was his job to make sure the show started when it should and that the performers were in the right places at the right times. This was no major problem, because most of them were as professional as Phil himself, and they always started showing up at the back door soon after Phil blew his fifteen-minute whistle.

Phil was thirty-eight years old, of medium height, black

hair, bags under his eyes, slightly prominent teeth. He looked several years younger than he was. He had a fine sense of humor, and he was extremely competent. Linda was very attractive, with blonde hair, and she was obviously very intelligent. She was handy, too. She was always sewing jewels on costumes, or making tiaras out of cardboard that she would cover with fabric and spangles, or working on her trapeze. Linda was hoping she could perfect a single-trap act in her spare time.

They lived in a twenty-four-foot-long, eight-foot-wide trailer, which they towed behind a three-quarter-ton pickup. The pickup had a built-up compartment in back, and that was where they stowed the props for the magic act.

Phil's parents had wanted him to be something along the lines of a banker or an accountant in Dayton. His father was a twenty-four-year veteran of government service, said Phil, "and my mother's been Harriet Housewife all her life." The family used to go down to Dayton's RKO Keith theater on Saturday nights to watch the vaudeville and to listen to the big bands. When Phil was a child, he told his parents he was going to do that someday. "And what was funny was that ten years later, when I got into the business," he said, there in Okeechobee, "I played that same theater. It made me very happy. I played the theater where I first really wanted to get into the thing."

Linda, too, was the product of a middle-class family. She was athletically inclined, and in the summers while she was going to college she worked as a counselor at Girl Scout camps. When she finished school, she became a high-school English teacher in Perrysburg, Ohio, which is near Toledo and also near her home town, Maumee. In the summer of 1971, King Brothers Circus played town, and Linda went to see the show. "They needed someone to work the animals," she said, "because some of the girls were going back to school at the end of the summer. So I went along, and I liked it better than teaching. I like the out-of-doors, and I like performing, and I like animals. It's better than being cooped up in a schoolroom all day." Linda's first act was with a flock of goats. She lived in half a truck, with two other people. In the other half were the goats.

"There was no running water," she said. "They did have air conditioning, which was nice, but we had to take bucket baths outside. It was very cramped, very crowded." The following year, 1972, Linda had her own compartment, in the office trailer. It, too, was mostly bed, but she had privacy for the first time. Then she made a total commitment to the circus, and bought a car and a trailer.

It was in 1972 that Phil first heard about Linda. He was doing magic in an indoor show, one that played various schools, and he was at a low point in his life. He was going through a divorce, and he was broke most of the time. Some of the other performers kept telling him about Linda Karl on the King show. In 1973 Phil signed for the season with King, "and two of my first projects were to get well financially and to get Linda." He had competition from a man who worked the elephants.

"He had about a two- or three-year head start on me," said Phil. "But he was kind of a floater. Not that *I* had that much to offer, having four children by a previous marriage and a stack of bills that high."

But Phil succeeded, and he and Linda got married, and Linda got a couple of new names. She had been Linda Karl all along; now she was Linda Barr (Phil's real last name) and Linda Chandler (the show-business name) and Renee, the Sweetheart of Magic (Phil's first wife used to assist him in his magic routine, and the publicity pictures and flyers still referred to the assistant as Renee). "Since I got Linda," said Phil, "I got rid of that stack of bills. I got myself together mentally, physically, and everything else. And I got a new truck and a new trailer this year. We decided we would either go first class or stay at home."

Now, said Phil, he was delighted with his wife and with the show. "I am, though, truthfully, a *building* showman," he said. "I love to play in buildings, like the Shrine dates and the Grotto circuses. But they are few and far between, and the hassle you have to go through is tremendous." He ex-

Linda and Phil in the magic act

plained that when you worked inside you often spent a lot of time just traveling to get to a two- or three-day date, and you weren't paid for the traveling time. And there could be long periods of inactivity between jobs. "Last year, when I was on the King show," he said, "the manager said something that was very true. He said the only way you can make money in this business is to get with one of these tent shows and stay the season with it.

"You have a nice long run. And you learn to live with the mud and sand and all that crap. If you stay the season with one of these things, you're not going to get rich. Not on the salaries they pay on any tent show. But it's *consecutive.* The pay comes every Saturday, and if they pay for your gas, you've got it made. You've got nothing to worry about. You can bank some nice money at the end of the season."

Then there's no question that you'll stay the season?

"Damn right. Because this is the best show. I've looked around. This is the best of the tent shows. Because the management cares."

"They don't just worry about making a buck," said Linda. "They worry about what the show looks like."

"Some of the corporation shows—the circuses that are owned by corporations—they could care less what the damned show looks like," said Phil. "This show, they *care* about the production. On the corporation shows, it's 'Get the people in, get your money, and run like hell.' That's their motto.

"And Hoxie. You know what I like about Hoxie? He don't stand for no shit. There is only one king, and he's it, and he's a damned good one. He runs the show like the show should be run."

Across the lot, on the bull line, a young man with long sideburns and a straw cowboy hat beat the elephants without mercy. His name was Cowboy Jim. When he was not beating the bulls he was threatening to beat them, and when he wasn't doing that he was talking bad to them. I found myself wishing one of them would get fed up and snap her trunk at him. Whenever Cowboy Jim made a menacing move toward

Myrtle, Myrtle would flinch and let out a little squeal, as if in fear.

"You do it mostly to keep them in line, you know," he said. "They know what the hook is, and they know what it does to them, and so you don't hit them so much as you draw back to. You draw back to scare them, and you scare them and they'll do what you tell them to."

When you hit them on the forehead, does it hurt them?

"No."

How do you know?

"Because if you hurt them, they'd holler, wouldn't they?"

How long have you been a bullhand?

"About a month and a half."

What'd you do before that?

"I've been with the circus about a month and a half. I laid asphalt in Ohio before that."

Jim was twenty-four, from Appalachia. He said he liked his work. "I'm going to stick to it," he said. "Get back!" He screamed at Myrtle, and he raised the bullhook as if to hit her, and she made her little squealing noise and backed up.

Both performances in Okeechobee drew strong houses, and there was something distinctively different about the evening. People came in late for the second show and didn't mind paying the full admission. Others, who had been inside, strolled out and walked around on the midway and then walked back in. Little crowds of people gathered on the midway and talked and then broke up. It was Friday night, and this was a night out on the town for a lot of the people, many of whom worked in the citrus camps. They were treating it more like a country fair than a circus performance.

Okeechobee also brought the first black people of the year. The suburban towns had been almost entirely white; now whites and blacks and Indians milled together in apparent equality, at least until the show was over and some of the whites got into the cabs of pickup trucks and some of the blacks and Indians got into the back and they started back to the farms. Many others stayed on after the show was over, standing and talking and smoking and watching the Big Top come down. There were no rescue squads, no policemen, firemen, or ambulance drivers, on the lot at Okeechobee. If you got into trouble here, you'd have to get out of it on your own.

An ancient black man with only one finger on his right hand tried to take down the marquee all by himself. He was doing it all wrong. I asked him how long he had been with the show, and he replied, "Six years." I had never seen him before that night, and I never saw him after it.

Because tomorrow was the Shrine date in Melbourne, and because it would be Saturday and the first of the three shows would be early, at one o'clock in the afternoon, we moved out of Okeechobee at night. Ordinarily, Hoxie's show moved early in the morning. It was a hundred and ten miles to Melbourne, and the rolling stock didn't start arriving at the new lot until one in the morning.

Hoxie got there at three in the morning. He had driven up from Miami earlier in the day, and he had checked into a motel and slept a little, and then he came to the huge shopping center to watch the trucks come in and to help lay out the lot. John Lewis was there, almost ready to go on the road with the Lewis show, and he drank some beer and talked about the tourist trap he used to operate. The cook truck came in, and the cook started to set up his tent, and John told him he was doing it all wrong. Then Hoxie came over and told John and the cook they were both doing it wrong, and he mildly chewed John out for drinking. John immediately became contrite and poured out the beer he had been drinking and said he was not going to drink any more that weekend.

The lot was the asphalt parking area of a large shopping center. The main store was a Montgomery Ward's, and there were maybe a couple of dozen smaller stores, and the back yard ended up being hard by the intersection of two heavily traveled roads. It was difficult to get clean without breaking some ordinance pertaining to public nudity. Most of the workmen got only three hours' sleep that night, but it didn't seem to bother them. It was a two-day stand, and when they finished getting the Big Top up they could rest a little. And it soon would be Saturday night, and there were two liquor stores within eyesight of the lot.

Jeff Woosnam said he had been terribly depressed. "I think the night we were—where was it? Davie?—I was so down that if somebody had offered me a ride off the lot I would have taken it. But since then I've had an opportunity to put things more into perspective, I suppose. I suppose I've really compromised a lot of my professional musical standards and have kind of settled for a lowest common denominator—realizing the situation that I'm in, and also realizing that things *are* getting better. The show is tightening up. The music is getting better. And I guess today, not looking backward, not looking ahead, I'm in pretty good spirits.

"You know, I think the neatest thing I've seen so far was the two full houses we had, last night in Okeechobee and then that second show in Coral Springs. Those, I think, have really made it worth while. I think we would probably play as well for half a house as we do for a house and a half, but it sure helps when the house is full."

Jeff said he had been pleased when he first learned that the Hoxie show moved in the morning, because "I thought I would be able to see some of the countryside. You know, 'Discovering America' and all that crap. However, I now know that we move out as soon as possible, before first light. So as far as seeing the country's concerned, I'm going to have to wait until the winter season and, if I still want to do it, see it the right way then, and spend some money at it."

How important is the condition of a lot?

"A dirty lot I don't like," said Jeff. "Primarily because I have not yet accustomed myself to the major aspect of this life, which is not being able to get clean all the time. I am very fond of this life out here." He gestured toward the parking lot in Melbourne. "I realize all the hard work it takes to pound these stakes into the asphalt and all that. But this is the first lot that I have really felt comfortable on. This morning I took advantage of the sunshine and the breeze, and I washed my hair, and I washed the rest of my body, and I touched up my beard for the first time in almost a week. And

Art Duvall getting water

that felt good. Kind of a basic kind of feeling. I felt good about myself. And consequently I could translate that into a good feeling about the lot."

Stash apparently blew the show during or after Okeechobee. Nobody remembered seeing him leave the lot, or even talking about leaving. The last anybody saw of him was at the tear-down after the final show.

Wahoo's name was mentioned only infrequently now, and then usually by one workman who had particularly liked her. The man said, "I wonder what Wahoo's doing now? Last time I saw her she was skinny as a rail." The rumor that Hoxie had given her to the dairy owner was confirmed.

There was a water shortage in this part of Florida. It had not really rained, they said, for more than six months. Art Duvall was complaining about how it had become more and more difficult to get the stuff. In the old days, he said, you just hooked up to the nearest fireplug; now some places said you couldn't. You had to go to the city waterworks and pay for it sometimes. Art's water truck held five hundred and fifty gallons, and some days he had to make as many as four trips to get enough water for the elephants, the other animals, the cooktent, and everybody's trailer. Hoxie said some of Art's complaining was a cover-up for the fact that he liked to take the truck off and stop in a bar for a few hours. If anybody else had done this, Hoxie would have had his hide. But Art was sort of a fixture; during the winter he worked on the Tuckers' yard in South Miami. Hoxie gave him old clothes to wear, but it didn't spruce him up much.

A man drove up in a truck carrying four portable donnikers, and he was looking around for a place to put them, and the cook, always ready with a humorous comment, said, "Hey, man, what're you doing with all those freezers?"

Hoxie ran around as if he had never had the heart attacks and nervous breakdown, doing everything, taking tools out of incompetents' hands and showing them how to do it right. There was some trouble with one of the electrical cords from the light plant, and Hoxie took out a pocketknife and expertly peeled the wire and made a new connection. He tied some of the seats down. He did smooth, perfect double half hitches, the basic knot of the circus. He held an iron stake steady while a workman hammered it through the asphalt, and the workman was terribly afraid he would slip and hit Hoxie's hand.

"You know how to do everything on this show, don't you?" I asked him.

"Well, I try to."

You've done it all before?

"Lots of times."

King Charles said he was not surprised that Stash was gone.

"All the workingmen are *headed* someplace," he said. "They're going to stay with the show until they get to someplace where they want to be. They weren't satisfied with Miami. That's why they joined us in the beginning. Some

King Charles: with it

wanted to get to Okeechobee, and some will want to get up
here in Melbourne, and then they'll split tonight as soon as
they're paid, because that's as far away from Miami as they
wanted to get. Some will want to go as far as Jersey, Milwaukee."

What about you? You stay here all the time. What place
are *you* looking for?

"Well," said King Charles, "I'm more or less what you call
with it." He winked as he pronounced the last two words,
which are the oldest ones in the circus business.

A TWO-DAY STAND

Stash walked onto the lot in the middle of the afternoon. Hoxie saw him and went over to him. Ordinarily, Hoxie wouldn't even know a workingman's name, or he would give him a nickname of his own that he made up on the spot. But Hoxie knew Stash, and he seemed to like him. Despite the trouble Stash had caused in Davie, he was a good worker when he wasn't drinking, and Hoxie liked to have him around. "What'd you do?" asked Hoxie. "Get drunk and decide to leave?"

"Hoxie," said Stash, "I *could* tell you I got drunk and was going to blow the show, but that's not the truth. I *could* tell you I got drunk and found some broad, and that wouldn't be the truth either."

"All right," said Hoxie. "Where'd you go?"

"Well," said Stash, "about the time we was loading the lumber in Okeechobee, I had this diarrhea, and I had a couple beers, and I went into one of the donnikers. And I fell asleep." Stash grinned broadly. He said he woke up about six o'clock in the morning, when the man came to pick up the portable toilets. The man had opened the door and found him there, asleep. The show was gone; there were just the toilets and Stash and the surprised man on the empty sand lot in the middle of Okeechobee. Stash had hitchhiked and walked to Melbourne.

Late Saturday afternoon, between shows, a lot of the

circus people decided to eat out. Eating out in the circus means going to the closest place that serves food. It does not have to be fancy; indeed, it should *not* be fancy, because the circus people don't have the space to carry many dress-up clothes.

In the case of Melbourne, the closest place meant the Eckerd's drugstore in the shopping center. The McGuire sisters sat together in a booth and caused a minor sensation among the teen-aged boys who were present, and the older ones, too. They wore tight bluejeans and flattering sweaters, and some of their stage makeup was still on. A middle-aged Shriner, with his fez and everything, came into the joint and sat with some friends at a table. He kept glancing at Maureen and Margaret as if nothing like them had ever come to Melbourne. One of his friends walked in, and the Shriner rose to greet him, and when they shook hands it turned out that the Shriner had a joy-buzzer in his hand. The friend nearly jumped out of his shoes. Later the Shriner did it to a second friend, and then a third.

Joe Hamilton sat at another table, eating a vegetable plate because he was a vegetarian, or at least he had been one before coming on the show. He pretty much had to eat what the cookhouse put out or eat nothing, so he had had to eat meat when he was with the circus. The vegetables tasted good, he said, although they were not very fresh. I asked him about his life.

"There's not really an awful lot to say," he replied. "I was born and reared on a farm in Clayton County, Georgia, outside Atlanta. And I stayed there until I turned nineteen, in '69. The draft notice came, and I decided it was advantageous, you might call it, to stay in school. So I went to West Georgia College, at Carrollton, but then I dropped out. As soon as I dropped out, I got dropped right into the army. I did a year and seven months, with a five-month early out for being in Vietnam."

There were eight brothers and sisters, Joe said, and they were all useful; the farm produced corn and wheat and cotton, and the children had to pick the cotton by hand. After the army, it became increasingly difficult to get along with his father because of his conservative views, and Joe took off.

"I traveled a lot," he said. "Probably the reason I got with the circus was that I liked traveling. I'm not traveling now in the sense that I was before. When I went to see a town before, I saw the town. I went by motorcycle for a while, and then it was hitchhiking. And then by Volkswagen bus, the one that broke down in Key West."

Have you had a good life up until now?

"I think it was good. I've enjoyed myself. I like to live by the philosophy that I may not live to be *old*, but I want to live while I'm here. I love to enjoy myself. Sometimes enjoying myself can be working, sometimes it can be partying. I'm realistic enough to know that there's a difference between the two."

Do you like the circus?

"I don't agree with the total setup of the social system. You've got three classes here—the performers, the people like the bosses, and then you've got the rest of the people. I'm in that last category. A prop man. It's three classes, and the only people who can go between them are the band members. And I just can't agree with that system. If I happen to get in a conversation with one of the Cristiani kids, I like to be able to talk to them without people saying, 'He's degrading himself,' or 'He's trying to act uppity by talking to a performer.'"

Has that happened?

"No, not really. But it looks like it *could* happen."

What about sex? Harry said there were a lot of opportunities for one-night stands.

"I'm not too big on the one-night-stand type things. I'm leery of social diseases, and I've never had them, and plan on never having them, and I'm careful. I've had a *healthy* sex life, I guess, but not an overly active one. It's not a full-time preoccupation with me. When it happens, it happens, and when it doesn't, I just don't worry about it." He laughed. "An occasional wet dream will take care of everything."

Are you still glad you came to the show?

"Yeah. If I wasn't, I'd of left. I'm not like a lot of these people. I can always find a job. But there's not much privacy.

You're never lonely. You're never bored. I think the circus is a great place for a guy who wants to forget about something—the proverbial broken heart—because he never has time to think about it. We've been going for—what? Since five o'clock yesterday morning. For an hour and a half I slept in my truck, and that's it. You just don't have time to be bored, because if you're not working or doing something that's important or doing something you enjoy doing, then you're sleeping."

Joe got to talking about his contact lenses (they had never turned up) and then about his childhood, and it turned out that when he was a child he was legally blind. He had an operation when he was six, he said, that corrected the condition, but before that he had a Seeing Eye dog.

"I kept the dog until I was sixteen. He died of old age. To him, I was always blind. Whenever I took him someplace, he took care of me. When I stopped, he just automatically laid down. And when we were at a red light, when the light turned green, he'd just automatically do his little double pull to lead me on. He died of old age. I don't think I could ever own another dog. His name was Prince. He was a black, long-haired German shepherd.

"I gave him a great funeral, too. I didn't put him in a dog graveyard or anything. I buried him at the farm. I put up a little cross and everything. It's still there. Metal cross. It's kind of rusty now. I made it in school."

When was the last time you went to the farm?

"Last Christmas. That's when the final argument between me and my father took place. If I ever go back again, it'll probably have to be when my father's not there."

The workmen got paid, and most of them left the lot. Many went to the liquor store; some went to a nearby motel for their first warm water in more than a week. One of them, a black man named Savannah, walked back on the lot in early evening looking like somebody totally different. He had become handsome. The difference was that he had cleaned himself up and shaved and put on good clothes. A workman said, "Savannah, you look pretty sharp," and Savannah replied,

"Man, it's been two weeks since I got myself any poontang. *Got* to look sharp to get poontang these days." Then he started walking down the road. He never came back.

A few other workmen left that night, too, but a few others joined. Two of them came from the citrus camp in Okeechobee. They had come to see the show, and they had stayed. Now they sat in the cooktent and ate voraciously.

The cook watched them eat, and he said that it did his heart good to see people who appreciated his cooking. I asked him why he was here.

"To see the country," he said. He was grinning. He was a pleasant-looking man in his twenties, with blond hair and a little overweight.

You don't really believe that, do you?

"No, not really. I like to travel. I don't like to be tied down to one place. I have a family. But every year—I don't know whether it's to break the monotony or what—I go away for about three months."

Does that mean you'll be here for only three months?

"Right. I've thought about sticking it out for the bonus. I was told there'd be a good bonus and all that. But I don't know if it's bullshit. At the end of the season they could renege on it.

"I enjoy the job. But it's too many hours. I like the hours I get as a roofer better. I make six dollars and ninety-one cents an hour at it. But now, with the fuel shortage, there's no asphalt, and no work. So I grabbed ahold of this."

He said he had worked at a famous restaurant on Biscayne Boulevard in Miami, but that he had been confined to a kitchen all day there. "At least, here you can see something," he said. "You see different people."

I asked if it wasn't frustrating because the equipment and the menu were so limited. The cook truck had a rather small stove, a freezer and a refrigerator, and inadequate counter space and storage and running water. Hot water was made by heating it outside, over the flame of a portable gas burner. The soapy water and rinse water for cleaning were hardly ever hot enough to destroy all the bacteria.

"Yeah, but what you turn out, with the facilities you have, it's rewarding. They ate beans three times a day here before I came. It's better now. They're going to get all the meat they want. You can't just overnight start putting out cakes and all that kind of stuff, but I think they eat pretty good. It's a balanced diet."

You seem to have a sense of humor about the whole thing.

"You have to. You know, I'll tell you something. I drink. I'm not what you call a bum. I don't drink wine. Well, I guess you don't have to be a bum to drink wine. But I can still do my job. I still have a sense of responsibility. It's not where if I get ten dollars in my pocket, or a hundred dollars, or a thousand dollars, I have to go out and spend it before I do anything.

"But these guys here, I'll guarantee you, half of them will leave tonight. You know, it's interesting to see these guys. I would like to open a place that's for rehabilitation for them. You know those missions? They're useless. All they do is feed them, sober them up for a night, give them a place to sleep, and then turn them back into the street. That's the same as a prison."

Are you paid enough?

"Ahh. We're in the middle of a debate about that right now. Mr. Hoxie told me to see him if I'm not satisfied, so that's what I'm going to do. Because if I don't get what I want, my pride won't let me stay. I feel that as a cook here, it's worth a yard and half a week. I'd *take* a hundred and thirty-five, and nothing under that. I'm making fifty right now. . . .

"You know," he said, interrupting himself, "this is hard to say. How can I say it? *The circus thrives on the weak.* I mean, you're paying piss-poor salaries, and you cater to their weaknesses. See, these guys are getting paid tonight, and they're all going to get drunk, and tomorrow morning, Sunday, they're going to wake up and find out they don't have no money left, and that means they'll have to stay around *another* week. They'll have to be here for tear-down Sunday night. They're trapped.

"Everybody drinks here. I drink, because I enjoy it. I don't drink to excess. If I have four or five drinks, that's it. I like, you know, social drinking. Not just socking it down for the sake of getting drunk."

The last show was over on Saturday, and many of the circus people had left the lot. Most of the younger performers had gone en masse to see *The Godfather,* and the workmen were off buying booze or getting clean in motel rooms or both. Johnny Walker didn't have much work to do, because the Shriners were handling the concessions in Melbourne. He sat on a folding chair outside Bert Pettus's trailer with Bert and Phil Chandler. Bert kept an eye on the elephants, who were staked out a few feet away. They were jackpotting.

". . . I've seen 'em take a guy for his bank roll and then send him home for more money," Bert was saying. "And they'd all gather outside and watch. They'd have one guy way down the road. And this guy would signal, 'He's on his way back.' And they'd get him back in there and fleece him."

Somebody asked how long ago this was.

"About '48," said Bert. "That's when it ended."

"Forty-eight was about the end of the grift," said Johnny Walker. "Around that time. That's when the sponsors started coming in. Before that, everything went on. They'd carry a little folding table around with them on the midway, for playing monte or the shell game, and they'd set it up right next to the sucker. They got a big man there in Georgia for fourteen hundred."

"They had to tear down the show and get the hell out of town after that one," said Bert. He remembered the incident, or said he did.

Johnny laughed. "They'd get the hay man. You know, the man who sold the hay to the show. He'd go by the office to get paid, and they'd lead him right by the joint early in the morning. They'd steer him into a flat joint before he got off the midway. Sometimes they'd get him, sometimes they wouldn't."

Bert spat on the pavement. "Oh, man, it was thick as shit and twice as nasty in them days."

Johnny went on, as if some other, simultaneous conversation had been conducting itself in his mind. "You know, we come back in the fall, me and that Dean. You know, Mickey borrowed about four hundred off me there. And me and Dean left in the winter, right after the horses died there. We left with Lumbo. And I went from there, Buddy wanted me to go back with Mickey, because he owned the sideshow props and Mickey and Cy was hot at one another and he figured—"

Bert, too, had been following another conversation. "When we got over to Sault Ste. Marie, Michigan, we went from Sault Ste. Marie, Ontario, to Sault Ste. Marie, Michigan, and just right after the matinee, you know, when they closed the office, I walked in and I just took all the goddamn money that they owed me. I got all I could get."

Johnny: "You know that fellow that butchered for Jim, right? I stayed with him that winter, and we didn't make *nothing*. We had to stay in that phony winter quarters there in Lake City, eat those leftovers from the slaughterhouse. Two fucking meals a day, and, man, that fucking meat! Them *lions* couldn't even eat it. Two meals a day is all we got. That was the roughest winter I can remember. Thank God for them slot machines. I'm walking out of the end of the building, see, and I see all them quarters on the ground. That Curly and that broad had busted them open, you know, and I picked up about sixteen dollars up and down that ditch. Shit, we went to the movies for a week. And remember when we were making that date in Macon? Sixteen of us staying in that *ho*-tel down by the railroad."

Bert: "One guy would go down and rent a room, and about fifteen or twenty of them would heel the joint. You know, all of them sleep there and only one pay for it."

Johnny: "You remember when the twenty-four-hour man would make connections and everything? Over at Kelly-Miller, ———— would put on a synopsis for us. Where the red-light was and everything."

Bert: "Years ago they used to pack aluminum quarters in the Crackerjacks. It looked like a quarter. And you'd get down in Georgia, you know, and down in this part of the country, and the guy would find these broads. They lived in little pup tents—they didn't have trailers in those days. These guys would promote these broads and take them out back, and one guy'd giver her a *good* quarter. And all the rest of them would lay her and drop a phony quarter in the hat.

"I was on the old Barnett show, and we were showing down there in south Georgia. Next day a merchant drove over with an old jig broad to where we was showing. And what happened was, this jig broad had laid all these guys and had just put her hat down, you know, and all the guys had put these aluminum quarters in there. And she had a hat full of aluminum quarters.

"The next day she went down to this merchant to buy a dress. She poured the money out, and the merchant said, 'That ain't no good.' She says, 'Yes, it is. That's *show* money.'" Johnny was anticipating the ending, and he was doubled over with laughter. "So he loaded her up in his car and brought her over to the show, and the old man had to pay ten dollars.

"You think he didn't call a meeting right away? He says, 'I don't mind you getting fucked around here, but I'm not going to *pay* for it.'" Everybody laughed. Bert said, "Yeah, she said, 'That's *show* money.' *Show* money. Them phony quarters."

Bert continued. "And many a farmer missed his can of milk sitting out on the highway waiting for the truck. That goddamned show had more empty milk cans around it than a dairy farm.

"And after they hit a grocery store, when that poor sumbitch took inventory, he was short. He was *short*. We were in—I forget the name of it, some place in Florida—and right on the front of the lot there was a café. And all these guys going in and heeling the joint, you know. So the owner, he got mad about it, and he had the cash register by the door, and he got him a chair and sat down next to the door and the cash register with the shotgun, and says, 'Now, all you cocksuckers pass the cash register on the way out.'"

Phil Chandler talked about carrying a couple of cockroaches with you into a restaurant. "You eat dinner and most of the salad, and then you put them in the salad. Then you let out a war whoop. It goes over real big in the high-line restaurants. They don't charge you for your meal."

Bert: "Course, none of this happens today."

Do you miss it?

Johnny said, "You never forget it, that's for sure. You never forget it."

Bert said, "You love to talk about it."

Does that mean you miss it?

Bert: "I have to realize that that part of show business is gone. It's not no more. Yeah, I miss it in a way. It was good days.

"What *is* life? Life is a case of one man eating another if he can do it. What the heck? That's all it is. You go downtown, and they're going to take you if they can. I mean, they may go to church and sing hallelujah on Sunday, and that's the biggest thieving son of a bitch in the world, as far as I'm concerned.

"The only thing is, with show people, they figure we're thieves to start with. When it actually comes down to the show people themselves, I would damn sight rather trust them than trust the people downtown.

"This is where circus people got their reputation from, from the grift and from the working class. Because the working class really weren't circus people. They were fly-by-night, here today, gone tomorrow. And the grift, they were just natural-born thieves. I mean, that's all they lived for, was to rob somebody. And the performers hated it. They hated the grift. See, the grift was always in the sideshow. It was never in the Big Top. And it made people mad at the whole show. It made people mad at show people. But there was nothing they could do about it. But that's what gave the circus a bad name, you know. And people still have that feeling, handed down from generation to generation."

Bert talked some more about how tough you had to be in those days. He sounded as if he missed it.

You've slowed down a little?

"Oh, you bet your damned boots I have. If they even *look*

Bert Pettus

tough, I turn around and walk the other way." Bert spit.

Is that you changing, or is it the world changing?

"Me. I had to change. Got too old."

How old are you?

"Sixty. I will be in September. I've seen a lot of water go under the bridge."

Strangely enough, and in contradiction of what the cook and a lot of others had predicted, not many of the workmen left the show on Saturday night. King Charles said it merely demonstrated that few of them wanted to get off at Melbourne; they were waiting for some other stop, farther up the line. (And yet, none of them knew where the circus was going. Only a few people in the office had an idea of the route the show would take, and even that was subject to changes.) Someone else said it was because they *couldn't* leave because they were now broke. As people woke and started moving around on Sunday morning, moving slowly, because there was not much work to be done, I tried to assemble in my mind what I had learned about the workmen.

Hoxie had said they all had weaknesses, and to him the weaknesses were elemental, classical ones: dope, booze, women. The cook, too, had talked about weaknesses. Bill Hill had spoken of traumatic shocks that could be found in each of their lives. Everyone seemed to agree that these men had had their brains disfigured in one way or another.

It looked as if all these explanations contained their elements of truth, and that something else should be added to them: the men, a lot of them, were *broken* in some way. Broken just as animals are broken in a circus act. When you break an elephant or a horse or a llama, you teach the animal the act. But you also, to a certain extent, break the animals' spirit. You make them understand that they are no longer, and never will be, their own masters; that they are owned by someone else. That is the way the workingmen seemed to feel.

Many of the workingmen had little pride in their work. It must be difficult to take pride in something that you know a moron can do; difficult to take pride in doing a job that you know was done equally well by some wino before you got there and that will be done equally well by a succession of other winos after you leave. And it must be difficult to have pride in your work when your employer denies you even elementary sanitation. The workmen seemed to actively solicit orders from those above them. They did not want to make up their own minds about how to do their work, because that meant taking responsibility for something. They wanted someone else to take all the responsibility, and as long as someone else would do that (being careful not to issue too many orders or take the men to the edge of exhaustion) the men did the work without much complaint.

And they did it for about thirty-five cents an hour. All they asked was a little money with which to buy some Mad Dog and beer and a few other necessities, and the right to avoid responsibility. And that is the way the system worked;

and when a man decided it had quit working for him, the man
blew the show and went someplace else, where he thought the
system might work better.

One thing that was uniformly missing in the men was self-
pride, and when that is missing, individuality is the next thing
to go. About all that many of the men had in the way of individuality was their nicknames—one of the men from the
citrus camp was already being called Okeechobee—and a few
eccentricities, and even those eccentricities were often sum-
marized in the nicknames. Wear a western hat, and you are
bound to be called Cowboy. Fall out of your bunk in the
sleeper often enough, and you become Hard-Butt. But survive
the system long enough, protect your brains from the scram-
bling process long enough, fight for your pride long enough,
cherish your one or two talents long enough, and you will
become, like King Charles and Gypsy Red, *with it*. And when
you are with it, the circus will never leave your system.

A man named Price Wilson, one of the canvasmen, sat in
the cooktent on Sunday afternoon, a little drunk because he
had saved half a bottle of vodka from the night before, and
he said, slurring it a little, "I've been to the top and I've been
to the bottom. And I'm going to get to the top again. I've
got a degree from Georgia Tech. I know you don't believe
that, but you can check the records. I worked on the Ringling
show. I got no family. By that I mean my family is all gone.
My children are all married and everything.

"And I love the circus. I'm on my own. I'll do anything
I can do to make this circus a success."

And yet, a few days later, Price Wilson blew the show.

Sunday night in Melbourne: For some reason, a lot of the
workmen had saved enough money so they could go across the
road to McDonald's for dinner, and the cook was left in an
empty cooktent. He proceeded to do some drinking. He picked
up my tape recorder, asked me to turn it on, and said the following:

"My name is ____ ____, twenty-five years old. I have a
wife, three children. I hired a dishwasher and made him second

cook. Whatever I asked him was too much. He didn't treat the people that I served as human beings. He didn't regard them as human beings because there was something—I say—mentally wrong with him. But I put up with it because I felt sorry for him. To a certain extent. But I've done time for fighting. This reporter knows me now. Am I a psychopath to you?"

I said I didn't think he was a psychopath.

"I'm going to tell you something. I'm an easygoing guy. Until you screw me. Then I'm dangerous.

"My job is to feed these men. My complete job is to feed these men. Hoxie comes by here, and he says, 'You're in charge of the kitchen. I don't want to hear no shit from your department.' So that means I'm in charge. Hire and fire. Well, I told this dishwasher to leave the kitchen. He said go screw yourself. I said Hoxie'll be back here in fifteen minutes to straighten you out. He didn't come back.

"So it made me look like a punk, hiding behind Hoxie. But let me tell you something—I have a family. Honest to God's honest truth, you know what I would have done to him? I would have creamed him. That's why I'm a bum now. I'm not a bum. I hold a pretty good position in the circus. But you know something? You get to be like an animal when you use your hands.

"Now, you see me laughing and everything all the time? You ever hear of *Pagliacci?* Well, that's what it turned out to be. I'm not really laughing on the inside. I'm crying. I'm not trying to be dramatic. I'm just not the happy guy you might think I am. You know something? Instead of those guys sucking on wine bottles, let's make this a circus!"

He went into a brief reverie. You could see it in his eyes. "You know," he said, "people think you're a bum if you work here. I went over to the grocery store yesterday and I bought ten cases of Bugler tobacco. I was going to sell it to the guys. The woman looks at me, and she says, 'You must be from the circus.' You know something? I got news for you. I take a bath every night. I take a pot that I don't use in the kitchen. I fill it up with hot water, which I'm not supposed to do, and I take my underwear off when it gets dark enough, and I take a

whore's bath. I want to tell you something. I had a man tell me
he was leaving. He didn't know where he was going. And I
took him in to work in the kitchen with me. Why don't somebody get ahold of these people? They're *human beings.* I'm not
a crusader. I stay here with the assumption of more money,
and if I don't get more money, I'm going to quit.

"You know something? It's not just food I feed these men.
It's also *affection* I feed them. You know, affection's a deep
thing. I'm friends with everybody here, and if you cross me,
I'm not your friend.

"You know, my rule is you eat all you want, but you take
all you eat. No. Take all you want, but eat all you take. And
that was my rule as a kid. Because my father used to come
home with five dollars. Two dollars went for his bottle of wine,
and three dollars went to make macaroni over taters for a week.
And I'm not ashamed to say it. Because you know what? Half
of the country learned how to eat that way. And my father,
when he died of a heart attack, he had nothing."

The next day, the cook asked for an answer to his demand
for more money. He was told there would be no more. He blew
the show.

RHYTHM

With each jump further away from Sweetwater, a rhythm was being perfected. The once seemingly impossible task of erecting a huge tent in a strange town, on an even stranger lot, every day of the week, regardless of the weather, was becoming more and more commonplace. Now the workmen could do it almost easily. Although it was only early April, nobody was first of May any longer.

For the performers, the acts became easier, too. They knew which prop hands were competent and which weren't, and they gave tips every weekend to those who were competent, to make sure the job would be done correctly. Their own winter rustiness was gone now, washed away by repetition, their muscles relaxed by practice, and they could spend a little time, when their temperaments and the weather allowed it, on improvisation.

The clown family varied its routine frequently. The Chandlers got their magic act down pat. The elephants (they are performers, too) slipped into their acts well, although occasionally one of them would get lazy and plod through the routine, making Bert angry. He was always working with the baby bulls, because they were still young and they had enough youthful perverseness to try to fool their trainer whenever they could.

The Cristianis were superb. They appeared four times in the show, not counting the walkaround they and everybody

The Cristianis performing: the trampoline act . . .

else did in Spec. The opening act was the trampolines, and the Fornasari family performed on one of them while the Cristianis worked the other. Tino and Armando went through a number of tricks, somersaults and twists, and then Lucio, who was in clown getup, mounted the trampoline. He bounced higher and higher, until, at the height of one of his leaps, he loosened his suspender straps so that when he hit the canvas the next time his pants fell off, revealing his long-legged pink underwear. It never failed to bring squeals from the audience.

Later, Lucio stood on the trampoline, with Tino on his shoulders, and Armando did a somersault to the top of the stack. The three performers ended up standing on each other's shoulders, and the sight was very impressive.

Later in the show, Armando and two other jugglers occupied the stages. Armando looked like a blond-haired miniature. The jugglers finished with flaming batons.

The cat act was Gilda's main performance. Prop men wheeled a large cage into the tent, and Gilda and Lucio attached leashes to the animals inside, and then they brought out two beautiful leopards. The cats stalked around the ring, looking self-conscious, and also looking as if they were considering —always considering, never really deciding on it—the chances of pouncing on someone in the audience. They jumped from pedestal to pedestal and over each other; one walked on its hind legs across the ring; one jumped through a hoop of fire.

Gilda rewarded the cats with kisses. The high point of the act came when both animals jumped to the tops of revolving, mirrored pedestals while King Charles signaled the band to play "Born Free." There was something about the music that always made the audience burst into spontaneous applause when the first few notes were played. It was as if they had been conditioned, by the music, to become emotional whenever they heard it.

Now that Luis Murillo and Jorge Del Moral were gone, taking their wire-walking and motorcycle acts with them, the Cristianis finished the show with their horses. They brought two horses to Ring Two, but ordinarily only one performed. Gilda put on a demonstration of bareback riding; she looked as light as a ballerina. The horse was put into a trot around the ring, and Tino and Armando took running jumps onto its back. Then Lucio came into the Big Top. He was dressed in ordinary clothes, usually grey pants and a white shirt, a checkered sport coat and a little hat. He acted drunk.

He wanted to get into the ring, and Phil Chandler warned him not to. Phil asked if someone would escort the man away. (Every once in a while, a well-meaning towner tried to comply.) Eventually, of course, Lucio got into the ring and rode like a dream.

For a lot of the audience, one high point of his act had nothing to do with riding. While circling the ring standing on the back of the horse, he would throw down his sport coat and hat. Gilda would arrange them loosely on the ground. Lucio would make one more circuit, then jump from the horse, hit the ground, do a somersault over the jacket and hat, and then

. . . the leopard act; the horse act

stand up, arms outstretched for the applause that always came. In the process of doing the somersault, he had managed to put his coat and hat back on, all in one fluid and seemingly impossible motion.

Lucio often reflected on the fact that that stunt, for a lot of the audience, was the feature of his act, although he knew that it was not nearly as challenging as the riding. A little later, he would turn the horse loose to trot around the ring and he would take a running jump at the animal's back, as Tino and Armando had done—except that Lucio would fly through the air over the horse, landing in a somersault on a scrap of foam rubber that had been placed just outside the ring. Then he would turn and start back into the ring, doing a somersault on the ground just in front of the horse's hoofs. The crowd always cheered lustily, and well they should have, for they had just finished seeing a branch of the most famous circus family in history. Most of them, of course, did not know this at all.

Even the arrivals and departures of people seemed to function according to some inner rhythm. The people who worked for the circus learned that nobody was indispensable, and that what really mattered was that the big piece of canvas got up and down every day and that the people who worked under it got fed with some regularity. Every once in a while you would hear someone complain about how his or her department wasn't treated with enough respect. The performers felt that too many of the other circus people considered them of low priority—as mere frills in a business whose main object was to sell cotton candy and flukum—and that the show paid more attention to the people on the front end than to those who did the performing.

The butchers who worked out of the concession wagon thought that they were wrongly considered to be close to the bottom of the status pile and that nobody recognized their own artistic triumphs in the field of selling things to people who didn't know they were hungry. The bosses suffered silently, for the most part, knowing that everybody was blaming everything, from the weather to a rocky lot to bologna sandwiches, on them. The canvasmen and workmen thought that *they* had ample reason to feel paranoid, and if you didn't believe them, just look at their living conditions.

It was a fact that in order to have a circus, although a not very complete one, you needed representatives of each of these departments: a piece of canvas and some poles to hold it up; somebody to put the canvas up in a new town every day; some elephants to perform under the canvas; somebody with a bull-hook to remind the elephants of the tricks they had learned decades before on some circus whose name even Bert Pettus was in the process of forgetting; and somebody to sell the tickets. That's really what it boiled down to.

Everyone else you could put in the category that Hoxie had put Junior it: if they were dead, you'd have to get along without them, so you just don't allow any permanent ties to form. If a dozen workmen blew the show one night after tear-down, there would be another dozen waiting to take their places tomorrow. Perhaps not *knowing* they were waiting; just sitting around in a mission or in a bus station—the circus does not always inform in advance those she is about to take.

And if a performer got hurt in tonight's first performance, or even was killed, the audience at the second show would not know that something was missing. Life went on. The Big Top went on. The elephants went on.

A new cook was hired to take the place of the man who left in Melbourne. The newcomer was not exactly a cook, but he had expressed an interest in cooking when someone asked him, so he was the new cook. The men ate a lot of bologna sandwiches for a while. Leo returned to his status as the chief critic of the cooktent.

Hoxie stayed away most of the time. He was with Lewis Brothers, because, he said, he had to keep his eye on every-thing. He left the running of the big show pretty much up to John Hall.

Joe Hamilton transferred to the elephant department. "They finally got a pacifist in that department," he said. "They got somebody who won't beat the bulls to death—me. I'm proud of that, because I get them to do what I want to without hitting them so much. I hit them hard every once in a while, but I don't have a hook on the end of my cane. Basically I just yell. You have to yell at them or they won't do what you tell them to do. Then they'll go ahead and do it." Cowboy Jim continued using *his* method, the violent one, in his dealing with the bulls.

The show moved to Ocala, then Jacksonville, the first city of any real size, and then came the first jump across a state line, into the Georgia red clay: Claxton, Sandersville, Swainsboro, then two days at the state mental institution in Milledgeville. During the season there would be a dozen dates at state institutions, dates for which the show would lose money or just break even. It cost at least three thousand dollars a day to operate the circus. Hoxie said the hospital dates were his only charity.

Gracewood, Georgia, was another state hospital. A man named Bob Mason joined the show there as its sideshow manager, freeing Phil Chandler to pay more attention to his other jobs. Then came another two-day stand, this one in Augusta, Georgia.

The lot in Augusta was next to a public housing project, and it was an unpleasant date. Kids from the project tormented the circus people something fierce, and they tried constantly to steal things. One of the men who had joined up in Okeechobee, the one who was named Okeechobee, decided to go to the store at night in Augusta and was mugged for three dollars. Next to the circus lot was an irrigation ditch, and some of the workmen found a plastic bag floating in it, and inside the bag was a tiny black-and-white puppy, half-dead. It was just a few weeks old. The workmen chipped in and bought some flea repellent, and they tied the dog to the sleeper and named it Big Top.

The circus moved farther north. I had read one time, in a newspaper filler, that someone had estimated that spring was moving up through Siberia at the rate of thirty-five miles a day. That was the approximate speed of Hoxie Brothers Circus, although a lot of its jumps were to the northwest, rather than due north. But the show was pacing along with early spring.

Two of King Charles's sons and a few of their friends from Ville Platte arrived to work with the circus. They were all good workers, and the best was John Weathersby, one of the bandleader's sons. King Charles kept money for the young men and made sure they had enough to eat. Sometimes this required marching into the cooktent and raising a lot of hell.

Maureen McGuire moved in with Bill Hill. There was a rumor that ten foreign students would be coming to work with the show for the summer. Bert Pettus said he was fed up and thinking about leaving. Jeff had something of a disappointment: In March, John Hall had told him he could make extra money, in addition to his salary for playing in the band, by driving a truck between towns. Jeff had done this, but he had never gotten any money for it. He had complained and been told that no money would be forthcoming. Jeff started riding in the mornings with Phil and Linda Chandler, and, because they left later than the trucks, he got to see more of the countryside. In the evenings, after performances, Jeff and the Chandlers and a few others gathered at the Chandler trailer and played Monopoly.

Clinton, South Carolina, was a state-hospital date. The ground was wet, and the bulls had to be used to pull some of the trucks on and off the lot. There were no evening performances at the hospitals, so the workmen and performers had the night off. Joe Hamilton checked into a motel in Clinton and took a two-hour bath. "If I can do this about once a month," he said, "you know, sleep between sheets and everything, and watch color TV, and just sit back with all the little relaxations, I think maybe I can survive."

Then came Columbia, South Carolina, and then Charleston. Jeff was very impressed with Charleston and with its newspapers. Almost alone among the circus people, Jeff tried to find a local newspaper each day, to see what was happening in the world and to see what the local journalism was like. Although the Watergate scandal was unfolding more and more each day, few of the performers, workmen, or bosses kept up with it. The lot in Charleston was next to a liquor store, and Stash got something to drink, and he started fighting again. He fought with workmen, and with towners, and finally with some of the young men from Ville Platte. The young men from Ville Platte stuck together very well, and Stash got beat up. The next day he left the show.

After Charleston there was Florence, and then the show crossed into North Carolina, to Fayetteville for a two-day stand. And then came Rockingham, and Mooresville, and then West Jefferson, up in the Blue Ridge Mountains.

The countryside reminded Jeff of home, although there were no real mountains in Ohio. Jeff said he was a little homesick. He missed not only the house and farm, but his family as well. Jeff and his family were particularly close.

"You know," he said one day, "I look back on my early years on the farm, and it occurs to me that we were really *poor* then. And the only reason we didn't starve—I say 'starve'; it's sort of a grandiose term—was that we planted a big garden every year. And of course we kids thought the only reason we planted a garden was so we would have to go out and slave in the hot sun. But we butchered a steer every now and then, and we always had milk from the goats, and we'd butcher a goat or a sheep every once in a while and we'd have some more meat.

"And I'm now realizing that my dad was really showing us something. He couldn't sit down and say, 'Look, this is why we're doing it.' But we were doing the same thing then that I want to do now. He took us back to the land and made a decent living for us, and he gave us some values that are really the only right ones.

"The farm, you know, is where I go when everything else has let me down. When I get into the trip where I feel as if there's *nothing* any more, or when I really don't want to do anything, that's when I go back, and I go walking in the woods with the dogs.

"Yeah, I want to go back to the farm. And I want to build a house there. I have plans for a dome house all set to go, a Buckminster Fuller dome. I've got my own little corner of the farm all picked out, and my folks know about it, and one of these days I'm going to build that house up there."

But right now you're working for a circus.

"Right. Right now I'm working for a circus. And I'm learning some things, about the circus and about myself. I haven't worked anyplace yet that I haven't found out something new about myself."

MOUNTAINS

"I came up through this same territory in nineteen and thirty-five," said Bert Pettus, "and we never saw the sun for eight weeks. I got three and a half dollars a week pay, working elephants on the old Barnett show."

Bert squinted at the sky, which was a deep mountain blue, almost turning to a sunset, and he spat tobacco juice on the ground. We were in West Jefferson, and Bert was waiting to take the babies in for their act. The best time to talk to an elephant man is when he and his animals are lined up outside the tent. There is something about the back door, and the music and the audience on the other side of it, and the waiting to go on, that makes them think about other circuses, other days, other kinds of weather.

"We opened out of York, South Carolina, the seventh day of April. Course, we didn't show these exact towns, but we showed the same territory. We showed like Hickory, Albemarle, and those towns. We showed Wytheville, the town we're going to tomorrow. We showed there in rain and mud—God how it was. And we jumped into Bluefield, and it rained. Rain, cold—course, the lot there wasn't mud. It was on the side of a mountain, so it was damned near all *rock*. That was one consolation you had. But you'd freeze to death. That was the last year we had the circus parade. Ho *Hoxie*, back *Hoxie*." Hoxie backed up; he had been going after some scrubby weeds to the side of the back door.

"We showed Maine, up in the state of Maine. We was in the state for thirty-four days, and thirty-two of them was rain. I seen them float the seat lumber out on the water. It was so deep in the Big Top they just floated it out."

Margaret Ann, Maureen McGuire's daughter, walked out the back door and petted an elephant. Bert noticed this out of the corner of his eye and he spat.

"In them days it was pretty hard for a young person to get on the show. They wouldn't have them around. If an act came on that had kids, they had to keep them in the trailer or whatever they had. Usually in them days they didn't have trailers. They'd make a house out of an old bus or something, or build one.

"But they wouldn't even allow the children to run around the lot. See, the circus people were clannish in those days. They took you a long time before you was accepted as a circus hand. They didn't just accept you like they do now. A guy can come on the show one day, now, and he's accepted. In them days, you wasn't." On the other side of the curtain, Phil introduced the baby-elephant act, and Bert went inside.

Bert had said, earlier that day in West Jefferson, that he was fed up. He had said that plenty of times before, but this time he said he had given notice to John Hall that he was about to leave the show. Bert said, though, that he was waiting to see Hoxie before he did anything. Hoxie was still spending most of his time with the Lewis show, and he hadn't been around the big show's lot for several weeks. He was due in Wytheville tomorrow.

"I told them when I came over here," said Bert, "that I couldn't do all the labor. I need an extra man to help work the bulls, but they won't give me one. It's just not very *professional* around this place. Take them ponies. You seen them in winter quarters. Look at them today. They're worse now than they were in winter quarters because look at that ring." The ring that the ponies performed in had a section of ring curb missing, and at the first show that day one of the ponies had run out through the opening and had paraded around the track, causing the audience to guffaw and Bert to become embarrassed and angry. "Once they start running out," he said,

"I've got to start all over again. I've got to start from scratch."

Bert said he was angry enough to leave, but that he wouldn't leave the show in the lurch. "I'd give them time to get somebody else up here to do the elephants before I left," he said. "I'll always give a man notice."

West Jefferson was in the mountains, but the lot was on flat land alongside a little stream. The town was prosperous-looking and was a few miles west of the Blue Ridge Parkway. It was doing what it could to attract summer tourists. The lot was made of red clay, but there had been no rain. In the afternoon, Armando and Tino Cristiani took a plastic bucket and went up and down the stream looking for crawfish. Armando said he wanted to catch enough so that his mother could cook them for dinner. They found one crawfish, and it looked soft and half-dead.

Cowboy Jim had gotten hurt the day before. He had approached Sue from the rear, and the elephant had whirled faster than one normally thinks an elephant can move, and she had smacked Cowboy Jim with her trunk. He had sailed through the air and landed on his back, and hurt it so badly he had to go the hospital. Some of the show people had said this was a case of Sue's getting even for Jim's violence against her and the other elephants, but Bert said it was because Sue was blind in her right eye and Jim had approached her from the right, and she had whirled in surprise.

"Sue is not a mean elephant," said Bert. "But then, too, they don't have to be mean to hit you. That's just second nature with them, outside eating. Eating's the first, and hitting you's the second. They'll take certain people. Like Jim. She wasn't *after* him. She was just probably asleep, and he walked up and she whirled and knocked him down. I think this is all. Now, if she had been a bad elephant, he wouldn't have been alive to tell it now. She would have stomped him into the ground and did a headstand on him and everything else."

Actually done a headstand?

"Sure. That's how an elephant finishes you off. Does a headstand on your body to make sure you're dead."

▶

Bob Mason and Linda doing the sideshow bally

The new sideshow manager, Bob Mason, was doing a good job from his platform. He was even honest: he managed to tell the tip that some of the things they saw advertised on the sides of the sideshow trucks were just representations of what the show had offered through the years, and that they would not see all of them here. Mason seemed to be drawing nice houses, but he complained a lot about how he wasn't really packing them in. His income came from a percentage of the sideshow take, plus whatever he could make by selling packets of magic tricks, at a quarter a throw, to the audience inside. Bob lived with his dog in a camper truck that he usually parked in neither the front nor the back yard, but alongside the sideshow tent. He was from Dayton, and he and the Chandlers were old friends. In the wintertime, Bob did club acts and packaged mind-reading illusions for other magicians and show people.

The next morning, as we were leaving West Jefferson, I stopped at what looked like the premier coffee shop to fill my

Thermos for the trip to Wytheville, and somebody at the counter recognized me from the night before. "You didn't have too good a crowd there last night. You know why not?" The man was smiling; he wore a lumberjack shirt and smoked a pipe.

"No. Why not?"

"Because they was streaking down at the supermarket again. In the parking lot. Done it three times this year. Gittin' to be a regular thing. Last night they got a good crowd. Damn near as good as yours. I would have gone myself but I'm too old." The man laughed heartily, and the other people in the diner laughed with him.

The run to Wytheville was half interstate, half back-country mountain roads that were absolutely beautiful. One of the things that the interstate highway system has done to Americans, in addition to training them to eat the most horrible slop ever perpetrated on a traveler, is to make it impractical and inefficient to drive along two-lane country roads through the mountains. The arrows led through mountain pastures, over bright rushing streams that must have held trout, up steep grades that promised a lookout at the top; and at the top, a view of miles and miles of hills and valleys and mountains and cows grazing on the sides of slopes. The circus people hated the mountains, no matter how beautiful they were, because they were so hard to drive with tractor-trailers and house trailers. Almost any time the show moved over mountains, you could be certain of breakdowns and sometimes accidents. But none happened today.

Wytheville was a pleasant town in the mountains, almost two hundred years old, named for a signer of the Declaration of Independence. Unlike a lot of Virginia towns, it was not self-consciously historic. There was an army-navy store, where I bought a cap and some cheap gloves, because there had been ice on the windshields when we woke at West Jefferson. It was April 27.

The lot was supposed to be at the horse track and show grounds, but the committee had failed to take John Hall's round tent into consideration, and there was no way to put it up without tearing out fences. So John got permission to set up the show on the front lawn of a community college. It was a beautiful lot, the way a lot should be, one that dignifies the Big Top. The college was far away at the top of the hill, and a grassy lawn sloped down from it, and at the bottom there was a large flat space; the logical place for the Big Top. It was like walking along a street in Manhattan, feeling that closed-in feeling that the city always gives you, and suddenly coming to a place where they had torn down a block of buildings: your eyes adjusted to the sight, and you found that you could see things in the proper perspective for a change. Hoxie's trailer was on the lot; he had driven in during the night.

When the last show was half over, Hoxie called me over and invited me to his trailer. His hatbrim was up, and he was in an expansive, humorous mood. When we got inside, he explained that he was through work for the day and it would be all right for him to have a drink. It was the first time I had heard him discuss alcohol in anything but negative terms. He unscrewed a bottle of Seagram's and opened a 7-Up and set two glasses on the table in his Airstream. He said he had just gotten in from the Lewis show, which at this point was in Kentucky.

"I enjoyed being over there with that show," he said. "I've had more fun with that thing than I've had in years. If this show had stayed small, I never would have thought about that other show. I wouldn't have thought nothin' about it. But I ain't no kid no more."

I asked him what he meant.

"Because I wanted another *little* circus, that's what I wanted. To go back into the hills and the crossroads. I started out with that kind of show, you know.

"I've had a lot of fun over on that show so far. We have no help on that thing, so I just give everybody a title. I've got majors, generals, captains, sergeants, buck privates. I've got everybody named around there. And when the show comes to town, I don't even have a layout pin and chain. I just walk it off and show them where to start driving the stakes."

Hoxie said he thought very little about the big show when he was away from it, because he knew that John Hall was running it well. "As you know, I don't have a son," he said. It sounded as if he regretted that. He had said this more than once. "If I had one, I'd want one like John Hall. John's different from most circus people. He's a *gentleman*. He has a very cool sense of humor. He doesn't get excited. I *have* seen him mad a couple of times. And I saw a guy bigger'n me and you either one go up to him one time, and John just says, 'Don't put your hand in my face again.' And when you make him mad, he'll get with you. I *ima*gine he'd be a pretty rough boy to deal with. John is a great guy.

"And Bill Hill's a very, very capable man. And Walker does a terrific job on that Big Top, and between the two of them and Gypsy Red, they do it all. They've got it figured out for the best system there is in the circus business today, I think. They've weeded out most of the drunks, and they've got capable people to do it now. And that's what Bill Hill has developed out of what he's had to develop it out of, and you know where the guys he gets come from, so I think the man has done a terrific job."

I remember what Bill Hill had said about how Hoxie ought to get a subsidy from the government for keeping so many people off welfare, and I mentioned it to Hoxie. "You do take care of some of God's children, don't you?" I asked.

"That's right. And you know, there's nothing in the world that thrills me any better than to get a bunch of guys that appreciate something, and try to help them. The greatest thing in the world is doing something for somebody else." Hoxie broke off and went to the window. He had seen a truck's lights moving outside, and he knew that a truck had no business moving at that particular time and place. "I'm glad I turned over the whole operation of this show to those guys and I'm taking it easy so I don't have to worry about where that goddamn truck's going," he said, and then he laughed at himself.

"You know, when my mother was living—my dad died when he was sixty-two years old, and my mother lived to be ninety-five—everybody was good to my mother. Everybody. Because she loved everybody in the world, and she never had a bad thing to say about anybody. You could shoot a man right next to her and she would never talk bad about you for doing it. I always thought that if people were always doing nice things for my mother, why can't *I* do something for somebody else? That's why I started playing them state hospitals so cheap—because I figured I was doing those patients some good. And I've never to this day regretted it, and I don't make any money doing it."

Hoxie fixed us another drink. "I tell you something," he said, in a confidential tone. "I have a big thing going right now. It may materialize in the next little while."

A circus thing?

"It all derives *from* the circus. I've got to use the circus and stuff to do what I want to do and what I'm trying to do. I ain't going to tell you what it is. I don't even tell John Hall about it, because if it doesn't happen, then nobody'll be hurt about it. Because there could be a lot of hopes built up and then everybody would be disappointed. I've been working on this thing for nearly three years.

"I sold the lions, you know, the other day when I was home. I sold them for two hundred apiece, just to get rid of them. I had just bought two of the young ones, and I paid *three* hundred apiece for them. Then I turned around and sold them all the other day for fourteen hundred."

So Junior made you lose money.

"Ah, what the hell do *I* care? It ain't no loss. They cost me at least ten thousand dollars last year, and I never used them. And I made up my mind that I wasn't going to do that again this year. I kept the arena, cages, truck, everything. I've got all that. But I ain't feeding no more lions all summer for nothing."

Hoxie got to talking about his daughter, Irene, who was in real estate in Orlando, and about what a fine daughter she was, and about how John Hall was sort of taking the place of his son. I mentioned that a lot of people thought of Hoxie in a paternal way; that he was kind of like the "old man" in an army unit, who was expected to hand out compassion and discipline and be a substitute for everybody's father, and who

was feared a bit. He said he was aware of that situation, and
that it didn't bother him. In fact, he sounded as if he enjoyed
being paternalistic.

"It's just like my will," he said. "I had as good a will
made as anybody in the world could have. But then John Hall
came to work for me, and I took the will to my attorney, and
I asked him to change it, and I have changed a lot of things
in it, and I'll tell you, if Betty and I die tomorrow, John Hall
will be pretty well off.

"That's right, yessir. And my daughter knows every bit
of it. And my daughter has power of attorney right now. If
she wanted to come up here right now and pick this circus
up, ain't a thing in the world I can do about it. And she's had
that power of attorney for I guess ten years, or fifteen. And I
know she ain't going to *do* that. But if she wanted to do it, she
could. My kid's a smart operator. She's smart. Just as smart as a
whip."

Hoxie said Irene had been concerned about his health
for a long time, and that once she had offered to buy the show
from him on the condition that he retire. "She says, 'Daddy, I'll
tell you what I'll do. I'll write you a check for three hundred
thousand if you'll let me burn that show to the ground. And
you take all the animals, and go give them to any zoo you
want to. But you got to *give* them away; you can't sell them.
But you can put in there the stipulation that any time you
want to come play with your elephants, you go ahead. But
you've got to *give* them away. You can't sell them. And I'll
write you a check right now for it.' "

Hoxie slapped his leg in admiration. He said Irene currently was finding herself in an enviable condition down in
Orlando. She had taken part in some of the land trading that
resulted in the construction of Disney World, outside Orlando,
and now she owned or controlled a good deal of land around
the attraction. Without even knowing it, he said, Irene had
gotten a lot of the land a little farther away from Orlando,
near Florida Highway 27, where Ringling Brothers had decided to build a year-round attraction called Circus World.
"She's a smart little cookie, buddy," Hoxie said. "And Dave,

her husband, he's the same way. See, my son-in-law's Jewish. And goddamn, he's a good boy."

Hoxie suddenly changed his pace of talking. He leaned over and said, almost in a conspiratorial way, "What I *would* like to do, really, is sell this thing, lock, stock, and barrel."

The Hoxie show?

"Everything. The whole show. Take John Hall and give him the Lewis show. Just give me a living. That's all I want, something to eat. And give it to him. That's what I'd like to do. Just give it to John Hall, complete. Do it right, give him good equipment and everything."

And you'd retire?

"Hell, no, I'm not going to retire, not until I *die*. And when I die, I want to die around one of these things.

"But I'd like to give it to John with the one stipulation that I've got to make a living out of it—and it don't take much for me to live, just something to eat, that's all. But that's what I'd like to do. And if I can sell this thing, that's what I'm *going* to do. That's right. Who the hell wants this thing to fool around with all the time? Hell, I can make just as much money with that little show as I can the big one. I won't *handle* near as much money, but when you get home it's what's down in that right-hand corner that counts, right?"

Hoxie said he had known, when he came on the lot in Wytheville, that a lot of people were hoping to present petitions to him of one sort or another. He knew that Bert Pettus especially wanted to see him, because John Hall had kept him informed, on the telephone, about Bert's complaints. Hoxie dodged all his petitioners successfully in Wytheville. "They tried it," he said. "I said, 'I ain't listening to none. Take your problems to John Hall. If I wasn't here you wouldn't be telling me, would you?' I ain't going to listen to their complaints. But I try to do it in a diplomatic way, to let them know that I'm kidding about it. If you have a *real* problem, I'll accept it. But until you do, I don't want to hear it. Now, Bert, I won't listen to him. He gripes all the time.

"You have to have rules of operating. Here's the way *I*

look at it. The way I've *been* doing it has been successful, so why should I change it? And I ain't goin' do it. Bert's had more help over there than I've ever had in my life around elephants. He should have advised that boy, by the way, *never* to walk up on the blind side of an elephant, unless you holler and talk so she'll know you're coming around there. Because if you don't, they're going to swing around—there ain't no way out of that."

Hoxie leaned toward the window. "There's some idiot going out there through the wrong place again. With the spool truck and no lights on it. No, that's the concession truck." He turned back and smiled. "I'm glad I can't see out of this trailer's windows," he said, and poured another drink.

Is the real lesson to be learned about the circus the fact that nobody is indispensable?

"That's right," said Hoxie. "And I'm going to show you why you have to believe that. The most important man as far as I'm concerned around this show is John Hall. Right? Now, if John died, I'd have to get along without him, wouldn't I? All right. There's your answer."

"That's the answer you gave when I asked about Junior," I said.

"It's the only way to put it. Now, truthfully, since I got rid of Junior, hell, things are ten times better. If he'd been here there'd been more problems because of his jealousy and all than anything in the world. You know why he left. He's afraid of them cats."

I told Hoxie I had been working on a theory about the workingmen. Everybody thought of them as essentially dirty people, I said, but I was wondering if that was only because the conditions of their lives *made* them dirty, not because they themselves wanted it that way.

"That is not right," said Hoxie.

What *is* right?

"All right. At one time on this show I had shower baths, I had rugs on the floors in the sleepers. I bought sheets for them. I've done everything you can do to make a gentleman out of them. And they don't *want* it that way. They want it just like as near nothing as you can get."

Why?

"Same thing I said before—the element where they come from. If they have had better, they have wasted it. They have got used to the other way of life, and they don't want nothing. I tried that, buddy, and I know *exactly* what I'm talking about. And if you don't believe me, you can ask John Hall what I just told you. He told me that same story, and I went along with him just to show him how wrong he could be. About fixing their trailers up, and getting everything just like they wanted it. And how long did it last? Not one week. *Not one week!*

"They throwed the sheets out of the way. They didn't want to have them washed. The blankets you put on their bed, they wouldn't clean them, they wouldn't wash them, they wouldn't air them out. Their mattresses—you'd think any *human* would take it out and sun it every once in a while. But that's too much trouble. They sleep just like garbage and that's the way they want it.

"We had showers in the trucks. With *rugs on the floor.* But it didn't mean nothin'. They wouldn't use them. They was too sorry to use them. They'd get a bucket and maybe wash their feet every once in a while."

Hoxie had been lecturing like a preacher. Now he smiled. "Did I ever tell you about Art Duvall, when we were in a town down in Florida? Art was going across the lot one day with a bucket of water. And this old boy we used to call Black Jim said, 'Look there, Art's going to wash.' Art says, 'Yeah, I'm going to wash and change.' He carried that bucket of water up into his truck, where he slept, set down on a bale of hay, put his bucket down, pulled his shoes off, took his socks off, turned them wrong side out and put them right back on, and he ain't never touched the water *yet!* That's why he got the name of Dirty Art.

"Now, you know any human can buy a bar of soap now just as good as you could twenty years ago when it sold for a nickel. If you want to wash, you wash. When I left home

A workman shaving

this spring, I must have taken twenty pairs of trousers, good clothes a lot of them, out to winter quarters and give them to Art. And twenty-five, thirty, forty shirts. Do you think he'd ever get one of them cleaned and washed? *Never* happen. I like the old bastard, though."

What was Art's weakness?

"Women and whiskey. Drinking. Every night he'll walk twenty miles to go to town and set up on a stool and drink beer and talk to somebody.

"I forget whether it was last year or the year before last, up in New Jersey, he went down to one of them bars one night after the show. He was sitting there drinking, and he sold my elephants. And a guy came down and knocked on my trailer door and woke me up and wanted to get permission to go to the truck and get his elephants.

"He told me that he owned them, and that I was just borrowing them from him. He had bought them from Duvall. I said, 'Man, let me tell you one thing. You better get away from here and go tell that Duvall that he better not come back because I'll kill the sumbitch tonight.' But he had sold them elephants, and I tell you, he laughed about that thing for weeks. I tell you, there ain't nothing like that Art."

I told Hoxie he had made a strong case against showers, sheets, rugs, and mattresses. But what about a place to go to the bathroom?

"Why, hell, what's wrong with the trees?" he said. He was serious.

What about places where there were no trees? Where there was housing all around the lot?

"What the hell, just wait till the next day, then.

"I used to carry toilets on this show, and those guys that drove the truck that hauled them, the first tree they could find to wrap it around, that's what they would do to get rid of them. They were just too damn lazy to keep the donniker clean. And I won't build another one. If the committee don't furnish them, we just don't use them, that's all.

"Toilets—" He laughed. "That's a bad name around here. John's on me all the time about building one. I ain't *never* going to build another one. Never.

"If I ever build another one, you know what I'll do? I'll put padlocks on it and set it way out, away from the tent. And then if people ask me do we have any donnikers, I'll say, 'We shore have.' But under my breath I'll say, 'But they'll never get to use them. They're locked up!' No, unh-unh."

A TOUGH
SCUFFLE

It was more than one hundred and fifty miles from Wytheville to Charleston, West Virginia, and almost all of it was through mountains, so a whole day was allowed for travel. The trucks moved out of Wytheville early on Sunday morning, and it took some of them all day to get to the lot in Dunbar, a suburb of Charleston. There was no performance on Sunday; the show would be Monday evening. Several trucks broke down. As usual, the mechanics left the lot last, so that they could catch any strays and repair them.

The pole wagon and the spool truck made it to Charleston unscathed, and they set up the centerpole and then laid the Big Top canvas out in two long ribbons beneath it. The tent would not be put up until Monday morning. The workmen and performers took half the day off; they lazed around the lot or went to Seven-Elevens; some of them found a Laundromat and took in their week's washing. Several people talked, now, when reminded of him, about how dangerous a man Stash had been, and about how they had not noticed it at the time. Joe Hamilton was working elephants for Bert now; he had plans to check into a motel Sunday night when his work was done and take his infrequent long hot bath and rest between clean sheets. Jeff Woosnam was helping with the punks, although he was not listed officially on the payroll as a bullhand.

Superchicken had practically nothing to do, since the

canvas was still rolled and he could not get to it with his big needle and waxed cord. He walked around on his wobbly legs in high black boots, stopping every now and then to survey the lot, as if he were judging it for a water color. Superchicken, whose real name was Pete Clark, was an artist as well as sailmaker. He occasionally did pencil sketches of scenes from his memory and presented them to show people who had been nice to him.

It was a lazy, warm day. Superchicken wandered over to my little tent, which they were calling Little Big Top now, and sat down on a rock. I asked him to tell me about himself.

How old are you?

"Who, me?" he said. "How good are you at mathematics? I was born in eighteen and ninety-seven. I'll be seventy-seven this year. And scratching like heck for eighty."

"I was on Zack Miller's 101 Ranch Wild West Show," he said, "and I was on Sells-Floto, and Christy, and I went to Europe, and I worked over there for about nine years with different European circuses. For some reason or another, the cowboy act pulls well over there." Superchicken, who was known as Supe for short, then said something disparaging about the intellectual capacity of Frenchmen. He talked about the cowboy shows, and how the Europeans loved to see someone shoot a cigarette out of someone else's mouth, and things like that.

"I done all that in Europe. I also done Russian riding. I was *supposed* to be a Comanche Indian, which is wrong. I'm not a Comanche."

He stopped talking and waited for me to say what I should say at this point. "What kind of Indian *are* you?"

"Who, me? I'm about half Chiricahua Apache. That's west Texas, and now Arizona.

"And I was in Morocco in '25, '26. I went from French Morocco to China. And the nice thing about that is, you got a salary plus all you could steal. That was understood when they hired you. You know something? I must have had glue on my fingers. I came away with such junk as Ming vases and jade and stuff like that."

Supe said his occupation at that time had been mercenary soldier, and that he had entered that calling several years before in America.

"I first went with Pancho Villa in Mexico. I was over there from sometime early in 1919 up until 1920. I was with him in Mexico one time, and I was having fun. A beautiful, willing girl, a young man—what do you expect? Villa had the town. I was having fun. The next thing I know, Villa hauled out and the town was full of federal troops. The whole goddamn town was full of soldiers. I left Mexico in a big hurry. I think they had about eight or ten federal cops right on my tail. And when they come to the Rio Grande, they didn't give up.

"I was traveling by horseback. I crossed somewheres near Presidio, Texas. I got up pretty close to the Texas-Oklahoma border. Empty gun, empty belly, and a hungry horse. And no money. And I rode up on this ranch. I rode in and asked for a job. Man says, 'Oh, sure, I'll give you a job. Can you ride?' I says, 'What the hell do you think this damn thing is under me?'

"He says, 'Well, I don't know. It's got four feet and it *looks* like a horse.' So he give me a job. And he offered me a tremendous salary, for me—twenty-five a week, room and board. That was damn good money. In those days, twenty a *month* and beans was good pay. I didn't know what the heck he wanted me for. It wasn't long before he loaded me, the horse, and everything else in a baggage car and we hit the road. This was Zack Miller's show. I didn't realize I was talking with a circus owner. I thought he wanted me to punch cows." The Miller Brothers 101 Ranch Wild West Show was a prototype of a peculiar form of American circus, the wild West show. It started in 1908, when a circus man joined forces with some Oklahoma ranchers. For a while, a few years before the time Superchicken said he had joined the show, its star performer was Buffalo Bill.

Supe perched on the rock as if he could be comfortable anywhere. "So you went from soldiering to circus," I said.

"I went from *outlaw* to circus," he said. "The next step was, I got pretty tired of the circus. It was the same old grind,

Superchicken

day after day, and I decided to quit for a while. I wound up in Morocco. I signed on as a sailor—ordinary seaman, on a freighter. I made a slight mistake when I got to Morocco. I forgot that French officers had thin skulls. I cold-cocked a French officer. I was walking down the street, and three of them come walking down there, and they knocked me off into the gutter.

"Well, I don't know whether you know what those gutters are. I got up, and I was covered with shit and pretty mad, and I hauled off and slugged him. He didn't get up.

"I didn't know where the devil to go. I headed over into native town. Some guy says, 'Hey, you want to work?' He says, 'You shoot?' I says, 'Yeah.' He says, 'You come with me.' He took me over to some skinny guy with chin whiskers and the usual nightgown, and he offered me five hundred a week and all I could steal. Oh, heck, who the heck wouldn't take that?"

What kind of a job was he offering you?

"Shootin' Frenchmen."

So once again you were a soldier.

"Once again I was using a gun," Supe corrected. "And after that was over, I worked with circuses for a little while in Europe. And I liked it."

You didn't say how many Frenchmen you killed.

"I don't know how many I killed."

Was it many?

"Well, I'd say, between you and I, I was young, and I was an expert marksman. Figure it out for yourself."

What were they fighting about?

"Freedom for Morocco. Freedom from the French. They was under French rule. I was on the side against France.

"Then I worked a while for circuses in Europe. I got an offer to go to Saudi Arabia. I went over there for a while. Same deal—shootin'. And then, from there, I went to China for a while. I was supposed to be training soldiers, but I got the training myself."

In what?

"Kung fu, before it was ever heard of in this country." It was interesting that Supe mentioned the current self-defense craze. I wondered if a decade ago his answer would have been karate.

"And after that I came back to this country and worked circuses for a while."

When you were a mercenary, was the main interest money, or was money just an excuse for shooting people?

"The idea was the money. I couldn't have gotten it anywhere else. Look, at that time I was uneducated. Let's say I had a minimum education, and the only thing that I knew how to do was ride and shoot. And they were offering me anywheres from five hundred to a thousand a week."

There had been a rumor that Superchicken had the most impressive bank balance on the whole show. I asked him about that.

"I probably do," he said. "Because I came back to this country in nineteen and thirty, when the standard stocks were selling for peanuts. I bought quite a few. In fact, I broke myself buying bonds. Now they've had pups about three or four times. So I think I'm doing all right. I own quite a bit of Texaco. I own a little bit of U.S. Steel. And I own *some* A.T.&T."

Supe seemed proud of this, but he also seemed to want to change the subject.

"I was in the Spanish Civil War, you know. I spent three months in the most beautiful prison over there. It was gorgeous. This cell was about maybe fifty feet square, and the only bathroom was a ditch alongside one side of the cell. In the morning, you got a piece of bread and a little water. At suppertime, we got some soup. Between you and I, being polite, a buzzard would have gagged over it."

Which side were you on?

"I was fighting with the Moors, because they was friends of mine. I was invited over there by them. But it was for money. I was in jail because I got myself caught by the other side. There was a few of us who was overrun. I figured surrender was better than what would have happened to me if I hadn't surrendered."

And since that time you've been mostly circus?

"I've been *all* circus. Except I made a mistake and I got married."

Where's your wife?

"Dead. She got hepatitis and she was in the hospital about three days and she died. I've been free, on my own, ever since. What was it? Nineteen—" He thought a moment. "Nineteen sixty . . . sixty-six, sixty-seven, something like that."

Do you like this life?

"Yes. But I'm coming pretty close to the end of the road. My legs are going. My back is going. And I don't think I can keep up more than one, maybe two more seasons."

Is there some sort of informal retirement plan for people like you?

"No, not as far as I know of. But between you and me, I don't need it. I have my Social Security, and my kids will have their education before long. So what have I got to worry about? I've got stocks; the dividends isn't bad."

How many children?

"Three. One boy and two girls. The boy's on Staten Island and my girls are on Long Island. My son should be going to college at present. My girls should be about halfway through high school. They're living with friends of mine. Plus I send them a little loot every week."

How did you get the name Superchicken?

"When I joined this outfit, I was the smallest man here. And I wasn't afraid to step into anything. The boss canvasman was named Birdliver, so he stuck Superchicken on me. It referred to my size. And my nerve."

You once introduced yourself as the sailmaker. Have you ever made sails?

"Yes. I was coming home from Europe one time and I got stuck in Sweden. There was a cordwood ship from Sweden and Norway down to Portugal. It was an old square-rigged sailing ship. This must have been, I'd say, '37, '38, something like that. I learned the business there. Splicing, patching sails, tarring rope. You was busy all day long."

"The Big Top isn't up today," I said. "Does it feel unnatural to you for it to be down?"

"No. Because I've run into this hundreds of times. On the old railroad shows, years back, we pulled in late and laid out. That's what you've got here, a layout. The only thing you have to do tomorrow is unfold it and get it up. What they've got here is called wind-rolling the canvas. Tomorrow they lace it up, pull it up, and you're ready to go. Then I can walk around under it and see where the rips and tears are, and next time it's down I can fix them."

But doesn't it seem like less of a circus when the Big Top isn't up?

"Not to me."

Are you happy?

"I'm not kicking. I'm not kicking at all. Because when it comes right down to it, I make about eighty, eighty-five dollars a week, room and board. Eighty-five and beans. And no taxes. All I pay's Social Security. And a lot of fresh air. Course, sometimes it's a little *too* fresh."

Once the rings were laid out, Lucio Cristiani went to them and surveyed the ground. There were rocks and holes all over it, especially in Ring Two, where the horse act would perform. He took a pickaxe and started smoothing out the ground. "You know," he said, "a high-wire performer, he has the same rigging every day. When the rigging is new, it takes a while for him to get used to it. But after that it's the same rigging every day. But we bareback riders, we have a new rigging every day." He pointed to the ground.

He said that for a few dollars the show could buy a load of dirt for bad lots and smooth the ring out. He had done that when he was the president of a circus.

"You know," he said, "there is a story about John Ringling North. The Ringling show was in Canada, and, as you know, the show train moved in four sections. The last section was the performers. Well, one day the last section got a hotbox, and the performers didn't make it to the date. Everything else was ready to go. The butchers were there, the Big Top was up, the people who sold the tickets were there, the sideshow was up. But the performers were not there.

"And John Ringling North, he called everybody together and he said, 'You see, we can't really get along without the performers.' I think that is a lesson that people have to learn from time to time." He picked up the pickaxe and chopped at the clods of dirt.

Jeff watered the baby elephants and took them back to the bull line and anchored them, and he sat with Joe Hamilton and Bert Pettus in the shade of Bert's trailer. I asked Jeff how his life had been.

"I've gone through several depressions," he said. "Primarily because I see so many things here that I would like to see changed, simply because there's so much wasted effort and misuse of people." Bert grunted in what must have been agreement. Bert had reconsidered his plans about leaving the show. "I suppose I've kind of pushed those feelings aside," said Jeff, "and I'm not as concerned with them any more as I once was.

"I've come to the realization that all my worrying about it in the world isn't going to really change anything. Up until the last few days I wasn't really doing too much of anything except playing in the band. I just didn't care any more. And then I got involved over here with the elephants."

I recalled that Bert had once spoken of being "amazed" at the elephants. Was that Jeff's situation, too?

"I suppose, yes, 'amazed' would be a good word to describe it. Also, I'm kind of curious to see whether the elephants will work without being beaten—whether it's absolutely necessary."

"I think it *isn't* absolutely necessary," said Joe Hamilton. "Since I started working in the bull department, I think I've learned that you can get them to do most of what you want them to do without really beating them. You have to use the bullhook to guide them, and sometimes you have to threaten them a little, but you never need to really beat them."

Bert broke in. "I don't want to interrupt your conversation," he said, "but you take these four old elephants. You see how hardheaded they are about minding you. You'll notice the young ones, when I cut down on them, how quick they'll move, whereas the old ones, you have to holler at them three or four times. And I'll show you how this comes about.

Jeff and the baby bulls

"On this show you have a lot of people, and you start across the lot leading an elephant, and you holler out, 'Come on, Myrtle.' There may be half a dozen workmen hollering at her at the same time. And pretty soon the elephant will get bullheaded, and they won't pay no 'tention to *nobody*. Now you got to crack him with the stick to make him notice you and get done what you want done.

"See, the elephants are like people. They like to goof off. And they're not going to do nothing that they don't have to do. And if they think they can get by without doing it, they play the iggie to you and get by. See, the damn elephant is so smart he knows before you do what you're going to do yourself when you don't even know it yourself.

"You think I'm kidding, but that's the truth. Like the guy says, 'Com'ere.' And all the time that elephant knows that man is going to turn and walk the other way and maybe be twenty, thirty feet away from him before he says 'Com'ere' again. And so the elephant says, 'I know that dumb bastard ain't going to make me do it,' and so he'll start going the other way, eating,"

Linda Chandler sat on the ground, splicing rope and covering it with canvas. It was Monday, show day in Charleston. She was putting together a trapeze, and she hoped that when she got it put together she could then put together an act. She was hoping that before the season was over she could have the device built and would have been able to practice on it enough, between shows, so that she could audition for John Hall. The Chandlers were hoping they would be invited back next year. She was wearing her sweat shirt that said "Libby Girls Staff." I asked her where she had learned to splice rope.

"I learned it in the Girl Scouts," she said.

And where did she get the sweat shirt?

"Libby's a Girl Scout camp. I was a counselor there about three summers ago. That was the summer before I joined the circus."

I asked Linda if, when she looked back on it, it seemed that she had been in some way destined to join the circus.

"No," she said. "I really didn't know until I saw the circus that day, and saw that they had an opening for somebody to work with the animals. Until then I didn't have any idea of going with the circus at all. Of course, I'd been dreaming about circuses all along."

Does this beat teaching English?

"Definitely."

I asked Linda where she got her athletic ability. Sometimes the young women who did web and ladder griped a lot about pulled muscles and sore backs and rope burns, but Linda never griped at all. She seemed actually to enjoy the work.

"I've been climbing trees all my life," she said, "and climbing up in barns whenever I visited my uncle's farm. I've been doing cart wheels and things like that all my life, as long as I can remember. And back when I was about twelve or thirteen, I had this circus dream. I wanted to have a trapeze act. And now maybe I will."

▸

Linda

The show grounds in Charleston was beside a busy road, but there was plenty of room on both sides of it. To the east there was a golf course, and to the west there was a patch of woods—tall trees and grasses and some thick vegetation. It was from these woods that the music came, faint at first and then louder. I walked through the trees to see what it was.

Claude Pasauer sat in an old stone amphitheater practicing his music. Claude worked in the band; he played a cornet. He looked perfectly at peace and at ease, sitting there in the glade practicing.

Claude was born in New Orleans in 1906. He pronounced it *New Or-LEENS*. I asked him how he got where he was now.

"My mother was named Payzzet Pasauer," he said, "and my father was named Hosea Pasauer. And the ancestors are from Haiti on my father's side, and my mother's father, he was from Santo Domingo. They came over—at least, they *brought* them over—to the United States in the early days of the French and the Spanish for the sugar-cane farming.

"I've been in music ever since I was around about twelve

or thirteen or fourteen. My father was a violinist, played a lot of country music, you know. And my grandfather, he played the old plectin' banjo, and I had another uncle and *he* played violin. In fact, the whole family was that way.

"They weren't in the show business. They were just farmers and country-music people. So I was about the only one that's branched out. And when I left home, I left with an E-flat clarinet and an E-flat alto horn. They was old-fashioned horns, you know. I paid five dollars for the horn, and the clarinet, I paid three dollars for it, and I used to pay fifty cent a lesson to learn how to play them. In the later years I came on out and I went from that to the cornet."

Were you what is called a Dixieland musician?

"Well, back in those days I was in country, but after I took the lessons, I learned to play the marches and the overtures and everything else. I've been in vaudeville, and on the stages, you know, and in the tent shows. And I've been in the circuses since way back in 1920. I came away from New Orleans when I was about four or five months old. My father was down there working the waterfront.

"From then on, that was just the way it happened. I just felt the music. I was out there in the field one day plowing with two mules, Red and Kate. I heard the calliope"—he pronounced it *KAL-e-ope*, the way many show people pronounce it—"from the circus, and I said, 'Now, that's it.' I walked off and left the mules and followed the circus.

"Yes, I had to go to work in the fields that day, and they wouldn't let me off to go to the show, so I left the mules in the field. You know how young boys is about the circus." Claude laughed a long time. "This was in Louisiana. In Opelousas, out in the country, on the farm. I was about twelve or thirteen or fourteen.

"After a while they give me a nickname, Jazz Curry. And my union first was five-ninety-one in Philadelphia. Transferred to Atlantic City and was playing on the Boardwalk way back in the twenties and then quit that and went into the burlesque and from that into the Lafayette Theater, where I had played previous, coming out of Boston, and it turned out I was breaking a strike, which I didn't realize what it was.

"And I worked around different jobs. Worked in coal mines, you know, and first one thing and then another. I worked sawmills and chopping wood. In fact, I had too much work. I just didn't get a chance to go to the schools like I should have. I had to cut out at the last of the third grade, and I had to pick up the rest on the road, and so here I am."

I asked Claude whether he liked indoors or outdoors better. "Well," he said, "I like indoors and night clubs and theater pits better. Because you don't have to go through so much *strain*. I've been up and down Broadway in the twenties so much it wasn't even funny, you know, with different bands. In New York. And that's the truth and you can't tell anything different from that.

"Yeah, a lot of fellows I met in bands and things, and they've all passed away, all the great names of them. Now, you take Louis Armstrong. Back home, when I first came back with a show in 1919, he give me a job. Didn't no one know me until I got out and started playing. They said, 'Where you from?' and I told them, I was native-born there in New Orleans. We got three dollars for gigs and funerals, and that's all they paid. Louis Armstrong, he worked on the boats, and I worked on boats, too. The pleasure boats."

Do you plan to stay here the whole season?

"Oh, yeah, I'm going to be here all season and quite a few more of them. I was off about eight years, and King Charles, he didn't know where I was until I wrote him a card. Boy, he thought I was *dead!* I could have been with him a long time ago, but I had this Social Security proposition to straighten out. So I got that all straightened out and I thought I might as well be out here. Just so I don't run over that limit, you know. See, you're allowed sixteen hundred and eighty dollars, and now it's twenty-two hundred, so what I'm making now won't hardly run over it.

"It's a tough scuffle out here, you know. But I'd rather be scuffling around out here than anyplace else." Claude laughed. "Yeah, a tough scuffle."

He looked around him in the amphitheater. It was a lovely day, and the birds were singing, and the Big Top was rolling with the breeze in the background. "Yeah," said Claude, "but with the fresh air, and the birds, it's not much of a scuffle today."

On Sunday the sun had set gently in Charleston, or at least it seemed gently, because there was no hurry to get ready for the show. The lot looked strange, the trucks and trailers sitting there without the Big Top up, without the hurrying and Phil Chandler's whistle, without the sideshow grind and the relentlessly repeated recorded message from the Himalayan Monster.

Cars moved along the roadway, slowing when the drivers saw the lot and the strange collection of purple vehicles and beasts, then speeding up again. Some of the performers unhitched their cars and trucks from their trailers and went to the movies. Some of the workingmen went to a motel for a bath and to sleep in a proper bed. Joe Hamilton was one of them. He asked Bert Pettus if the elephants would be all right overnight without him, and Bert said yes, and Joe said he would be back by eight o'clock in the morning. Then Joe and some others, an electrician and a mechanic (high, as Joe was, in the status of workingmen), went to the 60 East Motel, about three miles away.

Not long after they arrived at the motel, Joe and the electrician, who was named Sparky, called a cab and asked to be taken to a Laundromat. As they arrived, they saw the Laundromat was closing, and so they called another cab and returned to the motel. Joe took a shower and shaved, and then he went with some of the others to a pizza joint next door. The men ordered a pitcher of beer. Joe drank some, maybe the equivalent of two glasses, and then he fell asleep in the restaurant.

The others woke him. They thought it was unnatural, his sleeping like this. It was almost as if he had passed out. So they took him back to his room. Joe said he was very cold. They put him in bed and put blankets on him and returned to the pizza joint. When they came back, Joe was tossing and turning in his sleep.

"Now, I knew before that he'd been taking some medication," said Sparky later. "He had some capsules. I remem-

bered last time we stayed in a motel, he was wondering how
far we were from a VA hospital, because he wanted to get
another refill on his prescription. And I knew he had taken a
pill before we went to the Laudromat. I didn't know what
they were—I hadn't seen them that close. He never said anything to me about something being wrong with him. Now,
later I found out that he had a medical bracelet on. I don't
know what it said.

"Now, I have a type of epilepsy," said Sparky. "Temple-
lobe epilepsy. And I've been with patients that have epilepsy,
and he was exactly like they are. We left a call at the motel
desk for seven in the morning. I tried to get Joe for half an
hour. Finally, the last time I woke him up, I said, 'Joe, we've
got to go now. You're late already.' He says, 'I'm going to sleep
a little longer. I'll be back in a little while.' I went across the
street and got coffee, and then I came back and I woke him up
again and he still didn't want to get up. He was doubling his
arms up and shaking. And I came back to to the show. And
that was it. I've been with patients in the hospital who are
purely epileptics, and he was doing exactly the way they do.
They get the shakes, and they're so cold."

On Monday, Joe had not returned to the lot. Jeff
Woosnam noticed he was missing and asked around about
Joe, and he heard the electrician's story. Jeff was shaken. Joe
was his best friend on the circus, and had been since winter
quarters. Jeff knew Joe would not have blown the show without telling him. Jeff remembered that sometimes epileptics
suffered amnesia when they had their attacks. He wondered
if that had happened to Joe.

Bert Pettus heard all this, and he told Jeff, "He was high
on something. He didn't want to get up, and when he did get
up, he realized that it was too late, and he thought his job
wasn't no good with me and he was afraid to come out to the
lot. That's the whole thing. He got high on something, and he
just overslept."

Jeff said no, that Joe wasn't that sort of person. Bert
shook his head wisely. "You take the working class of people,"
he said. "Either they're drunks, or they're misfits of some kind.

A normal person of the working class could go out and make more money than you could on a thing like this. So why would he be here?" Jeff tried to interrupt, to say that Joe was here because he wanted to experience the circus; that he was not a misfit; that perhaps there were some exceptions to Bert's rule.

"The only reason he was here was that there was something driving him to this," said Bert flatly.

But wasn't there some room for wanting to be here just because it's a circus? asked Jeff.

"No," said Bert. "I don't think so. Not today. No. It used to be, yes. When I first come into the business, you *wanted* to be here. But today, when you look at them yourself around here—they're not wanting to be here. It's just a haven for them. Alcoholics, misfits of all kinds."

Someone asked Bert what he thought Joe's own particular trouble was.

"I didn't know him that well," said Bert. "I wouldn't say. He had the potentials to be a good elephant man, and I told him that. He had everything it takes to be a good elephant man. If he'd just accept the responsibility."

Was it alcohol?

"No. He didn't seem that way."

Pills?

"He didn't *seem* to be on pills, but there again, you can't tell too much about what these people do. He might have covered up when I was around him, and then when he got away from me, it would come out. I never looked at the guy that close. I did know that when he worked with me, he was a good worker. He could have been a good elephant man."

And there aren't that many good elephant men around?

"Hell, no. There're maybe ten of us altogether. Some old ones like myself who've already dropped out, and I'm ready to drop out, too. I *definitely* am going to make this my last season."

Jeff said that Bert was wrong; that what he thought might be applicable to many of the men who worked on the show, but not to Joe. Joe was different, he said. Bert said that not many people were different; that over the years you learned a few basic facts about people, and that Joe's disappearance could be easily explained. Bert talked firmly but compassionately with Jeff, as if he were a father trying to explain some of the harsher facts of life to his son.

Joe had gone on sleeping Monday morning and well into the afternoon. At two o'clock, a cleaning woman had opened the door to the room and had waked Joe up. Joe had expressed surprise at how late it was, the woman said, and he had dressed quickly and called a cab. He had asked the driver to take him to the bus station. But, on the way, said the driver, Joe had said he was going to stop by the driver's license office at a state building. The driver said he knew it sounded peculiar, but that was what Joe had said.

Leaving Charleston on Tuesday: It was dismal and dreary. All the factories had started up again after the weekend, and they had flooded the river valley with pollution. There was a temperature inversion, which held the pollution close to the ground. You could see for only a few blocks. The wooded edge of a mountain would come down out of the mist, and then a few blocks later there would be another one. The air was bad, the streets were bad, the people were angry-looking. The people who ran things in this part of the world must have taken more than their usual share. The mountains and valley had been raped, and now the air was dying. The people on the streets looked like mountain people, country people, who had been forced to live in a bad, stinking city and who had given up on trying to change things. It was an unnatural life.

These were essentially the same mountains that you saw in the Smokies and around West Jefferson and Wytheville, clear and blue and with the promise of trout streams, but here there was a difference. They were owned, here, by outfits named Union Carbide and DuPont, and they were horribly, irretrievably ugly. Even in the springtime, a time when beauty bursts involuntarily from the ground and is hard to repress, it looked bleak here.

On the way out I ran into Bob Brown. We exchanged

pleasantries, and I mentioned that Joe Hamilton had apparently blown the show.

"I saw him last night," said Bob. "He ended up with a little waitress. She's got a good job, taking good care of him. I was downtown trying to recruit some more help and I ran into him. He says, 'What should I do—stay with the show or stay with her?' I looked at her and I said, 'Stay with her. She looks better than that elephant you been working with.'

"He said he had the route card. He said he liked it in Charleston. He said he'd come back in case something happened. I told him he was welcome to come back."

I asked Bob if he was sure that was all Joe had said.

"He just said he had a shack-up with a waitress and she's taking care of him," said Bob. He was grinning. "Sounds pretty good to me."

SOMEWHERES ON THE ROAD

It was the real first of May now, and all the first of Mays were veterans, and the show was far from Florida. Up through the spring rains it went, quickly out of West Virginia and then thirteen days in Ohio, to places like McConnellsville and Zanesville and Heath and Eaton. In Cambridge, Cowboy Jim left the show. Then across the line to Greensburg, Indiana, for a day; then back to Ohio; back to Indiana for two days; Ohio again, this time Napoleon. One of the ponies foaled in Napoleon. The offspring was female, and they named her Josephine. Then nine days in the lower part of Michigan, where spring was not yet an accomplished fact at all. And two days across the top of Indiana and on into Wisconsin, where it was cold rain and hard work. Many times the elephants had to be called to drag the trucks off muddy lots. Superchicken said he had gotten "quite a few free baths." I asked him if the rain hurt his morale. "I'll just say that I don't have any, any more," he replied. "I lost it somewheres on the road."

Billy Joe left the show, as did a lot of other workmen. The combination of rain and cold weather and getting a great distance from Miami seemed to do the trick. New workmen came on the lot, men with Scandinavian faces and bodies heavier than those of the Southerners who had preceded them. They ate bread and meat and potatoes up here. Two cooks came and left. Leo stayed, and so did King Charles and Gypsy Red and Bert Pettus, although they complained a lot and talked frequently of leaving. They were *with it;* they stayed. Bonnie kicked Bert in the chest; Bert decided she was not trying to really hurt him.

In Greensburg, Indiana, it was so windy that they could not put up the Big Top, and the show was presented in the sideshow tent, with one ring. In the audience was a young man, seventeen years old, named Charles Stepleton. He liked the show. When it left Greensburg, he left with it.

At New Miami, Ohio, the Murillos returned. Luis Murillo's back had healed, and he and Jorge Del Moral had gotten in the yellow truck and driven to Ohio and rejoined. This time they did not do their wire-walking act. It was, they explained, too much trouble, and it took too much time to set the rigging for two separate acts; they were always hurrying, and when you hurried you cut corners, and cutting corners, they had decided, was what had made Luis fall in Sunrise in March.

The Murillos concentrated on their motorcycle act, which worked this way: They had a Honda motorcycle with no tires, just wheels. The motorcycle was mounted on a steel cable that ran from a low point near the sidewall up close to the top of the centerpole. It was about a thirty-degree angle. Beneath the motorcycle was suspended a metal cradle, and at the bottom of the cradle there was a horizontal bar, a trapeze. At the beginning of the act, Luis mounted the motorcycle and Jorge sat on the bar, and Luis raced the motor and roared up the incline, stopping just short of the centerpole. It was very spectacular, and it was made more so by all the noise involved. When they reached the top, Jorge hung by his hands from the bar, and he stretched out on it so he was balancing on the small of his back. There was no net.

Then Luis backed the cycle down the cable, stopped for applause, and raced back up. This time Phil Chandler announced that the pair would do the "butterfly spin," and Jorge started throwing his weight to one side and then the other, until the entire contraption was doing complete turns around the cable. There was a device to insure that the motorcycle could not slip off the cable. Still, it was exciting, and the crowd always loved it. The act was used to finish up the show.

Luis Murillo and Jorge Del Moral

The circus people got to know Jorge and Luis a little better, and they liked them a great deal. Both of them were always joking around. Luis, the older of the two, did not have a complete command of English, so he tended to pronounce the few phrases he knew well with great frequency. "Oppy New Year" was one of them. Luis tended to save his money and to stay away from frills, so people kidded him a lot about being a tightwad. Jorge, who spoke perfect English, was a handsome young man, and showed great interest in the few younger, unmarried women on the show. He was always playing practical jokes on people, and especially on Luis. He said that life was too short to waste it on being serious all the time. Now that the Murillos were back, the show seemed to be complete.

John Hall had picked up a new act, too. They were named Rosales. Ruben Rosales did foot juggling, and his wife,

Magalay, did a single-trapeze act that was very good. She stood
on her head on the trapeze, with no net, and then swayed from
side to side, touching the bar only with the top of her head.
Then she put juggling rings around her arms and legs and
rotated them while balancing. Ruben stood on the ground
beneath her, but he seemed too far away to do anything in
case she fell. They traveled in a small homemade camper with
their young son. They were from Mexico.

In Wausau, Wisconsin, Tino Cristiani was coming down
off the trampoline, and he was doing his tumbles on the
ground, as usual, and he slipped on a little rock and fell on
his arm. A bone was cracked. They put a cast on his arm, and
he went back to work the next day. Cristianis do not stay long
out of the act.

The show played Baraboo, Wisconsin, on a Friday, and
almost everyone went over to the Circus World Museum there.
Baraboo was the home town of the Ringling brothers. Bob
Mason, the sideshow manager, went, and he was looking at
the old circus flatcars, and on one of them was a float that he
had driven in 1948 on a circus. "It was the Mother Goose
float," he said, "and I got all choked up about it. I thought
about how young I was and full of hope, then."

The academic year was ending around the country now,
and a number of teen-agers and children, a great many of
them named Hill and Walker, joined the show, most of them
to work as butchers. Some of the other hands objected to what
they called this nepotism; it was an ancient problem that arose
every year in the circus and carnival businesses. Johnny
Walker's son, Johnny, Junior, seemed to be getting whatever
work he wanted. He worked as a butcher, but he also enjoyed
working with the elephants, and Bert Pettus and some of the
other bullhands didn't like this.

Milwaukee was the biggest city so far, and the circus
people were glad to be there, because it meant another two-
day stand. The shows were Saturday and Sunday, at the beginning of June. The lot was on the lakefront a few feet from

where the Milwaukee River emptied into Lake Michigan.

Linda Chandler finished her sideshow work for the first show, went through Spec, the magic act, and her other performances, and went to the trailer and changed into blue jeans and a T-shirt. She wanted to see what the lake looked like, and the dog needed walking. The Chandlers' dog was named Eustace P. McGargle, and was also known as D.O., which was short for D.O.G. It was sixty-six degrees in Milwaukee at that hour. The show was finishing inside the Big Top.

Linda climbed up on a cement pier and stared at the lighthouse for a while, then started back toward the show. At about that time, she heard a girl screaming, "My cousin's in the water!" Linda looked down and saw a child's head bobbing in the lake. The water was about seven feet below the surface of the pier, and the child was about four feet out.

Linda handed the other girl D.O.'s leash and lowered herself into the water. She reached the child quickly, put her arm around her in the cross-chest carry, and pulled her to the side. "It was very slimy on the side," said Linda, "and it was hard to get a hold onto it. But she was seven years old and didn't weigh very much." Linda pushed the child toward a ledge, and by this time her aunt and other cousins had arrived, and they helped pull her up. The little girl had not swallowed any water, but she did not know how to swim.

Linda found out later that the child had left the circus tent to go to the bathroom, and then had wandered down by the lake and fallen in. Linda carried the girl to her trailer and dried her off, wrapped her in a blanket and made some hot chocolate. Someone called an ambulance. Linda ran over to tell Bob Mason that she wouldn't make it for the next sideshow bally.

The people in Milwaukee referred to Linda's act as one of heroism, but Linda said it wasn't that big a deal. "It seemed like they were making a lot of fuss," she said later. "I just saw what had to be done, and I did it. Anyone would have done the same." Linda said her Red Cross training had equipped her to give mouth-to-mouth resuscitation, but that the child hadn't needed it.

Later, Linda received three plaques commemorating her act. One was from the Marathon County Deputy Sheriffs' Association, one was from the child's school, and one was from her parents. The school's citation was a "certificate of appreciation to Linda Barr . . . for your Gallant and Heroic Efforts . . . in saving the life of Pamela Rae Beach, Seven Year Old Student, from drowning in the Milwaukee River at the entry into Lake Michigan." The one from the parents said:

Linda Barr
Your Heroic Efforts
on
June 1, 1974
Will Forever Be
The High Point
in
Our Family's Life
Walter & Marian

Jeff Woosnam's occasional depressions continued as the show moved through the chilly Midwest, and the weather didn't help at all. Since Joe Hamilton had blown, Jeff had been working on what he called "a kind of permanent part-time basis with Bert Pettus," tending the elephants for free while retaining his position in the band. Jeff worked with the bulls all day, then changed into his band clothes late in the afternoon so he could play in the sideshow bally and the nighttime performances. King Charles did not like this; he thought Jeff was subordinating his band work, and that, after all, was what he was being paid for. And one night in New Miami, Ohio, two of Jeff's friends, who were students at Miami University, came to see the show and Jeff. "I hadn't seen them in quite a while," he said, "and they're both very dear people, and having to say goodbye to them kind of messed me up."

On the next day, the show was in New Castle, Indiana, and Jeff approached the sleeper at about five o'clock to change clothes. King Charles was cooking his dinner there, and he chewed Jeff out. "I got very annoyed at that point," said Jeff, "because several things had happened prior to that. I was upset about saying goodbye to my friends the night before, and earlier that day I had been robbed of fifty dollars. I was one of about half a dozen who got hit.

"So when Charles started in on me, I just got very hard, and I said to him, in a very loud voice, 'Don't give me none of your shit about being on time. I haven't blown a bally yet,' and so on. Because Charles had all day to lay around the lot. He didn't go anywhere, didn't do anything, but he waited until five o'clock to go to the sleeper and start cooking something on his electric frying pan. Which was one of the things Charles did. He'd wait until real late to eat, and then bitch because he ate too much and couldn't play in the band well. All I ever heard from him was excuses. Anyway, when I started hollering back at him, he jumped down out of the sleeper and told me to go on over to the office window because he was firing me.

"Ironically, that day and the day before that, Bert had said to me, on at least three separate occasions that I can recall, 'Why don't you put that horn down and come over here and let me make an elephant man out of you?' And I had said, 'Well, I don't know, I can't really do that, but I want to work with you, and I'll work with you as long as I can.' And in New Miami, Bert had said that he had finally convinced Bill Hill that every day I worked with the elephants Hill would slip me a fin. I didn't initiate that, but it was fine with me. I was happy just helping Bert and being with the animals.

"Charles went storming around looking for Mike McGuire and John Hall. Finally he found them. You've probably seen Charles when he blows his top. He's just totally irrational. You simply cannot communicate with the man, even to get him calmed down. Well, this happened in New Castle. John asked me what happened, and I very calmly explained. I told him that I didn't want to blow the show, that I was happy, that I was having a good time, and that I knew I could go over and work for Bert full time with no problem. And John said, 'Okay, fine, we'll do that, and we'll keep you on at your present salary,' which was eighty dollars a week, which is what band members get."

Jeff moved his belongings out of the sleeper and into the

elephant truck, and he became a full-time bull handler. Later one of the stock men left, and Jeff added the ponies, a horse, the llama, the camel, the zebras, and other animals to his list of duties.

"And I finally just got wrung out," said Jeff. "I was just too terribly tired. I was only getting four hours of sleep at night. I must make the distinction that the hard work was not what was hurting me. It was simply lack of rest. And what really put the cap on it was in Beloit, Wisconsin, when Johnny Walker, Junior, came around wanting to be an elephant man. He started giving commands to my elephant, Myrtle. I told him to get away. And he threatened all sorts of great bodily harm to me. And why I didn't beat him to a pulp right there, I don't know. I got very irate, because I was having enough trouble fighting the elephant without fighting the help, too. And I had my stock to be taken care of, and I didn't have any time to stand around and argue with the kid, and I was very upset. I handed my hook to Bert and I said, 'I can't take any more of it.' He said, 'Are you quitting now?' and I did a very quick reconsideration and I said, 'What the hell. No, I'm not going to leave today.'

"But I knew we were moving to Rensselaer, Indiana, the next day, and I decided then that I was not going to stay with the show any longer. So I called home, and I told them that when we got to Rensselaer I was going to get on a bus and I was going to come home. Mom said, 'No, I'll come over and pick you up.'"

And so Jeff quit the show.

Unlike a lot of other people who had left, Jeff did not just walk off the lot. He went around shaking hands and saying goodbye. The people he said goodbye to placed their own interpretations on his decision to leave. King Charles said it was because Jeff had found that he "didn't like the elephants." John Hall said Jeff had told him he hadn't had a good hot bath for a long time, and that "he just couldn't hack it any more."

I told John that Jeff had seemed to symbolize a lot of people of intelligence and ability who tried to run away with the circus. "Eventually," replied John, "most of them run away *from* the circus."

Why?

"The circus is a hard life. You have to really love it. You've got to be willing to put up with a lot of things to stay in this business. I think the biggest thing that would keep you here is your love for it."

And Jeff didn't have enough of that?

"I think it would be true to say that. I don't have anything against Jeff at all. He was a good worker while he was here. And he tried hard. But he just didn't have the *sufficient* love for the circus, I think, to stay. It was not that important in his life."

Jeff and his family sat around the big wooden table that dominated the biggest room of the farmhouse in Seville. Two sets of Sunday papers were on the table, and the family was dividing them up and reading voraciously and eating toast and drinking coffee and pouring glassfuls of milk and sometimes dipping the toast into the coffee. When one member of the family talked, the others listened as if they were really interested in what was being said. Often they broke in with additions or questions. Jeff's parents were about the age his parents should have been, but they seemed young and energetic and full of wisdom. I remembered what Jeff had said about his father's teaching them how to go back to the land. His brother and sister talked less, but they still were interested and respectful. Jeff looked as intense and thoughtful as ever, but he seemed a lot more rested. He had been home a week.

"What I ran into on the show," he said, "was constant obfuscation. If somebody went up to them with a problem, they'd throw something else up, or would constantly—to use a term that's currently in vogue—constantly stonewall. And they'd just beat you down. The treatment the animals received —it was awful. All those animals jammed into the front end of a truck. I said something about it to Hoxie, and he said, 'Oh, we used to carry five horses up there.' And the cookhouse. That cookhouse drove more good men away."

"You had something to offer them," I said, "that not many others did—dedication. You were sober, reliable. And they didn't reward you very handsomely, did they?"

"Well," said Jeff, "I wasn't looking for reward. It was just this thing about *caring* about what's going on. That just didn't happen. I had given them what I considered to be—what I *know* to be—just about everything I had, in terms of work and assuming responsibility. And it didn't help."

Hoxie said that everybody on the show had a weakness; that they were running from something. Did you find that *you* were running from something?

"No," said Jeff. "One thing that I contended ever since I started out with this adventure was that I was not running away to join the circus. I was just going to do something that looked like it might have some interesting aspects, and that not too many people were able to do."

What did you learn?

"I'll never forget about elephants," Jeff said with a smile. "And I know I can always go to Malakoff, Texas, and get a job working elephants. What I learned, really, was that you have to separate the actual show itself—the ninety-minute show and the people who are involved with that; the three hours a day that the show is on—from the other twenty-one hours a day that has the whole outfit going from here to there, the Big Top and the sideshow getting up and getting down and getting packed up to go away.

"I was lucky because I spent a lot of time in the back yard because of my involvement with the band. And the people in the back yard, I have great love and admiration for, and I've got to write them. Armando, especially. But I just couldn't put up with that *other* stuff any more—the other twenty-one hours."

Jeff paused a few moments, and his family watched him, as if they knew he was about to say something important, something that summed up his three months with the circus.

"I guess what I've learned is that things ain't what they seem to be," he finally said. He laughed because he knew it was a trite expression. "Or that all that glitters is not gold. Or something like that. I maintained from the day I decided to do this that I had no illusions about it. I knew what I was getting into. I wasn't expecting any glitter and glamour because I saw, when I did that newspaper story on my first newspaper job, that there really is no glitter and glamour. It's a lot of hard work. The people are tired. Behind the makeup, they're old, and their faces are worn. It's a rather grim life.

"But I had thought, or I had hoped, that the renowned Hoxie Brothers Circus was quality all round. And it's *not* quality all round. It's quality up to the extent of the show. The Chandlers, the Fornasaris, the Cristianis are three of the most beautiful families I think I'll ever meet. But the rest . . ." Jeff's voice trailed off.

I asked him what he had done when he got home. "I slept a lot," he said. "I took a long bath. One of the things I've noticed is that ever since I started working with the elephants, I'll wake up in the middle of the night—it happened again last night—and I'll be hollering orders to the elephants, or keeping people away from the elephants, or doing something with the elephants. It's some anxiety that I don't really understand. I'm not *worried* about it. It'll work itself out.

"But the first night I was home, I slept on the couch, and I remember waking up at one point and seeing an elephant lying down on the floor. One of the babies, lying down. Well, it took me about thirty seconds to realize that that was my *dog* lying on the floor, stretched out like that.

"And last night, I dreamed I was taking care of the elephants. In the dream, I wasn't *supposed* to, because I wasn't with the circus any more, but I was chaining them up and keeping people away from them. And I remember waking up and saying to myself, 'Why am I doing this? I don't even work for the circus any more. I shouldn't be messing around with those elephants. Let them *go*.'"

THE LIGHT

Close to a dozen years ago, John Hall and his first wife decided on a divorce as the best way out of their relationship. There was, as there so often is, a crisis, and each of the partners had to fall back on his or her own resources in order to deal with it. John's resources were those that had been instilled in him by a Southern religious upbringing, and he found that they were inadequate. "My church's teachings were that I didn't *believe* in divorce in the first place," he said a few years ago, "and it was a very difficult time. And my beliefs, my Southern Baptist beliefs, just didn't hold up."

So John started looking around at other churches. He did not limit his search to the more traditional forms of worship; he looked, too, at that broad category of believing that, often inadequately, goes under the name of *occult*. "I'd always had a strong interest in God," said John, "just like I'd always had a strong interest in the circus." So he explored God in books. The more he found out about occult and astrology, reincarnation and astral projection, the more comfortable he felt with it. Now John Hall was probably the only circus manager in the country who believed that he had once been an animal trainer in ancient Rome, who thought he had once lived on the lost continent of Atlantis, and who believed that his brain waves might have some influence on the weather.

After John had been reading about all this for a few years, and training his mind for an understanding of some of the complexities of his new religion, he felt he had made some progress. A few years ago, he said he knew enough to decide that all the things he had been reading were true. "One of the things I have come to believe in," he said then, "is reincarnation. I came gradually to a belief in it. It makes a lot more sense than a lot of the other answers, and I think there's a great deal of evidence—if a person looks for it—for reincarnation. And also, in the occult you have what is called 'out-of-the-body experiences,' where the idea is that your physical body is like a coat, or a vehicle, that you use. The *real* person is a spirit or soul that has used many different bodies at many different times.

"So, therefore, the spirit can leave the body even while you are here in this particular life, without dying. You can do this *daily*, and in fact, according to the ideas of the occult, everybody does this in dreams. Your dreams are out-of-the-body experiences. But through learning techniques and a lot of practice, a person can *consciously* do this at will. And to a certain extent I've done this. I've had the definite feeling that I was out of the body, floating around in the air."

I asked John, back then, whether any of this related to his work with the circus.

"It relates to living," he said. "It's a way of living, really. And I had one psychic to tell me that *I'm* a little psychic, and I think this is true. I think intuition, too, is a milder way of saying 'psychic ability,' and I have pretty good intuition—many times about the towns that we're about to play. In other words, I think what psychic ability I have helps me a great deal in planning the work that I do for the circus, or planning anything, really. I have pretty good intuition about things—about how good the sponsors are going to be. I have feelings that there are certain towns that aren't going to do well, and in almost every case I'm right.

"It extends to the weather. Also—I don't know exactly how to explain it—but you can use positive thinking, I think, to bring about a calmness in the weather around you. Because I think that everything Jesus did, anyone else can do if they develop the ability, including smoothing down wind and rain."

John had said all this back at a time when he was general manager of the show but when Hoxie was very much in personal charge of it. It was before Hoxie's heart attacks and nervous breakdown, and John did not by any means make all the show's major decisions. John had said, at that time, that one of his ambitions was to own his own circus, and that his feelings about out-of-the-body experiences and reincarnation were closely tied in with this ambition.

"I once had a very clear idea, going back to my childhood," he said, "about owning my own show. I would still like to have my own show, but it's not as important to me now. It's sort of like growing a tree. It eventually bears fruit. If I have thousands of lifetimes, as I now believe I have, having a large circus in *this* lifetime is not very important when you consider a wide span of time.

"But if there's something more important to life than having a very large circus, then that makes it different. I've become more and more interested in the occult and the certain *values* of life, which cover more than just one lifetime, because I think the talents and the skills and the knowledge that a person learns, through experience—he never loses them. He carries these with him, from one lifetime to another, and even in between lifetimes. Now the biggest goal in my life is to develop personality qualities, of a good nature, that go with me from one lifetime to another."

Through the years the circus grew, in size and in prestige. Hoxie's health declined, and John maintained his outwardly casual but inwardly intense approach to the show and to life in general, and he plunged deeper into the books and tried harder to stretch his capacity for the comprehension of life. He absorbed more and more of the responsibility for the running of the show; from Hoxie's point of view, he was perfect for the job. He did not drink, take drugs, or steal. He was competent, highly intelligent, and a hard worker. It made no difference to Hoxie that John was difficult to figure out by any of the usual methods or that his trailer's shelves were lined with books with strange titles.

Lisa

John was not a celibate, however, and he had several romances with women off and on the show, and some of the women he took up with were referred to by others as his "wives." Then John met Lisa. Her real name was Hermenejilda Gonzalez, and she was from Puerto Rico. Lisa worked at a printer's, and John met her one day when he dropped off a poster order for the circus. He invited her to come to see the show, and they fell in love.

Lisa was a strikingly attractive woman, with dark hair that flowed down to the small of her back, and with quick, intelligent eyes that were full of fun but that could occasionally narrow into anger. Lisa was practical, frankly spoken, and smart. She was scared of nothing. When she thought Hoxie was doing something wrong, she would walk up to him and tell him, even when his hatbrim was down.

Now, in the season of 1974, John and Lisa sat in their trailer in the middle of the Midwest and talked about life and the future and the past. Lisa cooked things while John spoke, in his slow, measured tones. Lisa was always cooking and offering the products of her oven to circus people. She was a Puerto Rican Jewish Mother.

↜

"The idea of reincarnation," said John, "is that a person can either regress or progress. It depends on how he lived in that particular lifetime. The whole ideas is to evolve *up*. It's an evolution-type thing spiritually, where you evolve up and become one with God. And this takes many thousands of years. It takes many lifetimes, either here in the physical dimension, or maybe in some other dimension somewhere."

John mentioned that years before, when he had talked about all this, he had used the word "occult." Now, he said, he thought the word was imprecise in describing what he was feeling. "It's not the right word to describe some of the experiences you have," he said. "Lisa disagrees with me. She still likes the traditional ideas more."

"It's not the traditional ideas," said Lisa. "It's just what I believe. I've had personal experiences, too, and I've tried to tell John about the experiences I've had, and sometimes he has explained them in ways that made sense to me. Like one time when I was a child in Puerto Rico I saw a woman who was possessed by a spirit. John explained it *his* way, and I said, 'Well, that's *possible*,' but then I said, 'Wait a minute, let me ask someone else.' I asked God. I said, 'God, if this stuff that John believes in is true, then why aren't there more people spreading the word around?' I said, 'Give me some kind of a sign,' and that night, when I went to sleep, I dreamed that I was in space somewhere, and that I was talking to something almighty, and this huge something or other—I can't really describe it now— said 'No!' And that was that, and I was convinced. The thing was very bright, like a light."

John smiled his little smile, as if Lisa had just proved his case. " 'The light' is the basic word we use," he said. "It is used in the Bible. It is used in myths and religious writings and teachings, and it can be compared to the Holy Spirit.

"You see, you have the physical realm, which we're in now. The astral realm is next to the physical, and then there are many other realms and dimensions that go on up. When you go down below the physical, you get into the nature spirit, but your physical dimension is the lowest dimension that the human soul deals with as a full soul. And when a person dies, normally they would go to the astral realm. You have many books out now on astral projection, and some of my friends at will can do astral projection. That's projecting your consciousness into the astral dimension and being *aware* that you are there. Many of the dreams a person has are actual experiences in the astral realm or maybe in some realm above that.

"Lisa dreamed about seeing a lot of light, and seeing figures in a bright radiance. In many of the books that I read, they talk about these beings, and of course in the Bible you have these beings, too. A person dressed in white may be an angel or something, but sometimes a person *radiates* a very bright light. They're *clothed* in this bright light. Well, on a very high dimension, this is the way highly evolved beings *look*.

"You see, what happens is, a physical body is like a suit of clothes. There's a spirit, the soul, that resides in these physical bodies, and when the physical body stops operating, that spirit still keeps operating, and it takes off into the astral realm or somewhere. Its frequency changes, and it continues to exist, whereas the physical body will start to decay. But in the physical body, which is a *vehicle*, the soul can sort of shift to a neutral position, release its control of the body, maybe step out of the body. And this allows another spirit to step into the body. And that spirit which steps in may be a good spirit, and it may be a bad spirit.

"It's possible for two or three spirits to reside in the same body. And that person is really mixed up when that happens. It *is* possible to cast a bad spirit out of the body, so that the *home* spirit has full access to the body and can function properly."

I asked John how he described his own home spirit.

"Well," he said, with that little smile, "I think mine's pretty good, because a lot of my friends who are psychic can see that I carry a great amount of light. Also, the Bible says, 'By your fruits you know them,' and a lot of people like me. I think hardly anybody *dislikes* me. People respect me, and this is the fruits of what I do. But I make some people feel good just by being around them.

"When I see problems, or when I see people on the show or anywhere being in difficult straits, or being at odds with each other, or arguing, or when I see an accident along the highway, I send them the light. It's something like saying, 'God bless you.' It's just a *thought* of sending them the light, and the light is very powerful. It's the power of the Holy Spirit, you might say. And when I've used it, I've seen, maybe nine times out of ten, at least, that the situation will calm down. I solve many of the problems on the show in invisible ways by using the light."

I remembered that terrible day in Davie, at the beginning of the season, when the police wanted the show to move off the lot and when the workman was beat up. Did John use the light then?

"Yes," he said. "The police didn't take Stash away."

That didn't help the man who was beaten.

"It helped some. It helped the policeman calm down.

"There are so many ways you can say it. You could say maybe the light had this particular lieutenant on duty at that time. And you can look at the *results* that I get by using the light. I get the results I want. Basically, those people calmed down. They didn't do what they said they were going to do."

John leaned back in his chair. Lisa made a little face, as if he hadn't convinced her completely. "I use it all the time," said John. "It's called 'calling in the light.' It's a sort of praying. But it's a more positive thing. Praying shouldn't be begging, and most people, in the old traditional way, beg God for something in their praying."

Lisa said, "Tell him what you were."

"No," said John. "It's not really important."

"Come on," said Lisa. "Tell him."

"Okay," said John. "I'll tell you a few things. I was in Atlantis in one lifetime, which was probably maybe fifty thousand years ago. Of course, I knew that anyway. I can guess some of these things. Because Atlantis covered maybe fifty thousand years; it lasted until about ten thousand years ago. That was the last destruction.

"Supposedly, Atlantis ran from the Mississippi all the way

across to the Mediterranean Sea, and it crossed the whole Atlantic Ocean. Atlantis is rising again. People who are psychics can see this, not in the physical, but in the *etheric*. The etheric is a dimension where everything that ever happens, happens there first. And then if the pattern holds, it later comes into the physical. If that mold or pattern breaks up, it won't happen in the physical.

"So it's not *guaranteed* that Atlantis is going to rise in the physical, although it's very likely it will. Anyway, in Atlantis I was an animal trainer. I used to go out and catch animals—more or less creatures that don't exist now, but that existed then—and bring them back and study them and also exhibit them. I used to do the same thing in Rome. I used to train animals for the wealthy Romans who liked them. And one lifetime in Rome I was a Roman soldier. I was a captain there, and I didn't meet certain responsibilities in that particular life. I was a little weak. I went along with an order from somebody—I can't remember whether it was Caesar or not—but I was told to kill some people who I really didn't want to kill, and I went along and did it. I didn't do what I knew I should do.

"And that has a reflection in this lifetime. This lifetime, I finally did what I knew I should do, which was to join the circus and be in the circus. Even though everybody thought I was crazy to do it. My family was completely against it. My family still doesn't like the circus. My mother doesn't; my father never knew I was in show business. I was in the business for one year before he died. My father would have disowned me if he had known it. But this lifetime is with the circus, with making people happy. I'm very happy with this lifetime." Outside, an elephant trumpeted in the night.

MOVING EAST

The show was moving east now, almost imperceptibly because its route was zigzagged and far from a straight line. But it had come down out of Wisconsin, which was as far west as it would go, and it was back in Indiana on the tenth of June, and a few days away there would be Ohio again, briefly. Summer would come in Chardon. And then there would be the long trip eastward across Pennsylvania. And not too far away, then, would be New Jersey, a state that traditionally loved circuses and hot dogs and flukum and sideshows. Johnny Walker said he had seen people in New Jersey buy a hot dog, take two bites, throw it away, and then buy another one. New Jersey was like the pot at the end of the rainbow. And the spring rains would be someplace far behind, and in New Jersey you could afford even an occasional thought about the end of the season, because after New Jersey came the long descent back down South.

The Midwest was flat, and the land was farmland, but it was not the red-clay farmland of Southern poverty. It was the black earth of Midwestern well-off. The sun was still low in the south, but it put good heat on the land in the daytime, heat that the winds took away at night. When the season got a little more advanced, they said, the heat would continue at night, and the corn would grow around the clock. The winds came across the flat land from Nebraska or Iowa or someplace else, maybe even Colorado, and they picked up a lot of the black dirt and put it in the air, but it did not sting or hurt you.

The roads were very straight, because the people who had built them had had no natural obstacles to avoid. Every few miles, after you got off the interstate, you crossed a railroad track, and it was always headed east-west. There was a certain amount of thrift showing in the way the farms and homes had been laid out. Here you saw three-story brick homes that would have looked natural among row houses in Baltimore or brownstones in New York, but they sat in the midst of prosperous-looking farms. The barns and outbuildings seemed to be actually functioning, not the skeletons that they are in other parts of the country. Islands of trees, tall and old and beautiful and deep green, grew in the fields. There were King Edward Cigars signs along the roads, not giant and oppressive like billboards, just small reminders that the King Edward people would like you to remember their name. Dunkin' Donuts and Seven-Elevens were gone. Arthur Treacher had not yet arrived with his Fish 'n' Chips, and even McDonald's was missing. There were more signs advertising fertilizer and strains of corn than there were signs advertising Coca-Cola. And sometimes there were signs saying "America: Love It or Leave It" and "Get US Out of the United Nations." Coming from the East to join up with the show again, you passed through a little town called Wolcott, Indiana, and the sign there said WOLCOTT, WHERE THE PRAIRIE BEGINS, and you headed west across the prairie to Rensselaer.

The circus pulled into Rensselaer after a two-hundred-and-some-mile jump from Wisconsin, and there was no show that night. That was the night Jeff left, and it was the night that a lot of the performers and workers and bosses rested up, primarily because it was what was left of an off day, but also because Wisconsin had been a lot of rain and cold, and because this was the first jump toward the East and things should start getting better now.

Bert Pettus looked older. It was as if the season, and the demands it made on him, physically and emotionally, had put extra wrinkles in his face, had closed his eyes a little, had formed his mouth into a straighter line.

"You know, I quit the show the other day in Wisconsin," he said.

Bert's quitting the show, or at least his talking about quitting the show, was getting to be an unremarkable event. I asked him why he was still around.

"Well, Bill Hill talked to me. And I've been a very funny guy all my life. I won't leave nobody when they have nobody to work the elephants. If they came up here now and said, 'We've got somebody,' I'd say, 'Hoo-ray,' and walk away. But as long as they ain't got nobody, I'll stick around and work the elephants for them. I'm just not the type of guy who'll get up and leave them stuck."

I asked Bert if he still thought of this as his last season on the road.

"Who knows?" he said. "I'm never sure of anything on one of these shows. I'm still thinking of them live-oak trees down there in Texas. Already I got three people who want me to train baby elephants for them when this thing closes

Bert and the bulls

or when *I* close with the show. I don't have to worry about a job. I could go sit on my butt for the rest of my days if I wanted to, but I don't want to do that, either. I've been *raised* in this business. Git back *Irene!*"

The weather had hurt the spirits of the circus people, and the performers were among them, but they tried not to let it show. The performers were professionals, and they had learned many years before that weather was one of the factors when you played under canvas. The bosses knew this, too. "I never let the rain bother me," said Bill Hill. "Because if you let it bother you, it's got you whipped. I always get that in my mind—that I ain't never going to let it whip me. I love it. Because unless it rains, we ain't going to have no tomatoes. No corn, right? So it's got to rain, so you got to expect it. We're gonna get it. We got to get it. If we *don't* get it, we're in trouble."

King Charles said it wasn't the cold and wet so much as it was the food. He was beginning to replace Leo as the prime critic of the cookhouse. "Bologna, bologna, bologna!" he shouted that day in Rensselaer. "Bologna. That's all we have. A man has bought the circus out. He's paying three to four thousand dollars a day, and what do we get out of it? Bologna."

What Charles meant was that a promoter, in this case Mearl Johnson, of Central City, Pennsylvania, had paid Hoxie a flat rate for the show's performance over a period of several days. The flat rate was always in excess of Hoxie's daily expenses, or "the nut," so Hoxie always made a profit this way. This was called "buying the show," although it was actually more like renting it for a while. Johnson then contracted with his own local sponsors. They and he sold tickets, and Johnson's profit depended on how much more he made in ticket sales than he had spent in buying the show.

Johnson was what was called a "phone man." That is, he hired people, in advance of the show's arrival, to staff a "phone room," or an office equipped with many telephones. The people picked numbers out of the local telephone directory (in the case of a small town, they went through the entire book) and called residents, asking them if they wanted to buy tickets for the circus. Almost invariably there was a local sponsor of some repute—the Jaycees, a fraternal organization, the police or fire department, or the local rescue squad—and the phone men and women would mention that they were calling on behalf of the sponsor. This helped reduce some residents' anger at being subjected to telephone solicitation. It helped, too, that the local sponsor usually was putting on the show for some local charity. Sometimes the phone people told telephone subscribers that, if they didn't want the tickets themselves, they could purchase them so that an underprivileged child might attend. In the case of the phone promoters who worked with Hoxie, this deal was always on the up-and-up, but some localities had grown tired of telephone solicitations (some of them by organizations that were not as respectable), and they had outlawed the practice. If a resident said yes to the telephone pitch, tickets were sent in the mail, along with a bill.

"Bologna, bologna, bologna," said Charles. "They've got a cook that's drunk all the time. It's too much. I mean, it's too much, man. I know at least forty, fifty men who've left. Every day since this show has been out, from one cook to another, we've had at least five cooks, and it's always been bologna, bologna, bologna. The cook we got now, he calls himself cooking liver, but it's more like boot leather. When Betty Tucker was here, buying food for the show, it was good. And if she heard anything bad about the food, it was *hell* raised. That's why you see the band going along as sloppy and nasty as we are, because she's not here. Hoxie has just shifted his entire interest to the other circus, and we are just left out alone.

"John Hall is a great businessman. John Hall is an educated man. And, as I say it, *John Hall has never seen a circus in his life.* He's seen the performers, and he's seen the front end. But when he leaves the office, to come through the front door, past the rings, and go out the back door to the back yard, he doesn't know anything about it. And the cookhouse always sets in the back yard. And John Hall knows nothing about it."

I asked Charles about the cook who had started out with

the show, the one who had left in Melbourne. Hadn't he been
all right?

Charles thought a moment. "I don't even remember," he
said. "You know why? Because we've had so many." Then he
smiled. "Oh, I remember. He was beautiful. He was one of the
beautiful people. Even if the office brought him some bologna,
he knew how to make a good bologna soup. He knew how to
make a good bologna roast. Bologna cacciatore! Understand
me? It's not funny. That guy was a *cook!* The only thing this
guy who's with us now claims to be is a bigger drunkard than
I am."

If we had been anywhere other than a grassy lot in Rensselaer, Indiana, and if King Charles had been in any other
business in the world, I would have asked him why he didn't
leave, since he was so unhappy. But it seemed that bitching
about the management, and about the food, and about most
other things, was about as big a part of circus life, for some
people, as anything else. Charles was a chronic complainer, but
that did not lessen his ability to lead the band through its com-
plex maneuvers each night, and it did not lessen his ability to
put up arrows with precision and, sometimes, even grace. I had
heard Charles's complaining before, and it had always fallen
into the same category with Bert Pettus's complaints about
how the new days were not like the old days, and I confess
I tended to discount it.

King Charles Weathersby was born in Bonham, Texas, and
he had studied music at Langston University in Oklahoma.
"And I finally wound up on circuses," he said. "How I did it, I
don't know."

His grandfather had been a cook for Jesse James, Charles
said, "and he run away from Jesse James many years ago. Six
months ago, the governor of Missouri pardoned my grandfather
after all those years." Charles produced a newspaper clipping
with a story about the pardon. "And he ran away from Jesse
James to join the circus," he said.

"The first circus *I* was on was back in 1948, the Kelly-
Miller show. I've seen that circus blow down at least twenty

times. And this circus, Hoxie Tucker, we had a blow-down two years ago. We were playing a hospital date, and we had a lot of retarded kids in there. And the top fell on those kids. Some was in wheelchairs. We cut the top with knives and things to get the kids from under the tent. Not a kid was hurt.

"Hoxie saw that one. Hoxie told me, he says, 'Out of all my years in circus business, I've had blow-downs. But this is the first time that I've ever been here to see it.' So he immediately went into one of his heart attacks. But I have been on the Hoxie show when we have had blow-downs other than that, and Hoxie was not there. If you were here tonight"—he pointed at me—"and a tornado comes and blows this thing down, I don't think you'll write about it. Because it's detrimental to circus business."

The sun did not come out that day in Rensselaer, and a hard wind blew from the west, across the prairie. The American flag on top of the centerpole pointed straight toward the east. Late in the afternoon, though, the sky got very dark. All of a sudden the flag started pointing toward the south, and a strong rain hit. There were big drops of rain, and they were cold.

The rain soaked the ground for an hour or so, and just before the first performance it stopped. The ground, with its cover of wiry grass, became the color and texture of collard greens that have been boiled for hours, as in Southern cooking. The circus people walked around in rubber boots, not complaining, and just before the performance the sun came out, briefly, and then it set.

Gypsy Red turned up for the sideshow bally in good, strong boots. He said he was sorry that Jeff had left, but he did not sound tragic about it. Gypsy Red had seen a lot of people come and go.

He said the bear had been particularly active lately. "The bear done walked on everybody," he said. "He's gone now. He was some colored fellow out of Savannah." It sounded a little strange, Gypsy Red saying this, because Gypsy Red himself was colored. He was a very light shade of brown, but his nose

The rain coming in Rensselaer

Gypsy Red

and features and hair made him an American Negro. "But then, you never can tell who the bear is. Unlessen he *tell* you who he is. *I* could be the bear."

Have you ever been the bear?

"Oh, yeah, and I'm *still* the bear if the right thing's laying around. That come natural. Natural with *me*. I told King Charles when I was sick with the flu, I said, 'If I die, Charles, you write a letter to *Billboard* and tell them that Gypsy Red said he had only one regret—that he didn't make Alcatraz or Sing Sing. He made all the rest of them.'"

Which ones had he made?

"Oh, three or four. Joliet. Bismarck, North Dakota. Angola, Louisiana."

What were you in for?

"Robbery, burglary, sodomy. Illinois it was burglary—Rockville, Illinois, one to life. Angola it was one to twenty for robbery. In Bismarck I got five to ten for sodomy."

But you're a gentle person, aren't you?

"Oh, yeah, until somebody bothers me. It's a funny thing.

I've been in jail a lot of times, but I've only been in jail once for stealing. Twice. That's pretty good for a thief, isn't it? Not a thief, a *bad fellow*."

I asked Gypsy Red when he was born.

"I always thought September the twelfth, 1912, but I found out from the government that I was born in February, 1914. I was adopted. Some people in Memphis *Tin*-a-see raised me."

Do you consider yourself black or white?

"I consider myself black. I was raised by black people, so I consider myself black. If I'd been raised by whites, it probably would have been different. It's the early environment that's ingrained in me.

"You see, I never did know my mother. My real mother. Or my real father. But the people that raised me, they was both black. And I went to a black school in Memphis. Now, if I would have had a mother and father adopt me who was white, and I went to a white school, well, naturally, as I grew up, I'd of been a white man.

"A lot of people tell me I could pass. I say why pass? It doesn't help *me* none."

Gypsy Red paused. "I might be leaving this place on Sunday," he said. "You know what they say about me—here today and gone tomorrow."

I asked him what he would do.

"Oh, I don't make a move unless I have another job in sight. And I've got another job in sight. I'm only making eighty a week here blowing trombone, and they take out ten in Social Security and income tax. That leaves seventy. I go over there, and I'll get two hundred and fifty a week."

Where?

"I'm going to the Vargas circus. I'm not afraid to tell anybody where I'm going. *I* don't owe nobody nothing. It's no disgrace to quit one job and go to another job to better yourself. If I had a ten-piece band, nine of them and myself, and nine of them left for a better job, I'd set right up there and play by myself. And the show would go on."

▶

It was Bob Mason's last night as sideshow manager. When he had come on, in Georgia, it had been with the understanding that his work with the circus would be only temporary, because he had other work that had to be done in Dayton. Now a replacement had been found—a husband-and-wife team that had been in the business a long time, and that was leaving Sells & Gray, for some reason—and Bob was free to leave. There were no hard feelings. After Bob's last sideshow pitch and performance in Rensselaer, John Hall gave him a nice bonus and thanked him.

Bob put on a windbreaker and walked around the soggy front end after the second performance started, and he said goodbye to his friends. He said he was sort of glad to be leaving. Business in general had not been too good, although in some towns it had been spectacular.

"The sideshow had potential," he said, "but business is just off this year. I think it's the financial scene. People have a limited amount of money to spend. Some of them bring their own popcorn from home. And I get them inside, and I give them the lecture on the snake, and then I start the magic pitch. Often I make just nothing on it." Bob had offered the sideshow crowds a three-item packet—a three-card-monte trick, a magic-paddle trick, and another trick card. "And it just costs a quarter, which is really the cheapest thing they can buy on the circus grounds," he said.

I asked him what he blamed his depression on.

"On the nature of things," he said, "and bad weather. This happens constantly. I've never been on a show where it didn't develop. Little petty jealousies and lack of business, bad weather, cold night, lack of sleep, many, many days without a day off. Yesterday was a day off, but we traveled two hundred miles, so it wasn't really a day off. It's just like day after day after day of this. Like I've had a cold now for about two weeks at least. So you don't feel your best. But now this couple is coming and I'll go home." He sighed. He seemed both happy and sad about his leaving.

I asked him what he had done before.

"I've been an in-again, out-again circus man," he said. "I

was born September 5, 1924, in Lakeland, Florida. My real name is Stenner. And I started in show business as a film actor in 1943. I worked for all the studios. I did bit parts—never under contract.

"I had the satisfaction of being a German soldier who died in Hitler's arms before he had risen to power in what is known as the worst movie ever made about World War II. It was called *The Hitler Gang*. Bobby Watson played the part of Hitler. I guess that was the biggest name in the whole damned picture. But it reached people. I saw it at the Egyptian Theater in Hollywood, and a foreign lady who sat in back of me was cursing out loud during the Nazi scenes. Evidently she had lived through parts of this, because she was sitting there saying, 'You sons of bitches.' She was very emotionally upset.

"I made a lot of cowboy shows where I rode the horses. I'd ride as a bad guy and I'd ride as a good guy. I was just one of the gang. And there was a picture I enjoyed because I did have quite a bit of footage in it. It was called *Are These Our Parents?*

"So I did nothing important in the film world. I migrated into the outdoor-show business, in a trampoline act with a friend of mine, and then I went into the circus scene. I started out as a clown at forty dollars a week, which is ridiculous, but I wanted to do it. And then, after I had done it for a couple of years, the railroad shows disappeared. So I was part of a history of the circus that'll never be again.

"I've worked with the Eagle Circus, which was the one and only circus sponsored by the Fraternal Order of Eagles. And that was my first one. And then I was with Cole Brothers, and I was with Hunt Brothers, and with Hoxie Brothers four years ago, and I was with a tiny little show called Bond Brothers Circus, out of New Jersey. It was so small that all the performers went home at night, except me. I had a bunk in a sleeper that had a hole in the roof.

"And then I was with a little circus around Chicago about 1950. That was the first time I worked in a sideshow. It was very small—just a one-ring, dog-and-pony type show.

"So it goes, on and on. It's a pretty small world, you know.

Tomorrow I'll get in the camper and drive to Dayton. And then I'll get ready for an international convention of magicians. I create magic. I'll build anything to order. I started out with illusions. But basically I create small, intimate things for mind readers."

Do you think the people were pleased with the sideshow they got for their fifty cents?

"This year they were," said Bob. "Because everything they were promised they got. Absolutely everything. The only thing that wasn't there that was on the bannerline"—he referred to the advertising signs that were painted on the sides of the sideshow trucks—"was the Punch and Judy show. I had a little puppet show with me, but there wasn't time to present it. And the fire-eater. But I understand that at the beginning of the season there *was* a fire-eater."

I remembered Harry for the first time in three months.

"A lot of people came and told me afterwards that they enjoyed the sideshow because I lectured on the animals." It was true. Bob had gone out of his way to explain the animals to the spectators, and I had always thought it was kind of him to do that. "After all," he said, "what can a snake charmer really do?" Linda Chandler was a gracious and attractive snake charmer, but all she could do with the show's six-foot boa constrictor was take it out of its traveling case and wind it carefully around her neck and display it.

"So the more I could find out about a snake, I tried to tell the people about it. Tonight, for instance, I was telling them about how a boa constrictor gives birth to live snakes, not eggs, as most reptiles do. And that they have no ears. And these are things that the average person doesn't know. People are basically not too intelligent, and you have to take them by the hand."

"This is a pretty good life, isn't it?" I asked. I had the feeling that Bob really enjoyed it, despite the frequent bad houses.

"It's an *interesting* life," he said. "Actually, for a fellow like myself it's a rather lonesome life. Because at night, when it's all over, and even in between shows, there aren't that many people to hobnob with. The Cristianis are a family unit, and the

Fornasaris are a family unit, and they're eating dinner and they're busy. And of course Phil Chandler and Linda and I are old friends. So we visit, and it's fine. And I'm on good terms with John Hall and his wife, and we would visit and sometimes go out and socialize once in a while. I took them out to dinner to celebrate John's birthday, and many times Lisa would fix some goodie and give it to me. So there's a bit of socializing. But basically you end up all by yourself."

I asked Bob if he would miss the canvas. His plans called for the rest of the year to be spent in constructing magic and performing in indoor shows.

"Oh, not at all," he said. "The circus to me isn't the Big Top. It's the people."

I told him I had a half-baked theory that the Big Top was sort of representative of the world, and that the circus people were merely temporary visitors on it, like hitchhikers. What really mattered was the Big Top and maybe the elephants.

"Well," said Bob, "it represents *our* world because that's where it's all done. You'll notice performers who're tired and depressed and dragging along. But when the band plays their music inside the Big Top, there's a certain charge of adrenalin or something where you're another person for a few minutes. The world is yours, and now you do your thing. And the laughter and applause really does get to a performer. That's not really *me* up there on the bally platform—I'm simply portraying a stereotyped part. I'm providing what people expect from the man they call the barker, which is the wrong name."

After saying goodbye to his friends, Bob went to his camper to heat a can of chili and go to sleep. The next morning he woke early, walked his little dog, climbed into the cab, and started off for Dayton, leaving the world of Hoxie Brothers Circus behind him on that muddy lot.

A NEW ADVENTURE IN LIFE

Mearl Johnson, the promoter, had a partiality for fairgrounds, and the lot in Logansport, like the one in Rensselaer, was the site of the annual county fair. It was known as the 4-H Fairgrounds, and it was neat-looking, with the usual open barns and exhibition buildings. There had been rain there, too, and the ground was damp, but it was strong enough to hold the Big Top's stakes, and when we arrived in the morning there was no sign of more rain. There was a faultless blue sky, like a winter sky after a storm has passed through, or like an ocean sky sometimes.

A lot of people came to watch the show go up. In some towns they did that, and in others they didn't, and one of the reasons, according to the people who knew, was that some towns were well known in the trade as good circus towns and some weren't. A good circus town meant that there were a lot of people there who liked the circus, and who could be counted on to come to one—in fact, to come to all the circuses that might pass through in a given season. Show people remembered which towns were good circus towns and which ones weren't, and they tried to play as many of the good ones as possible each year and to stay away from the bad ones. Every once in a while a circus owner would let temptation get the better of him, and he would book his show into a notoriously bad circus town, and sometimes the results would be surprisingly good, but more often they would be bad. Logansport was a certified good circus town.

Tino Cristiani

There were several circus fans on the lot when we pulled in. A lot of the people who fall into the general category of circus fan are members of one, two, or all three of the organizations that cater to those who love the circus: the Circus Fans of America, whose motto is "We fight anything that fights the circus"; the Circus Historical Society; and the Circus Model Builders, Incorporated, International. Members of the last group, as the name implies, construct scale models of circuses, just as John Hall did when he was a child and, later on, when he was designing the new tent. This morning, in Logansport, John was spray-painting a piece of plywood with green paint. It was to serve as the base for a model of a new tent he was designing for next year.

Tino Cristiani continued performing with his arm taped up, and the injury seemed to make no difference to him. He could have laid off for a few weeks, but he didn't. I asked him why, and he said, "Because I wanted the satisfaction of saying when I grow up that I caught a triple on the trampoline with one arm." At that point he had made the catch fourteen times without missing.

That night, the Cristiani men were doing their three-high stack on the trampoline when Armando went too high and came down at the wrong angle on Tino's shoulders. This pushed Tino forward, and the entire stack collapsed. Lucio fell on his leg and stayed there, on the ground, for a moment. "He was paralyzed for a minute," said Tino later. They got up and tried the trick again, and fell again, so they bowed and came out of the ring.

The new sideshow managers arrived, the husband-and-wife team, and they worked feverishly. While the man was talking from the platform, the woman, an attractive blonde who was approaching her middle years, walked down the midway to the marquee and literally took people by the arm and turned them around and walked them back to the sideshow platform. The old-timers watched this and marveled at it. "Man, that's literally turning the tip," said Phil Chandler.

Bert Pettus stood at the back door, ready to take the big elephants in. He stood tall and erect and dignified, waiting, two acts beforehand, the way he had been taught in the old days. "The people that run the circus go on the assumption that they can run it like they did back in the twenties and thirties," he said. "And it just don't go that way now. I mean, things have changed. And these circuses have not changed with it." He spat. "Ho *Myrtle.*

"You've been around here. You see how they treat the help. Well, those things have changed. You don't *treat* people that way no more. That's the way they did in the twenties and thirties. They would shove you around, push you around. Short pay. Bad food. No sleep. Work, work, work. Work today has been changed.

"And the circus don't mean that much to the workingmen today. Maybe one out of fifty of them would come on because it's a circus, because of the thrill of being with a circus. But these guys today, they're not here because they *want* to be. It's cause they're forced to be here. By that I mean they can't go out and hold a normal job."

Inside the tent, Phil Chandler was starting the introduction of the elephant act. Myrtle rocked back on her hind legs and urinated on the ground, just as she had been taught. Bert patted her on the trunk. "Many a time in the old days," he said, "I raked an elephant before a performance. They didn't want no elephant shit in the ring during the show. So you raked them. You roll your shirt sleeve up, soap up your arm, and stick it up there and pull it out.

"I spent the greatest majority of my life in circuses. Anybody can tell you that. And I love it. I think it's a wonderful institution. But as I look back, I see that they had one philosophy. Be *with* it, be *for* it, but don't ask me for anything, especially money." Bert spat again, opened the curtain for himself, because the back-door man was missing this night, and led the elephants into the Big Top.

Charles Stepleton was the seventeen-year-old kid who had seen the show in Greensburg, Indiana, and joined it that night. Now, one month later, the show was approaching Greensburg again and Charles was leaving. Charles was always smiling through his long blond hair. He had been put to work in the sideshow when he joined, but now he was helping the electrician. He was a good worker, but he said his month with the show had been a bummer.

"There isn't any fun in it," he said, in Crawfordsville, Indiana. "It's like it's something new for a day or two, like a thrill, and then after you know what you're doing and everything, there just isn't nothing to it. It's like working in a factory—you go in and you do one thing all day and that's it.

"I mean, like, if this was back in the fifties, it would have been something. But now, circuses just aren't as big as they used to be. I mean like I've heard my grandmother talking about when she was a little kid the circus would come to town and they'd close up the whole town. Everybody'd be up at the circus. Now just a fourth of the people come to see it. You meet a lot of new people and see a lot of new places, but that's about it."

That night, after the second performance, Charles's mother appeared on the lot. She waited until he had helped tear down the Big Top, and then she drove him back to Greensburg.

Logansport and Crawfordsville were to the west of Indianapolis, and Shelbyville was to the east. The lot in Shelbyville was, again, a fairgrounds, next to a grandstand and a harness-racing track. Men were running the sleek brown horses when the show pulled in.

A man stepped out of a tiny Datsun camper when the first trucks arrived, raised a camera to his face, and started taking pictures. He seemed especially delighted to see the show. His camper had California license plates.

His name was Arnold Sherman. He was from Los Angeles, and at the age of fifty-three he was running away with the circus. He wanted to be a clown. In real life, he worked for the Los Angeles water-and-power company as an electrician. He had six weeks of vacation, and he had decided to spend the time with the circus.

Earlier in the year, Sherman had written letters to five shows, asking if he might join for six weeks in the summertime and be a clown. He had done some clowning with his Shrine club back in California. He got a reply from only one show. John Hall had written him, saying come on.

And so Arnold Sherman had packed his costumes and makeup and a lot of canned food into his small camper and had driven east from Los Angeles. There had been a mix-up over where the show was going to be, and Arnold had gotten more or less lost for three days. Finally he learned that the circus would be in Shelbyville on the fourteenth of June, and he had driven to the lot and waited. "Every time I heard a little noise last night," he said, "I'd wake up and look out the window and see if the circus was here yet. And at six-thirty, a truck came in. And I jumped out of bed and ran out with my camera, and I've been out here ever since."

John Hall introduced Arnold to Phil Chandler, and Phil

more or less took Arnold under his wing and walked around the lot with him, explaining how the show worked and introducing him to the various people. Sherman was a tall, robust man, covered with California health and sunshine. I asked him why he was here.

"Well," he said, "for about eight years I've been clowning with the Shrine clubs I belonged to. My first clowning was done with the Woodland Hills club, and then later I joined another one, called Show Business Shrine Club, in North Hollywood. And that's where I got my first training and my first love for doing this kind of work. I clowned mostly in hospitals for children. I played in a real circus twice—just one afternoon. And I just fell in love with this type of work. And I decided, well, I'm going to take my vacation this year and go join a circus, and learn more about clowning and makeup and life in a circus. I thought I might retire in another year or so, and this would be another life, another job, and I think I would enjoy it." Arnold said he no longer was married, although he had a woman friend, and he had little tying him down, and if his vacation experiment worked out he might well spend the rest of his life with circuses.

"The camper I have now is obviously too small to live in. I'm going to build up a rig that I can travel in, and start a new adventure in life," he said. Arnold said he was very nervous. "I haven't eaten a thing all day," he said, "and my stomach's a little tight. My first performance will be tonight. I think my main concern is that I want to please, and I want to do the job right, and of course I'm not a professional, and everyone here is, and I just want to do right. I want to act like a clown, and be a clown, and this is all I'm thinking about. I think that explains my stomach problems."

I asked Arnold how he planned to determine whether he had made the correct decision.

"I think applause would satisfy me," he said. "And, of course, I hope I have friends here who will tell me what I do wrong and advise me what to do the next time. People like Phil."

Suppose it worked out terrifically?

"I couldn't cut off my job immediately. I'd have to go back. There are things I'd have to straighten up at home. I just couldn't do it overnight."

But you think that at the end of six weeks you'll know whether this is the life for you?

"Yes. I think I know *right now* that I'd like to do it. It's just a matter of becoming more proficient in doing the job that's expected of a clown on a circus."

Phil asked what kind of clown he was.

"Not a tramp clown. I would like to think I'm a happy clown. That's the way I classify myself."

Phil told Arnold that a lot of people thought of the circus as a kind of "closed society," and that to a certain extent it really was that, and that Phil would help Arnold any way he could. "This business is very close-knit," said Phil. "And if you're accepted by—let's call it 'the family of show people'— you've got it made. But if you're rejected, it can be tough. There are some little tips that I'll give you as we go along. For instance, you just don't copy another clown's gag. You just don't do it. That's his gag. That may have been in his family for generations."

"The same with a face or a costume?" said Arnold.

"Right," said Phil. "You just don't do it. As another example—Armando Cristiani, who you'll see tonight, is a kid. He's sixth generation. I mean, they were a circus family back in *Roman* times! And *nobody* copies their routines."

Phil leaned back in his folding lawn chair. It was a beautiful lot, with nicely kept grass and tall oak trees, although the sky was clouding over. "Here's the thing," he said. "I love people, and I love acts. I love show people. Somebody breaking into the business, such as you are, man, I'll bend over backwards to do what I can to help. If something's good, I'll tell you it's good. If something's bad, I'll tell you it's bad and try to tell you *why* it's bad.

"Sometimes I may not tell you why it's bad because I may not know. I probably know more about acts and the working of them than a lot of people, but I can't do them myself. A friend of mine does a wire act. And when he was first doing it, he said, 'Now show me how to style.' 'To style' means to take your applause. I said, 'I know how *I* would do it. But you just don't *teach* somebody to style. You have to do what's natural for you.' Which really you don't have to worry about. Clowns can get away with murder.

"Anyway, I tried to show this friend how I would style a wire act. And I couldn't walk a wire—hell, I'm lucky to walk across this ground without falling all over myself. But I've seen the best wire acts. I can tell you how to do a cat act, can tell you how to break it. But whether I could do one myself, I don't know. Deep down inside, that's what I'd really love to do. Except I don't want to clean up all that shit and feed them and all that stuff."

I asked Phil what his motivation was in giving Arnold all these hints. Was he looking out for the good of the circus?

"No," said Phil. "For the good of him. I want to see people in this business. I can't see why *everybody* isn't in show business. Except if they were, who would be our audience?

"I cannot see in this world why anybody would not want to be in this business. How anybody can stand to have a foreman who's probably dumber than they are saying, 'Hey, you're five minutes late for work.' Punching that time clock. They can have it, man. Not me." Arnold smiled.

"I admire the people who can do it," said Phil. "I don't knock them. It just isn't my cup of tea. I've tried it. Hell, I could have been a stockbroker today. I worked at it for five years. Didn't work *at* it—if I'd worked *at* it, I'd still be in it. But I love this.

"Now, if you take circus people out of this realm, they're dead. I'll give you an example. What happens when we're close to another circus and we have a day off? Everybody visits. It's like the busman's holiday. But how many times, when a stockbroker's got a day off, do you see him going to another stockbroker's firm and visiting? He runs like hell to go fishing."

I asked Arnold what he had seen so far.

"I see a lot of freedom," he said. "Personal freedom. Mental freedom. And there's a great deal of togetherness. People want to help each other, and they're kind. I haven't heard a

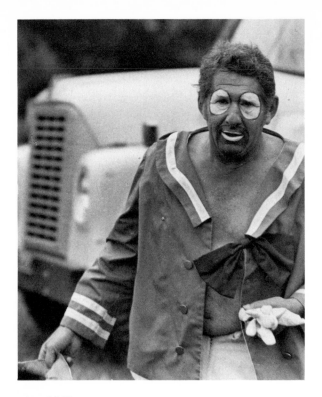

Arnold Sherman

harsh word yet. And people enjoy being together. That's the first thing I noticed here. I imagine that much more will become evident as time goes on."

"The secret of this business," said Phil, "is that you've got to *love* it. You've got to eat, sleep, and drink show business. I know of no other subject. Oh, I can talk to you on other subjects. You name a subject and start talking about it, and if I don't know anything about it, I'll tell you and shut up and listen. But when I'm out in, say, mixed company, at a party or something like that—maybe one guy's a doctor, and another guy's a lawyer. I can sit a while and talk with you about the medical profession. But I don't really dig it. I'd much rather tell you about a jump I made from here to there, or my asshole prop crew, or something simple-minded like that.

"You've just got to love the business to be in it. To me, this is all I ever wanted to do from the first day my folks ever took me to see a big-band show. I told them then, sitting in the balcony, 'Someday I'm going to do that.' I was watching a comedian or a juggler or whatever the hell it was on stage. And I was lucky enough to play that same theater later. And it was a great feeling."

"What were you doing?" asked Arnold.

"My magic act. My tired old magic act. It kept me out of poolrooms and all that shit. I also dressed in Victor Jory's dressing room. He had been there the week before with *Cat on a Hot Tin Roof*. And that and thirty-five cents will get you to downtown Brooklyn on the subway."

Arnold Sherman laughed, but as he did his eyes swept over the Big Top, and you could tell that he was really thinking about tonight and his first performance with Hoxie Brothers Circus. Before long he excused himself and went to his camper to put on his makeup for the six o'clock show.

"This part of Indiana and Ohio used to be known as the Graveyard of Circuses," said King Charles. He had his trumpet in his hand, ready for the first show at Shelbyville. "If you could ever get through here, okay. You'd become a millionaire. But the risks you were taking on having your equipment torn up by the elements were very great. A lot of circuses didn't make it out of here. Hoxie is apparently making it out of here this year."

The crowd went into the Big Top for the six o'clock show, and Phil sent Arnold Sherman in to clown around with the audience before Spec. It was called "meeting and greeting." Arnold was in a typical clown costume. Then he came out and disappeared into his camper to change into his Spec costume.

Phil blew the five-minute whistle, and Arnold didn't show. The other performers lined up at the back door. At the last moment, Arnold opened the camper door and waddled out. He was in a duck costume, with gigantic yellow feet and a papier-mâché head and a fluffy little tail. The other performers smiled and laughed. They liked him. When Arnold walked around in Spec the kids loved him; several flash bulbs went off in his face. After the first performance, a kid came into the back yard and asked for his autograph. That does not happen all that often. Arnold signed his name "Donald Duck."

"I felt very flattered that a little girl noticed me in what was my first professional show," said Arnold a little later. "I'm very gratified. I know I can do it now. And I know I like it. This is going to be my new life." He was as happy as a child.

That night a huge thunderstorm struck. The lightning

Arnold waiting for Spec

danced around the metal centerpole until they got it down.
The workmen took the canvas down in the middle of the down-
pour. It was heavier than usual, because it was wet. Arnold
Sherman sat in his little camper and watched it all through a
tiny window.

CONNERSVILLE, ASHTABULA, AND MOUNT NEBO

Gypsy Red was happy. He was sure he was going to blow the show, now. He was in Connersville, Indiana, on a Saturday, and he said that by Sunday he would be gone.

"I can't think of nothing else I'd rather do than the kind of work I'm doing right now," he said. "Here today and gone tomorrow."

You'd rather do this than sit and fish?

"Let's put it this way," he said. "I was born in the business. I was born on the biggest carnival in the United States. It's called the Royal American now. My parents, my real parents, were minstrel-show people. That was sixty years ago."

Those were the days of the grift, weren't they?

"There was a lot of grift."

Do you miss that?

"Yes, I do. The last grift show I was on was with the Dailey Brothers. We came into town 'daily.' Oh, yeah, I miss it. I just like to see them robbing a sucker. A sucker come out to the show with twenty thousand dollars in his pocket—what's he going to buy? You *know* it's because he's hoping for some action."

Do you think you'll ever retire?

"Yeah. When they bury me."

What about leaving this show?

"Well, I told everybody. I don't keep it hid. It's a free country. I ain't stole nothing lately. I ain't running from the *po*-leece. There ain't nobody looking for me. I'm going over to the Vargas circus."

You said before you were hot in several towns. Now you say the police aren't looking for you.

"Yeah, well, I mean, there's different places where—what I mean by that is, somebody's daughter might be looking for me."

How will you get to the Vargas show? (It was due in Chicago in a few days.)

"I go by bus. See, when I go, I don't go unless I have some of this stuff." Gypsy Red produced his billfold; it was crammed with money.

Have you got a lot of money saved up?

"Not too much. I had a little property, and I lost it when I got into that trouble on Long Island. But that's all over now. I'll start again. And you never can tell. I'm just sixty. Maybe by the time I get sixty-five I'll have another ten thousand dollars."

I had heard that Gypsy Red carried a gun, although he had said before that a circus was a bad place to have such a weapon. I asked him about it.

"Oh, yeah, I have a little barking dog. He barks here and bites way over there someplace. I carry one." He made no move to show it to me.

"I'll show you what else I carry. I'll give you a little secret a lot of people don't know." He produced from his pants pocket a spoon and a pocketknife. He held up the knife. "I keep one in my pocket since I was fifteen years old. And I've had *much* occasion to use it. I've had three-hundred-dollar days and I've had days when I didn't have the poke-and-beans to eat with the spoon, or the sardines to open with the knife.

"The spoon is to eat with. See, I like ice cream. And I like poke-and-beans. That's why I carry the spoon. And the knife is for peeling apples or something."

And those are your worldly possessions?

"Well, they're my *prized* possessions. Any time you see me, if I ain't got that little barking dog in my pocket, I shore got that knife and spoon. I can have on a herringbone suit, or a

Hickey Freeman, and I got a knife and spoon in my pocket. And don't nobody know it but me. Unless I show it to them. And most of the time I got the little barking dog up in the bill of my cap, too."

On the next day, Gypsy Red left the show.

The show made it through the Graveyard without too much damage from the elements. What damage there was, Superchicken repaired every morning with his needle and cord and little canvas patches. After Connersville, the circus moved across the line into Ohio: Greenville, Urbana, Bucyrus, Mansfield, Richmond Heights, Chardon, Ashtabula. Three days after the husband-and-wife team came on the sideshow, they blew it. John Hall called Bob Mason and asked him if he wanted to return. Bob said yes, and he loaded his belongings and his dog into his camper and started out again from Dayton. In Ashtabula, Bert Pettus left the show. He did not talk about it beforehand; he did not offer to stay around until a replacement was found; he just blew the show.

Beaver Falls, Pennsylvania, came next, and then Mount Nebo, a suburb of Pittsburgh. The lot at Mount Nebo was a race track, like the one at Shelbyville. The show played Mount Nebo on a Monday, the twenty-fourth of June.

Bert Pettus's replacement arrived in Mount Nebo. He was a young man named Gary Jacobson. Gary had been working at Circus World, the Ringling Brothers' year-round circus park near Orlando, as an assistant to the chief elephant trainer, and Hoxie had called him and asked him if he wanted a job. Gary had jumped at the chance.

On Tuesday the show moved out of Mount Nebo and headed for a date at the state hospital in Polk, Pennsylvania. As usual, the trucks left early and the performers slept later, waking after the sunrise and methodically hitching up their trailers and setting off. When they were all gone, Arnold Sherman's little Datsun camper stayed on the lot.

It stayed there Tuesday, and Wednesday, and on Thursday the people who worked at the race track knocked on the door. There was no answer. They figured the truck must have broken down and that its owner would return for it. On Saturday the decomposition was advanced, and the men knew that there was someone inside the camper. They got the police, and they forced the door open, and Arnold Sherman was inside. He was dressed for sleep. The coroner ruled that he had died of a heart attack.

By this time the show was in Clearfield, Pennsylvania, and most of the circus people had assumed that Arnold had decided to blow the show. Many of them had never learned his name; he was known only as "the new clown" to them.

Supe patching the tent

3 IN THE EAST

BALTIMORE

We were in the East now, in Baltimore for a three-day stand, and the season was half over. The halfway point had been reached the day before, in Lemoyne, Pennsylvania, on the Fourth of July. Halfway does not sound like much, but in the life of a circus it is a lot. A big part of the first half is spent just getting on the road: getting out of the perpetual summer of Florida into the real world of windshield ice and deep mud and mountain roads; learning how to put the Big Top up and take it down; learning who would stay and who would leave; getting past the spring rains; learning the interior dynamics of an hour-and-a-half show, what made it click and what made it drag. The military ponies were out of the program now; they spent their time exclusively in the sideshow tent. Some acts were shortened; others were lengthened.

It was a real circus now, an entity. The Big Top went up and came down on schedule, and it seemed, to me, more than ever to be symbolic of the world. It carried its performers and workingmen and bosses and the elephants in its womb down the highways, from town to town, almost oblivious of the feelings, the lives and deaths, of those who traveled on her. Arnold Sherman, Bert Pettus, Jeff Woosnam, Gypsy Red, Joe Hamilton, Harry—they left, and others came to take their places, and the transition was so smooth and effortless that sometimes hardly anyone knew it had taken place. In Baltimore, on the smoggy first morning, a man walked on the lot,

carrying his belongings in a paper shopping bag. He applied
for a job as a butcher, and he was hired, and the show went
on. But it would have gone on if he hadn't come, too.

The lot was in downtown Baltimore, on an urban-renewal
site right next door to the inner harbor. The centerpole was
less than thirty yards from the water. It was a spectacular
place to have a circus, but some of the show people were
skeptical about it. They didn't like playing large cities; they
were annoyed and sometimes threatened by the small bands
of adolescent black boys who roamed about the back yard,
and they believed audiences would not be large in a city.
"Sometimes, the smaller the town, the better the prospects,"
said Lucio, and it was a fact that the show had had one of its
best dates in a tiny town a few days before. Mill Hall, Pennsylvania, had a population of about seventeen hundred people,
but Hoxie Brothers Circus played a two-day stand there and
drew something like ten thousand paying customers.
Big cities also have big bureaucracies, and big bureau-

cracies mean a lot of inspectors, and John Hall was having his problems with inspectors this day. One of the city's inspectors had come around and found a lot of electrical wires that were not grounded. He ordered that every trailer on the lot have its wiring connected to a stake which would be pounded into the ground beside it.

Hoxie was expected on the lot in Baltimore, and several of the workmen were passing around the rumor that he was going to clean house when he got there. They all got to work. John said Hoxie had had another heart attack. He had been with Lewis Brothers, in Cannonsburg, Pennsylvania. On that date, June the twenty-sixth, the Hoxie show had been in North Warren, Pennsylvania.

"They say he passed out for fifteen minutes on the lot," said John. "He had been doing some physical work that day, which he shouldn't have done. You could predict that if he does too much physical work, he's going to get himself down, or he'll pass out. He just has to learn not to do that. His doctor told him that if he didn't stay away from the circus a while and stop the work, the next heart attack would kill him.

"If he was an average person, he'd probably be dead from his heart attacks. He's a very tough person. He's an extremely strong physical person in his *will*, and probably inside. And he just doesn't give up that easily."

Does Hoxie have the light?

"I wouldn't say he has the light," said John. "But I *send* him the light, which helps a little bit."

Back in the spring there had been a rumor that some foreign students would join the circus for the summer, and now the rumor was fulfilled. Nine of the students, brought to the United States by the Council on International Educational Exchange, had arrived from Europe in July, and they were living in a separate sleeper, which was much more attractive than the one the workingmen lived in. The students worked in various of the circus's occupations—the sideshow, Big Top, animals, props. John Hall paid the students pretty much the standard circus wages, but he had promised them a bonus at the end of the summer, to offset the cost of their transatlantic transportation.

One of the students, Jan Bronkhorst, from Sittard, in Holland, was in Mill Hall, Pennsylvania, the day Arnold Sherman's woman friend arrived from California. She did not know that he had died. By that time the circus people did know.

One of Jan's jobs was driving the sound truck. The truck, which was equipped with loud-speakers, a tape player, and a public-address system, was usually driven through a town on the day of the circus, and its operator broadcast the news of the show's arrival. Jan, who spoke excellent English and who was studying philosophy at the University of Amsterdam, did very well at the sound-truck job.

He had been driving around in Mill Hall, and he parked the truck briefly in a parking lot at a baseball field. "I was getting out of the truck," he said, "and there was somebody in a white car sitting there, and she asked me, 'Do you know where the clown Arnie is?'

"And I asked her, 'Is he the clown who's about fifty-five years old and was only with the circus for a couple weeks?' and she said, 'Yes, that's him.' And I said, 'Well, I have some pretty bad news for you. The police have found him in his camper near Pittsburgh, and he was dead for a couple of days.'

"And she was shocked, and she said, 'No, it isn't true! What kind of car was it?' And she tried to ask all kinds of details I couldn't answer. Then I went around to several people asking for details—what the name of the clown actually was, and everything, but most of the people didn't know and didn't care. But I found out some things, and I went back to her and told her all the things I knew, and then when John Hall got in, he had more information for her.

"I tried to talk to her a little. You can't say much. It's something you have to deal with yourself, emotionally. And there's no other person who can help you except for maybe to be there and just make you feel at ease a little."

Jan had been speaking in a low voice, as if he were respecting the life and death of Arnold Sherman and the shock that the woman had had to absorb. "It's strange the way people take things here," he said. "Life goes on here, you know, even though something like this is happening. They don't really seem to care. They seem to take it like they would take the news that, well, the truck broke down. Okay, the truck broke down. So let's fix it. Or we lost this or that. So we lost it. So get something new. I told Bill Hill—the girl was sitting out there in the car, and I told Bill Hill, 'Well, the clown's girl friend is sitting out there, and she doesn't know what to do.' And Bill Hill said, 'So what, let's set up this tent.'"

Hoxie pulled his Airstream onto the lot at Baltimore in midmorning and surveyed the midway. His hatbrim was up. The mayor of Baltimore, William D. Schaefer, was there, and he and Hoxie conferred, and I was struck by how at ease Hoxie was with the heads of governments. It happened several times a season: a mayor or some other official would visit the lot, and if Hoxie were there they would walk around the midway, talking as if they had a great deal in common. Hoxie did, in fact, have a few things in common with Schaefer, one of them being elementary sanitation. Baltimore was in its ninth day of a wildcat sanitation workers' strike. Also, the police were in their third day of what was called a "job action." About three thousand city employees were out. I wondered how Hoxie would react if someone walked up to him and announced that a union of circus workers had been formed and that one of its first demands was new donnikers.

The mayor went away, and Hoxie patrolled the back yard. He walked for a while along the water, which lapped at an artificial bank made of cement and riprap. He spotted a waterlogged two-by-four floating not far offshore. "Come here, son, and get that piece of lumber," he said. A young workman ran down the bank and grabbed at the piece of wood. "That's worth two dollars," said Hoxie. "There's plenty of places we can use that piece of wood."

I told Hoxie I was sorry to hear about his heart attack.

"I am, too," he said. "Because it makes you feel like *hell*." He laughed.

Hoxie pointing

Did you go to the hospital? (On some of Hoxie's collapses, he had neglected to go to the hospital.)

"Oh, yeah, they sent me in there. They carried me to the hospital in an ambulance, and I was up there three or four hours. I told the man I wasn't going to stay when I come to, and he give me a shot, and I was feeling all right—I wasn't feeling *all right*, but what I mean was I wanted to go home."

To Miami?

"No, no. Back to my trailer. Which I did. I went back over there."

Was it officially a heart attack? Three or four hours in a hospital—

"That's what they said it was. That's what the man told me. That's why I ain't doing nothin' any more. John Lewis and this friend of mine who was visiting with me, they went to the hospital with me, and the doctor told them, 'You better stop him, because if you don't do it, he ain't going to be here for another one.' That's the way he put it."

That's which one for you?

"You mean how many? Four."

A little later, I saw Hoxie with John Hall, and Hoxie was actually pointing toward some work that needed doing. Betty used to say that if Hoxie would just learn to point his finger he'd last longer.

King Charles was bitching, as usual. He said that if he had good sense he would quit the circus and get some guys together and play in a night club. There were several clubs within a hundred miles of Ville Platte, and Charles could drive home on his days off.

Why, then, I asked him, did he keep coming back to the show each spring?

"It's the circus that's in you," he said. "It's just the circus that's *in* you. Once you get it in you, it's hard to get it out. You know, it really is true what they say about 'the show must go on.' Plus when you get on the road it's hard to spend the hot summer in one particular city. Like this place. I'd hate to spend the whole summer here."

Phil Chandler was sitting in the back yard drinking a beer, although it was well before noon. Linda was sewing jewels on a costume. Phil's young daughter, Robin Anne, had arrived a few days before, and she would spend the summer with Phil and Linda. At the moment, she was off playing with Armando Cristiani.

I started to tell Phil what King Charles had said about wanting to start a night-club band, but Phil finished the statement for me. "And it's only a hundred miles from home and he could come home on weekends. I know. Charles has been trying it out on everybody. He'll never leave."

Phil said there had been an increase in the tensions that were caused once all the young Hills and Walkers got out of school and joined the show, but he added that he was trying to stay out of that argument. "I try not to pay attention to what goes on in the front yard," he said. "That's not my department. I just try to keep my little play actors happy in the back yard. What happens out front, I could care less. They could kill one another and I wouldn't notice. Everybody in the front yard makes fun of me, I guess, for worrying about my play actors, but that's my job. I like to see everybody happy back here."

Bert Pettus's replacement, Gary Jacobson, was a young

man with long blond hair and light blue eyes. Gary was twenty-four years old. He was a pleasant fellow, but he also seemed to have a kind of chip on his shoulder, and it was difficult to figure out the chip's origin. Gary said quite openly that he had been a dope freak before he had gotten amazed about elephants.

"I came from a small Midwestern town," he said, "and I got involved in the drug scene at a pretty early age—by the time I was out of high school. I went to college for a year and a half. My family more or less expected me to finish college, but I didn't."

Did the drugs get you into trouble?

"Well, hard drugs aren't necessarily good or bad," he said. "There's an even line. If you can stay on that line, you can pass yourself off in society. But there's a point where you can either quit or go on. And if you quit, you're better off."

And you quit?

"You bet. You don't have any time for hard drugs when you're out slogging through the mud eighteen hours a day."

Gary said he regarded his position as chief elephant handler for Hoxie Brothers Circus as an extremely good opportunity. "I'm probably one of the youngest elephant men in the country right now," he said, "with a herd of ten elephants. It was just a coincidence and an accident that they were handed to me, and if I do well, it's a good start. And if I do badly, well, I suppose I'll be back in Orlando, waiting for another chance."

Gary said he had found the elephants in "completely fucked-up condition," and that especially the babies had become surly and were refusing to take even the basic commands. "But I've got a method for dealing with that," he said. He pointed to his bullhook and a cattle prod. He said he had been using the instruments mercilessly, trying to get the elephants back into shape.

I asked him if it really was necessary to use force and electricity. "It sure as hell is," he said. "Don't let nobody tell you any different. It's the only way to deal with an elephant. Right now I've got Hoxie so upset he shrieks when I even

Gary working the babies

come *near* him with these things." Gary waved his weapons.

A pretty young woman walked up and took Gary's hand. She was wearing shorts and an old blue work shirt, and she bounced deliciously with each step. "This is Vickie," said Gary. "She's my girl, more or less." Vickie smiled shyly.

When they went to get the six-foot boa constrictor before the sideshow performance, they found it dead in its traveling case. Mike McGuire, who kept the snake in his trailer, suspected mites and mouth rot. A young workman was told to take the snake away and bury it.

The superintendent of the Maryland Society for the Pre-

vention of Cruelty to Animals, David M. Stewart, was on the
lot. Stewart looked over the animals, and he watched a performance, and he said he was pleased with what he saw.
"This is the most co-operative circus I've dealt with," he said.
"And I've dealt with about three a year for the past twelve
years, plus carnivals and stuff like that. Every suggestion that
I've made, this show has complied with."

I asked about the elephants. Gary Jacobson, I said, talked
about how tough he had to be with them.

"He came across to me as a very humane trainer," said
Stewart. "He might come across to some people as a very
tough guy, but when he's working with the animals he's not
as tough as he sounds."

On the second day in Baltimore, it was decided that the
jaguar in the sideshow should have its claws trimmed. Bob
Mason had noticed that the claws were curving inward on
themselves, and that meant that before long the animal would
be in great pain if something were not done. The claws were
becoming ingrown because the cat did not have enough room
for proper exercise. Bob told John Hall, and John arranged
for a veterinarian, Fred Garrison, of Reisterstown, Maryland,
to come and do the clipping.

Garrison wanted to tranquilize the animal in its cage and
then pull the legs over to the side, to the feeding slot, and
trim them. Hoxie thought this was a needless waste of money
and medicine, and he went to the sideshow tent with a piece
of rope and proceeded to try to do it his way.

Hoxie's plan was to lasso one of the cat's legs, pull it
over to the feeding slot, and trim the claws, all while the animal was awake. Fifteen people watched while Hoxie tried to
catch the cat's leg. "I've done it that way with the same
animal about three or four times at least," said Hoxie. "No
tranquilizer. Just catch him with the rope and drag his leg
back, and you get *one* leg back, and while you're holding it
you get the rope on the other one and pull it out and cut
them both while you're at it." The vet stood by and watched
while Hoxie tried his method. The lasso kept falling short,

and Hoxie's face got redder and redder, and it was hot, and several people suggested that Hoxie take it easy for a moment. He did not.

After a while it was agreed that the vet could use his dart gun. He fired the tranquilizer into the jaguar, looked at his watch, and waited. Ten minutes later the big cat started stumbling around; then it lay down; then it passed out. Two workmen got the cat's legs over to the slot, and Garrison clipped the claws expertly with a scissorlike device that looked like a heavy chain cutter.

Garrison told Bob Mason that the cat should have rest for the remainder of the day. He suggested that Bob hang some canvas over the cage, so that the cat would not see the sideshow spectators. Bob said he would do that.

A few hours later, just before Spec, someone looked in the jaguar's cage and noticed that it was lying very still. He looked closer and saw that the cat was dead. Gilda Cristiani came and looked, and she started crying. Phil Chandler blew the five-minute whistle, and Gilda crossed herself and ran to the back door, still crying.

I asked Hoxie how he felt about the cat. "I don't feel anything," he said. "What you worry about is things you can *do* something about. You can't do nothing about that."

That night, the crowds were thin, and the performers said it was because none of the people who worked in Baltimore had the courage to come back into the city on a Saturday night, and none of the people who lived there had enough money to attend the circus. A thunderstorm came up during the second performance. You could see the lightning coming closer and closer along the cityscape. I was going back to my tent to get my raincoat, and I saw Vickie sitting on the embankment. Her head was down. She was crying.

I told her that was a bad place to be in a thunderstorm. Some of the lightning seemed to be playing across the water just a hundred yards from her. Her feet were barely six feet from the water.

"I don't care if I *am* struck by lightning," she said. "Noth-

Hoxie and the vet, trying their own methods

The jaguar

ing matters to me any more. Gary told me he didn't want me here any more." She sobbed. "I suppose I'll just go home now to my husband."

They cut the second performance short because of the thunderstorm. By nine-thirty the crowd was gone out of the Big Top, but the storm passed by without causing any harm. The performers went back to their trailers, and the elephants went back to the sideshow tent, and small bands of small black boys roamed the lot in the darkness. After the storm passed, the lightning bugs came out.

The next morning the SPCA man, David Stewart, came with his son in a pickup truck, and they loaded the jaguar's body into the back and drove off. Stewart said that ordinarily the city would have disposed of the animal, but the sanitation workers' strike was on.

HOW DO THESE PEOPLE *Live?*

After Baltimore, the show moved around Maryland and eastern Pennsylvania for a few days, playing towns like Ephrata and Sinking Spring and Lehighton, and then giving a two-day stand in Philadelphia that none of the circus people enjoyed. Then Doylestown and Coopersburg, and somewhere along in here the Cristianis and the Fornasaris had a falling out. It had something to do with the children. People from both families said they were sad that the feud had started, but after it started it stayed. For the rest of the season, the Cristianis and the Fornasaris did not speak to each other.

Spring City, Pennsylvania, was on the seventeenth of July. Spring City was a hospital date. The sponsor had previously been called the Pennhurst State School and Hospital, and it had been a fairly typical state mental institution, but now the social scientists and the euphemists had gotten hold of it, and it was known simply as the Pennhurst State School. "The emphasis is on the education and training, rather than the medical model," said the school's assistant superintendent, Robert Smilovitz. Smilovitz's training was in special-education administration, and he had a Ph.D. in education. "We're the first institution in the state to have leadership by doctors of education, rather than by psychiatrists and medical people," he said, as he watched the Big Top going up.

They left the sidewall down, because the show was on the school's property and there was no point in keeping people from seeing what was going on inside. Large sections of seats were not set up, so that patients in wheelchairs could come in. The sideshow tent was spread out on the ground, and Superchicken spent the day patching it. The pit show and the concessions trailer did not operate here. It was just a pure-and-simple circus, with everything going on inside the Big Top. The people at the school seemed entranced by the show. The tent went up in the middle of a huge lawn that stretched out beneath the main administration building, and all morning people were walking up and watching and trying to engage the circus people in conversations.

"We call them 'citizens with retarded behavior,'" said Smilovitz. "They are primarily severely and profoundly retarded. We don't use IQs, but, to give you some perspective, eighty per cent of our population are from zero to thirty IQ— the severely and profoundly involved. Multiple handicaps. That's wheelchairs, cerebral palsy, blind, deaf, and retardation combined, in all combinations.

"The emphasis here is on the normalization principle, coming from Sweden and Denmark, which says that every individual, no matter what their handicap, has the right to live as normal a life as possible. It's that simple. So there's a vast number of people in institutions who never should have been there in the first place, and we have citizens here who've been in here forty, fifty years, and never should have been here in the first place. So they're all going out into the community—to group homes, shelter departments, halfway houses, and so on. And what the institutions are receiving in terms of a population now are the more severely, multiply handicapped individual that the community still can't deal with.

"The medical model would say, 'Give them good custodial care, keep their clothes clean, and put them in a nice, clean bed.' *Our* philosophy is an educational model—every single person can learn. There are a number of citizens who you won't see here today who are so profoundly involved that they can't come. But we're educating them, also."

The sky was a beautiful deep blue, with a few clouds. The temperature was in the eighties. A great portion of the audience was in wheelchairs, and some of them wore protective helmets. Many of them looked intently at the acts; some stared off into the distance.

As so often happened in hospital dates, a lot of the performers seemed to be working just a little harder than usual, perhaps because they knew the circus was one of the few bright spots in a somewhat dreary institutionalized routine; perhaps because they knew they had to work harder to capture the attention of some of the members of the audience; perhaps because there was a feeling of "There but for the grace of God go I." Gilda Cristiani said, "I feel very sad, very depressed. Some of them enjoy the circus, but I think that some of them don't know what's going on." She said it had been difficult for the horse act to try a little harder today, because the ring wasn't level. "There was a little bit of gravity," she said. "But we do try harder, for some reason. We feel so sorry for these people that you want it so much for them to enjoy themselves."

During the second performance, an aged woman in a wheelchair caught a circus person's arm as he walked by, and she pulled him in close to her. "I'm *damn* glad I came here," she said. When the show ended, some of the audience did not want to leave, and some of them were screaming and some of them were weeping. The Big Top came down in the afternoon, and what was left was a circle of trucks and trailers, and a smaller inner circle of empty lemonade containers. Johnny Walker sat around talking about the old days when Ringling Brothers went to great pains to tell the customers that Cokes sold for fifteen cents. "They had signs up all over the place," he said. "The butchers'd try to charge a quarter, and most of the time they'd get away with it. Every once in a while a customer'd ask about the fifteen cents, and you'd say, 'Oh, we get a dime extrey for bringing them to your seat.'" As evening fell, the lightning bugs came out, and the windows of the trailers gave off a faint bluish glow as the circus people turned on their television sets.

In the morning, the trucks pulled out early and left for Hatboro, and some of the performers slept a little late. Three residents of the state school came down to the lawn and walked around the trailers. They were attracted to the Cristiani horses. Lucio was outside early, as usual, feeding them and getting them ready for loading into the truck. One of the citizens took a bread-and-butter sandwich over to one of the horses, and the horse ate it.

"I sure liked your circus," the man told Lucio.

"Thank you," said Lucio. "I enjoyed playing for you."

The jump to Hatboro was not very long, but the roads in that part of Pennsylvania were from the last century, and it took the show a long time to move. On the map, the little towns seemed to be deep suburbs of Philadelphia, but as you drove through them you saw that they were individual communities, some of them quite attractive. In the town of Spring City the front porches were decorated with hanging baskets of geraniums. Farther down the road there were signs advertising roadside produce stands, and although the corn was just starting to come in, there was the distinct feeling that the real summer had arrived. The gasoline crisis was over, but occasionally there were reminders that it had been very much with us a few months before: King Charles's arrows took the show past one gasoline station that had been turned into a bicycle shop, and another one that had been turned into a dirty-book store.

The lot was next to the parking lot for a large shopping center—not a modern one, but a huge barnlike building that housed many small shops, like a public market in Mexico. The circus people parked their rigs and drifted over to the market, driven, as always, by the need to buy food, wash clothes, and browse among the shops like typical American suburbanites. Linda and Phil planned to hit the shopping center after breakfast, but Linda had an accident.

She splattered hot bacon grease on her right arm. It was extremely painful, and she applied ice cubes to it, but the pain did not go away. Phil said Linda should take the day off; Linda said she didn't need to. Later in the afternoon, the pain got so bad that Linda went to a hospital.

The doctor diagnosed Linda's injury as a second-degree
burn, and he wrapped her arm and hand in a huge bandage,
gave her a prescription for some painkiller, and told her to
come back in a few days. Linda got back to the lot at six
o'clock, just as Phil was blowing his fifteen-minute whistle,
and she hurriedly changed into her costume for the magic
act. It was obvious that she could not do web and ladders,
but she thought she could do the magic act. Phil said no, and
Robin Anne took Linda's place during the levitation trick.
But Linda was out there in Ring Two, anyway, styling and
helping with the act.

"That's a performer for you," said Phil later. "She hurt
like hell, and that painkiller made her dopey as the devil, but
she was out there trying. Unlike *some* of the broads on this
show."

Jorge Del Moral walked up on the outside of the Big
Top each day to set the rigging for the motorcycle act. There
was an adjustment that had to be made at the very top of
the centerpole, and the easiest way was for him to do it from
the outside. Sometimes when Jorge got to the top he would
do a handstand on the centerpole, fifty-five feet up. Jorge
was young, and full of energy, and sometimes you had the
feeling that he was uncomfortable with the show, because
there were not many people, and very few unattached women,
his own age.

Jorge's family went back for three generations in the
circus business. His uncle was the manager of Circus Atayde,
one of Mexico's largest shows under canvas, and Jorge was
hoping that he could find employment with that show when
winter came. Jorge had done a lot of things in the circus,
including selling Cokes with the butchers and clowning, but
he liked aerial acts the best.

"I like the wire," he said. "I like the motorcycle, also. But
I think what I'd really like to do now is the perch act that my
father did. It's a pole about four inches in diameter and about
thirty-five feet long. My uncle supported it on his forehead
while my father went up the pole and did one-armed hand-

stands, and two-arm, and headstands. And then my cousin went up and did other tricks at the top. That's what I'd like to do next year, that and a balancing act. But I don't think I'll be able to do a balancing act next year."

Why not?

"Because I'm not practicing at all. Don't have the time to, and I don't have my props with me. It takes all day just to set the motorcycle rigging."

How long have you been a performer?

"Well, actually getting paid for it, this is my first season. But I've been in a circus family all my life. I worked in the concession department at Ringling Brothers, and I went to school, and I was in the army for two years, seven months, and five days."

Jorge was born on a circus lot in Macon, Georgia, twenty-two years before. He remembered hearing his family say that a member of the famous Zacchini family, the family that specialized in being shot out of cannons, took his mother to the hospital. He did not remember the name of the show.

Jorge Del Moral

It was nighttime, after the show was over, and the Chandlers sat in their trailer and ate—not much, because Linda's arm was still hurting and Phil wasn't much of a cook. That evening, between shows, a town woman and her kids had come through the back yard and stared at them and their trailer in something approximating disbelief. Phil called it the "How do these people *live?*" syndrome. Towners were always looking at them, he said, and wondering, sometimes out loud, "How do you circus people live in all that filth and mud and everything. How do you keep *clean?* How do your kids get an *education?*" The truth of the matter, said Phil, was that they lived very well.

I asked them what they had to do, living in a trailer, that they didn't have to do if they lived in a house.

"Pack carefully," said Linda. "Keep everything down to the bare essentials. You don't need ten dresses, because you don't go out that often. Just basic living clothes, basic dishes, basic pots and pans, basic bedding. Just the basic things, because there isn't room for everything." As Linda spoke, she was trying to sew jewels onto a costume with her one good hand. She kept the jewels, graded by size and color, in an egg carton, and she kept a lot of her other sewing apparatus in thirty-five-millimeter film cans.

Did basic living extend to food, too?

"Definitely," said Linda. "We have to go to the store about three times a week, because there just isn't enough room to buy up a lot of things at once. We can't buy a lot of meat at one time, or a lot of milk, because there isn't any room in the refrigerator. There's plenty of room for canned goods."

What about keeping clean? I realized I was sounding like one of the towners.

"We have a shower, so we don't have any problem. Except we were keeping the boa constrictor in there for a while, and that didn't leave much room. We have hot water. I go to the Laundromat about every two or three weeks. I hate doing laundry, so I try to make it last as long as possible."

The Chandlers' trailer was twenty-four feet long. The front part of it was given over to beds and storage, the middle was kitchen and bath and storage, and the rear was a living and dining room and storage. There were seats along the sides at the rear, and a table that came down in the middle. On one occasion Linda had gotten herself, Phil, Robin Anne, the four Cristianis, and me around the table for a meal.

I asked what they did about privacy. Robin Anne was sleeping in a bunk bed above theirs.

"She's a sound sleeper," said Linda.

"Or we send her outside and lock the door," said Phil.

Linda said that if she were giving someone advice about living in a trailer, she would suggest that they throw out half the things they thought they would need. "We're even carrying stuff now that we don't need," she said. "And, of course, we have to carry winter clothes as well as summer clothes, and that takes up a lot of room."

Linda said she did almost all of their cooking in an electric frying pan. They got electricity from the show's light plant from the time they pulled into a lot in the late morning until late at night. Their lights and their television set were rigged to work both on the voltage supplied by the light plant and on the power that came from the trailer's own battery.

"A person going out to buy a trailer," said Linda, "should look for storage space. A lot of cupboards, and especially closet space. Underneath storage, too. And the frame. A trailer must have a good frame, especially in this business, going over these rough lots. It'll bend if it's not a good, solid frame. And an electric blanket is great for the wintertime."

"We asked for an electric blanket for a wedding present," said Phil. "And some other things—a small electric heater, a TV antenna for a trailer, one hundred feet of power cord, and a case of ten-forty motor oil."

"What was your silver pattern?" I asked.

"*What* silver pattern?" said Linda, and she smiled.

ALL ACTORS
ARE CHILDREN

All of the trucks and most of the performers had pulled off the lot in Hatboro when a small boy appeared, pushing a bicycle. He looked around and he said, "Where did the fair go?" A solitary man walked back and forth across the place where the Big Top had been. He was swinging a metal detector along the ground.

The circus went to Thorndale, to the west. It was another place where eastern Pennsylvania had tried hard to be rural, but where it couldn't bring it off, because there were simply too many people, too many highways, too many cars. The lot was pleasant, in a big old field that was bordered by tall old trees. Gary Jacobson staked the bulls out by the trees, and they went to work eating the grass. Vickie sat with Gary on the ground near the elephants. He had not sent her home after all.

It was hot. By early afternoon it was one hundred degrees in the sun against the side of the Big Top. It was windy, and that helped some. The Big Top billowed gently in the breeze. Radios played in the trailers. There was always an early-afternoon lull on a circus lot, except when there was an early performance, but today, in the heat, it was quieter than ever. People were staying in their trailers. One of the McGuire sisters walked around the tent and off to her trailer, and it was amazing, seeing such a vision of loveliness out there in a grassy field.

Art Duvall was complaining because, he said, he had to drive twenty-seven miles to find someone who would sell him hay for the elephants. But then, he always said something like that. Sometimes the mission was hay and sometimes it was water, and sometimes the distance was twenty-seven miles and sometimes it was fourteen.

Across the road was a busy railroad track. Commuter cars kept shuffling back and forth from Philadelphia.

It was inevitable that one of the workmen would be nick-named after the monster in the pit show. They called the man Pongodies, and it was amazing how closely the two resembled each other. When you asked Pongodies his name, he reached in his pocket and produced his Social Security card, because he had difficulty spelling it himself. It was a very ordinary name.

Leo sat in the shade under the big trees, close to his elephants. His full name was Leo Entwistle. Few of the circus people knew his last name. He was just Leo.

"You have a family, don't you?" I asked him.

"Yep. Haven't seen them in about fifteen years."

Children?

"Two. Married. Got a daughter and a son. My son, he's been to Vietnam and back."

Why haven't you seen them?

"They married and moved away."

Do you like this kind of life?

"The best kind of life going. The best life going."

King Charles had arrowed the show into Thorndale and then had pulled his station wagon under a tree where he knew there would be shade in the heat of the afternoon. He woke in the middle of the day, got out, stretched, and opened a soft drink he had carried with him.

I told Charles that I had particularly enjoyed his arrows on the way from Hatboro. There had been a couple of diffi-cult turns, and Charles had shown, with subtle inflections in the way the arrows were stapled, the right way to go.

"Well, I guess you would say there's an art to putting

them up," he said. "And an art to *lying* to get to putting them up, too. This morning, on the turnpike, I was putting up two arrows, and I know they don't allow you to put them up. So a state policeman stopped, and I knew he was going to tell me to take them down. So when I saw him coming, I tore the arrows down.

"He said, 'What are you doing?' I said, 'I'm taking these arrows down.' I said, 'I put them up yesterday for the trucks to come through, and I promised I'd come back and take them down, so tonight I'm taking them down.' And he says, 'All right.' So that's one of the things you have to go through. Course, I put them back up later."

I said it looked as if Charles really loved the circus.

"Well," he said, "it's a part of show business. And I'm in show business, *period*. But I've been just a little bit of everything. I've been a hotel porter, I've worked in bakery shops, I've been a bootlegger. You might even say I was a pimp, which I didn't want to be, but I was working in a hotel, and back in those days there wasn't any streetwalkers. There were girls that would travel around the country, you know, from hotel to hotel. In others words, they had a circuit they would make. So, naturally, if you were a porter there, you would just take the men up to them. So therefore I was, I guess, what you'd call a half pimp.

"In other words, I've had a lot of experience. And while I was working in this hotel I met a man, and he paid for my first trumpet. This was down in Bonham, Texas. And the first band I played with was a fellow's band over at Fort Worth. And after that, I went with the Sugarfoot Green minstrel show. This was back in 1943. Back in those days there was quite a few shows named Green. It meant black show."

Are you discriminated against because of your color?

"I don't know. It may be so, but I don't know it."

What's the funniest thing that happened to you when you were putting up arrows?

"Well, I can't call it too *funny*, but there was one time in Georgia, down close to Edison, Georgia, I was putting up arrows, and I stopped in front of a house. And all of a sudden

I heard some screaming and hollering, and here comes a naked woman, running out the door. And right behind her comes a naked man. And right behind *them* comes a man with a shotgun. I figured it was a family triangle or something. And after I got down the road about three miles the sheriff caught me and he asked me what did I see. And I told him what I saw. He said he'd have to have me for a witness, that this man was attempting these people's lives with a shotgun. And I explained to him that I was with the circus and that we'd be about thirty-five miles from there, so the next day he sent an officer over to take a statement, a signed statement of what I saw. I don't know if you'd call that funny or not."

How many years have you been putting up arrows for Hoxie?

"I've been with Hoxie since 1967. And I've been putting up arrows ever since."

That's a lot of arrows.

"Well, I'd hate to have someone stack them up on top of me, after all these years."

I looked at the station wagon. Its back was filled with arrows and masking tape and cartons of staples. "How much sleep do you get a night?" I asked Charles.

"Well, out of twenty-four hours, counting good sleep, I might get three hours. Usually, when you come into town, it's a hot night, and you're in the car, and maybe you're next to a pond or something, which breeds mosquitoes, so when you come in you have to leave your windows up, and you sleep until the sun comes up, and then you're all hot and stuffy and you're sick the rest of the day. So not much sleep. Not good sleep."

"You can't live on three hours of sleep a night," I said.

"*Circus* people do," said Charles.

We sat in the shade next to the Little Big Top, drinking a beer. It was an hour before showtime, and it was not as hot as it had been. Phil was wearing walking shorts and an old pull-over and the wooden-soled slippers that circus people liked. I asked him about other work he had done.

Supe again

He was, first and foremost, a magician, and a magician who preferred the large, old-fashioned illusions. Phil was hoping he could make enough money this year so that he could purchase, in the fall, a buzz saw that would appear to cut

Linda in half. But he had done practically everything else, too. He used to work horror shows—stage shows at a movie theater that often were coupled with horror movies, and in which Phil would come on in a Frankenstein or werewolf suit. He also did the "buried-alive" routine, appearing at drive-in theaters with a small troupe, which would bury a man in his coffin and then leave him there for several days. Spectators could look down a viewing tube at the man. Supposedly the man had no food or water during the period of his burial, and once the Chicago bunco squad came and warned Phil and the others that if they caught the man being fed the police would consider the troupe in violation of the law. "We fed him right in front of their noses," said Phil.

"And then I sold insurance once," he said. "During one of my lean times, my ex-wife talked me into getting into the insurance business. I went through two weeks of school. They paid my way up to Chicago, plus giving me two weeks' salary. I went to the school, and I came back, and I had a series of club dates, and that was that." He laughed.

What did your parents expect you to be?

"Oh, an insurance man, bank president, government worker—a white-collar worker. So they could say, 'That's my son the bank president,' or whatever."

I asked him about his name. It was really Barr. Was there anything wrong with Barr as a show-business name?

"No, but Chandler looks better in type. It's easier to pronounce. Just a good name. Found it in the phone book. It just looked nice. But there's another reason, too. I never had any encouragement from my parents, never any encouragement to go into show business. So I thought, by God, if I ever make anything of myself, I'm sure not going to use my family name. And that's the reason I adopted the name of Chandler."

Phil popped open another can of beer. "You know," he said, "I consider myself an enigma. I'm many different people. The person you're talking to now is one person. That's the one you see most. The person in the Big Top is another one. That's the Amazing Mister Chandler. And I even have a touch of the devil in me that comes out every now and then."

You mean you're possessed in some way? I wasn't taking Phil's comment too seriously. *The Exorcist* had come out recently.

"Slightly. But I keep it in check."

I could see that Phil was serious about this now. He wasn't just making a joke. I asked him if he really wanted to talk about it. I suppose I was afraid that he would tell me something about himself that would alter my feelings about him and Linda.

"It doesn't make a damned bit of difference to me if I talk to you about it," he said. "It's just me. Now, after telling you what I tell you, you either like me or you don't. If you do, that's fine. If you don't, then what the hell.

"What's funny is, I see the devil. He doesn't *appear*. He's just there. He changes my whole personality."

Does he make you mean?

"No."

Vindictive?

"No."

Does he bring out any of the negative qualities in you?

"No. It's kind of hard to explain. I don't know how to explain it to you. Oh, he don't come out *too* often."

Well, what happens when he comes out?

"He just has to come out, and that's all there is to it. And once he's there, it's like a Jekyll-and-Hyde personality. Like in my entire life, I have only been mad three times. One time, I was beating up on my ex-wife. And my grandmother, who had been dead for many, many moons—her voice told me to stop, that she wasn't worth it. That's when it was bad between us. I was literally throttling her, and my grandmother's voice came to me and said, 'She ain't worth it, Phil.' And I stopped."

What other personalities do you have?

"I've got the businessman. I can be just as hard-nosed as anybody else. Make good deals, and this, that, and the other. The one you're talking to now is the one you see the most. I'd like to be known as a nice guy. Which basically I am, because I like people, and I like to see people happy. In fact, my first wife used to tell me that I probably went too far to try to make people happy, to the extent of even hurting my own family. In other words, if I had only five dollars in my pocket, and a friend needed that five dollars, I'd give it to him.

"You see, I'm a very sentimental person. I have to watch my emotions very, very much. I'm tough on the outside, but in some respects I'm like Hoxie Tucker. You can hurt me just like that"—he snapped his fingers—"but I'd never let you know it."

What do you think of Hoxie?

"I love him. I think he's the most marvelous man there is in this whole world. He is the supreme being, the final word, on this show. He controls the sun, the moon, the weather, and that's it. He is the head kazooki. When he says 'Poop,' you better be straining. And that's it."

All the things you just named are things Hoxie tells you to do. What's the pay-off for doing them?

"I'm very happy. I've never been so well off in my life."

You're not just talking about money?

"Money, everything. I'm happy. I'll come back here just as long as he'll have me back."

How much do you make?

"Three and a half a week. Plus Linda gets extra for doing sideshow. Plus he pays for my gas. It's not a whole lot of money. But it's every week, and I know there's going to be a Saturday. And that's what counts."

What about John Hall?

"I think he's a marvelous man. When I was first around this show, in 1969, I didn't understand him. I just thought he was sort of an office man. But now you might say that I guess he relies on me to keep the show moving and keep everything cool back here in the back yard. He gives me responsibility, and I think he respects my opinion and my word. If I tell him the Cristianis can't work because the ground isn't right, maybe he doesn't always *like* it, but he takes my word for it. Like I said before, I got to look out for my play actors. I may want them to work tomorrow."

Phil Chandler

I told Phil some of what John had said about sending the light to people. I asked him if he knew what I meant.

"Oh, yes. Sometimes, man, I'm going in there with problems, and this and that and the other, and his cool, calm, collected manner, it just gets to me. I asked him one time, I said, 'John, do you ever get angry?' He says, 'Yeah, but not too often.' Thank God for that. He's sort of a security blanket. I enjoy it when John's around, and I *especially* enjoy it when Hoxie's around—to watch the people jump and try to cover up this, that, and the other. It is a scream, man. I just stand back at my little trailer and watch it all."

You can afford to do that because you don't have anything to cover up?

"Right."

Except occasional visits from the devil?

"Don't we all have them, though? Think about that."

I still don't understand what you mean. Do you mean you become violent?

"No, no, I'm not a violent person. I'm far from a violent person. I can't afford to be."

Hoxie said everybody in the circus had a weakness. If that's true, what is yours?

Phil looked at the sky. "I want to make my family, and my ex-wife, so fucking jealous that I can just go like this." He stuck out his tongue. "That I can say, 'I don't need you for a fucking thing.' I'm going to make my children so proud of me that it isn't even funny."

Is it that you want to be *better* than somebody?

"No. I just want to show a few people some things. All those that said I couldn't do it. All those who laughed and scoffed."

Isn't that an essentially childish attitude?

"Yes. I'm a child. *All* actors are children. Surely you understand *that* by now. You take us out of this world and we're dead. That's why we don't get involved in politics and all that debris. Who needs it? The reason most actors don't get involved in politics is they see through all these phonies that these towners, man, are too fucking dumb to see through. All politicians are old carnies, really. You put a business suit on them, but a carnie's a carnie no matter how you dress him, man. Think about what I just said, man."

Phil looked at his watch. "I hate to do this," he said, "but I've got fifteen minutes in which to scrape my face, get myself lovely, get the mortician's wax into all the cracks and crevices, and go in and do Children of All Ages." He got up and struck off in the direction of his trailer.

John Hall saw to it that the six o'clock show was started properly, and he walked back to his trailer for dinner. The western sky had gotten cloudy, and the wind had picked up a little, and there was the possibility of some rain. John went inside the trailer, where Lisa had been fixing one of her excellent meals. She made him a cup of tea and put the food on the table.

John was halfway through the meal when there was a knock on the door. Bill Hill was outside. "We better cut it short," he said. "It's getting bad out there." From the trailer door you could see the Big Top; it was tossing mightily in the wind, and it looked as if the wind had become much stronger. John silently left the trailer, and Lisa put the food back into the oven.

Workmen struggled with the sidepoles, trying to keep them from dancing when the wind picked up the tent above them. The real danger in a windstorm comes when the wind blows in under the tent and has no way of blowing back out. The wind has no recourse, then, but to blow up against the canvas, and this causes the canvas to lift, and when it lifts, it also lifts the poles that hold it up. That is why the jumper ropes are so important. If they are not tied down properly on their poles, a gust of wind can lift the Big Top and its sockets right off the sidepoles and quarterpoles, and the poles can fall and injure someone. And, worst of all, the tent can collapse.

The wind in Thorndale

Tonight all the sidepoles on the western side of the tent were dancing, and occasionally one of the quarterpoles would try to dance, but all the jumper ropes were secure.

John surveyed the situation for a moment and then went to the center ring. He took the microphone from Phil. "Ladies and gentlemen," he said, "we are having to cut the show short tonight because of the wind. Will you please hurry on out, safely?" The audience left without panic. Outside, the clouds seemed to have drifted on, and you could see the sunset.

Someone asked Bill Hill how bad it was.

"You never can tell," he said. "Why take chances? We spend billions of goddamn dollars on the weather bureau, and they still can't tell us what the weather's going to be."

The windstorm was over about as quickly as it had started. It had been dangerous for about fifteen minutes. John Hall went back to his dinner. I asked him how he decided something like that; like asking the people to leave.

"From experience, basically," he said. "It's much better to be safe than sorry. That's the rule I go by. You try to give the people enough of a show so that they're satisfied, but basically you've got to be safe. And it's safer to have people outside of a tent than inside it if it's going to collapse."

The second performance went on as scheduled. A few minutes before, King Charles drifted back to the bandstand, and he just started talking, as he often did.

"I'm a musician," he said. "I've played everywhere. Strip parties, gangster parties—in fact, Jack Ruby was a good friend of mine. In Fort Worth, he opened a club, and he told my brother and me, 'Look, I'll make stars of you guys.' He had three or four clubs around Dallas, but he opened up a club in Fort Worth, and he happened to hire my brother and I. We were youngsters, you know.

"But you saw this evening, when the wind was blowing, the danger that was in it. You know those big stakes out there, one can pull and konk you on the head. Well, I parallel that with playing in a night club, musically speaking.

"There's no difference. You have dangers on the circus.

You've got dangers in the night club. Because when ——— ——— killed a man about his wife, the man was dancing with his wife in front of the bandstand, in Fort Worth, Texas, and we were playing. He walked on the dance floor and shot the man in the head right on the dance floor. There was bullets flying everywhere. The bouncer was shooting at him, too.

"I've been on circuses during tornadoes, hurricanes, cyclones, and everything else, and so, as I say, I parallel the whole damn thing that way. There's danger on either one, and the circus is show business, the night club is show business, a boxing match is show business, show business is show business. That's why being on the circus is no different from being in the night club. I'm equally at home in either one. And I'm equally as confused and everything else. Because you get slugged in a night club, and you can get slugged by an elephant on the circus. I'm worried with drunks in the night club, I'm worried with drunks on the circus. So that's it."

At the end of the performance, Phil made his usual announcement about young people who might want to make some extra money helping to load the seats, and the usual complement of young boys stayed behind. And the usual complement of parents stayed to wait for them. One man, who had four kids out there loading lumber and picking up trash, stood and gazed at the scene, and I knew, from the look on his face, that he was remembering.

"Did you do this when you were a kid?" I asked.

"Yes, I did. Carried water for the elephants."

Do you remember which circus?

"Ringling Brothers and Barnum & Bailey. It was in Philadelphia."

Did you get paid very well?

"I didn't get paid at all, really. What they did was they just let us into the circus for nothing on the following night. Because usually they stayed for more than one night in those days."

Do you think this is good training for a kid?

"Absolutely. It teaches them a little responsibility, and it teaches them values."

CRISTIANI

The Cristianis finished their riding act and ran out of the Big Top, and Phil directed the audience's attention to the slender cable that would carry Luis Murillo and Jorge Del Moral to the top of the tent. The leopards had already been wheeled in their cage back to the red-and-white Cristiani trailer. Gilda went inside to change out of her costume and finish cooking dinner. Lucio and the boys covered the leopard cage with a tarpaulin, against the night air, and they changed clothes and came back out and made sure the horses were all right for the night. The family was starved. They always performed on empty stomachs, and tonight Gilda was making spaghetti with red clam sauce. In just a few minutes they were inside the trailer and sitting at the little table that turned later into Lucio's and Gilda's bed.

Lucio opened a half gallon of red table wine and poured us some, and I asked him about the family.

"Well, it started in about 1840," he said. "See, my great-grandfather, he was a blacksmith in Pisa. He used to go to gymnasiums quite a bit. He loved acrobatics and gymnastics. And his son became a fairly good tumbler. And one day the son met a girl from a circus, and they got married. He went with the circus.

"And then later he came back to Pisa, and the father got interested, and he sold the blacksmith shop and joined the circus, too. And he put some money in, and it became a combined circus with Cristiani. And that's how the circus dynasty started. It really originated out of Pisa.

"And then it started to be handed down from father to son. My grandfather, he was a daring man. He was a man of courage. In fact, he was the first one to put electric lights in the circus in Italy. Before, they used to have these torches and so on. But he was always daring. He was a real showman. Never had too much money, but he always had a good-looking circus, and he used to attack big cities, which not many circuses did. He wasn't afraid of anything. What I'm driving at is that he wasn't afraid to be full of debts, too." Lucio laughed.

"But he was a showman. And he had two wives in the meantime. You see, in Italy there was no divorce, and he had about twenty-four children between the two wives. The family got so big that my father decided to branch out by himself. My father was a good performer. He was one of the best tumblers of the day. And he went everywhere—France, Spain, Yugoslavia, everywhere. He was Ernesto. And then, of course, the family got big, and it was too big to travel around as a performing group, and my father was the kind of a guy who didn't like to work for somebody else if he could help it. So he went back to Italy and started a little circus himself, with his little family. And the circus grew with the family. We grew up and the circus became big, until it was the largest one in Italy. But then the war clouds started gathering."

Because Lucio's father was not overly sympathetic toward the people who were running Italy, people like Mussolini, he started finding it harder and harder to get working permits in that country. A friend in the Fascist party warned the Cristianis that things were going to get worse, and so the family left for France in 1931. They joined the Cirque Medrano, in Paris, one of France's most famous circuses.

"We stayed in France for the season, and from there we went to England, and then we went to Germany," said Lucio. "And we didn't finish the season in Germany, because we had a bad experience. There was a little midget, and he was Jewish. He was a Hungarian Jew, and he used to go out with me all the time. Going back, let me say that when I was in Italy I joined the Fascist party." Lucio made a gesture that indicated that he had done this merely as an expedient measure, not because he had any partiality toward the movement. "And when I was in Germany, I carried my Fascist papers with me. Good thing, because the Nazis came in one night. I asume that somebody must have squealed that the little midget was a Jew. Because we were sitting at a restaurant, the one we always went to after the show, and a couple of storm troopers came in. That was 1933.

"And the storm trooper comes in, and he says, 'Heil Hitler.' I said, 'Heil Hitler.' He says, 'The little one. He's a Jew, isn't he?' I should say it in German. It makes it more dramatic that way." Lucio then said it in German. He spoke five modern languages and Latin.

"So I tried to be smart. I said to him, I said, 'You believe that a Fascist like me would associate with a Jew?' He says to me, 'Are you a Fascist?' I took out my papers, and I showed them to him, and I said, 'Here I am.' He says, 'You, sir, are the *real* Fascist.' Then he says 'Heil Hitler,' and I say 'Heil Hitler,' and he walked out.

"Anyway, I told my father this story, and he called Medrano in France. Medrano said, 'Send him over here and I'll give him a job.' So this Hungarian Jew packed up and left because he saw the danger."

You may have saved his life, I said.

"Probably. I don't know. Anyway, let's eat." Gilda brought a huge bowl of spaghetti and clam sauce to the table, and she set down a loaf of supermarket Italian bread, apologizing because it was not the real thing, and Lucio poured more wine, and we dug in. Tino and Armando ate furiously.

"Anyway," said Lucio, "in the winter of 1933, Pat Valdo of the Ringling Brothers came over looking for us. In those days he was the talent scout. And he hired us for 1934. And we came to this country in 1934."

Ringling Brothers at that time owned the Big Show and also several smaller ones. The Cristiani family, which was doing tumbling and riding, went to work for one of the smaller ones, Hagenbeck Circus, for two seasons. Then it went to another Ringling-owned property, the Al G. Barnes show. In 1938 the family made a short-subject movie, one of the Pete Smith Specials. By that time John Ringling North, a nephew of John Ringling, had acquired the leadership of Ringling Brothers, and he happened to see the movie.

"And he said, 'Where in the hell is that family?'" said Lucio. "And Pat Valdo said, 'Well, they're with Al G. Barnes.' He said, 'What are they doing over there?' Valdo says, 'They like them there.' John Ringling North says, 'Well, I like them, too. Tell them to come over.' So we joined the Ringling Brothers in 1938." The Cristianis were the stars of the show, and they stayed that way for close to a dozen years. Those were the years of the private railroad car that said "The Cristiani Family" on the sides.

"But then the family got so big and so wanted that John said, 'I can't pay you any more, because I need *many* families, and you make me go over the budget.' So we started going from one show to another, but it was tough to get that money. We asked for a lot of money. So one day I told the family, 'Either we split up or start our own show.' Well, we started our own show. There was a show broke in Texas. I went over there and we put some money in it. We called it King Brothers–Cristiani. This was 1949.

"In 1954, we dissolved the partnership with King. He bought me out. And we went and put on our own show, because I wanted to go to Alaska. Alaska never had a circus before, so we went to Alaska with ten elephants, a lion act, the biggest show they ever had in Alaska. And we had Hugo Zacchini with the cannon. Go get the route slip, Armando."

Armando, who had eaten a copious amount of spaghetti, slipped out of the trailer and ran to the office and ran back with the slip that showed the route for tomorrow's jump. It was useful if you blew an arrow, and it showed the mileage to the next town and the composition of the lot. This time, it was fifty-eight miles. "Pappa," asked Armando, "what kind of a lot is it? A shopping center?" "It's a shopping center, Armando," said Lucio. "Oh, boy," said Armando.

"And then we did two years with the indoor, but we really

didn't like it. The atmosphere wasn't the same. So in 1956 we started a show of our own, Cristiani Brothers. It lasted from '56 to '61. And then, Ringling took a show to South America, and they wanted us to augment the show, and we went there on a partnership. The tour was successful, but the show was too heavy. Too expensive. So you didn't make any money. Then when we came back to this country we went out again, but things didn't go too good, and dissension in the family started, and that was it."

I asked how many Cristianis were performing in the United States now.

"Except one brother, the six brothers are still performing, in one way or another. One's got elephants. Pete is the manager over at Lewis Brothers. One, he builds rides for carnivals. All the rest, in one way or another, are connected with entertainment."

With all that history behind you, does it become certain that Tino and Armando have to be circus people?

"We don't force them. The only thing is that I can see talent in Armando and Tino. And I feel that through the life *I* had, I think they have the opportunity to have a good life and to be good entertainers. I guess in a few years they will probably decide, for themselves, to do what they want."

Now Armando says he wants to be a juggler.

"And a bareback rider," added Gilda.

Well, when you ask him, he says juggler.

"Right now that's true," said Gilda. "He *is* involved with the juggling. Even too much, sometimes. And we worry because he does practice too much, and he gets tired."

Lucio cleared his throat. "See, juggling is a kind of a business where the ability of your juggling doesn't amount to much. It's the personality that counts. How you sell it. How you present yourself. And if Armando's got that type of talent, why not?"

If Armando decided to be something other than a circus performer, would you feel bad?

Both of them replied, "No, no, no."

"Not at all," said Gilda. "And the same with Tino. We're

not going to force them. In fact, you can remember, Lucio, we really didn't want the children to be in show business. The first couple of years we were married, we were thinking about that. Especially on the bareback riding, because, you know, it's hard. And there are not too many bareback riders around because it is such a hard act. And we didn't think about juggling or trampoline or anything. If they were going to learn anything, it would be bareback. Then the children grew up, and they started doing these things, and they liked it, and they *wanted* to be performers. It wasn't really that we decided or that they decided. We decided all together."

"You know," said Lucio, "the circus business today is in the hands of the promoter and the businessman." Talking about the difficulties of bareback riding had reminded Lucio of this, one of his favorite themes. "They don't know too much about the circus itself. What they know is how to make money. Which is important. But the performer, the one that is born and raised in the circus business, who loves this business, he realizes that it's hard for a man to ride horses. Because a horseman like me, he's got a new rigging every day, which is the ring. And nothing is done about it. Whether it is crooked or not, they expect you to go into that ring. Now, years ago, the owner of the show was probably an ex-performer himself, or an ex-rider. And he *knew*."

"They would use the hoe to fill the ground," said Gilda. "Like tonight. There were holes in the ground. You would be afraid that she would stumble."

"One thing about this show," said Lucio. "They tell you to do the best you can. But for a performer, he wants to go in there and he wants to do his work, see. Because if I really didn't care, I wouldn't be here."

The spaghetti and clam sauce was gone, and Lucio poured more wine. I started to thank Gilda for the excellent meal, but she turned around from the stove, and she had a large bowl of veal in wine sauce. She put it on the table.

"I can't possibly eat any more," I said.

"I can," said Lucio. "This is my only meal." It turned out that I could eat some more.

I asked Lucio how many times he had been hurt.

"Well," he said, "very seriously, a couple of times. I had concussions. I fell on my head. But I must say that I was lucky as far as falls were concerned. I have had many falls, but not many bad ones. I was lucky. Considering my line of business, especially the bareback riding, I have been lucky. I never got hurt seriously enough to quit."

I asked Gilda, "Is he an interesting person to be married to?" She replied with great enthusiasm.

"Yes, he is! You know, we've been married sixteen years."

Is this a classical Italian family, where the pappa is the strong man?

"I wouldn't say that I agree with that," said Lucio. "I believe that children and wife have to have a voice in the family. And I never did like the command of the father and the mother on the children, that dictation. I always believed that a child should be brought up with *reason*—to tell him the reason why you do something. But that authority that used to exist during my day—"

"And mine," said Gilda.

"—wasn't so bad in my family, but I saw other families where the father was really the law. And when he said something there was no talk back. You see, it comes from the Romans. A woman had very little rights. In fact, they say that when the wife was a good wife, you could put on the grave, 'She stayed home to make wool.'" He said it again, in Latin. "*Casa mazi lana ficis.* That was a great honor. She was a good woman, so they had the right to put this on the tombstone, that she stayed home and made wool."

Gilda was born in Trento, Italy, the daughter of a circus family named Zamperla. The family was as old in the circus business as the Cristianis were. She came to the United States in 1958, although her father was still running his circus in Italy, "because we wanted the glamour of America. I came as a bareback rider," she said, "and my brother and I worked for these people who had a big troupe of bareback riders. And then, after we split with this group, I met Lucio. And the year after, we got married."

Lucio

Gilda

I asked Gilda when her leopard act had started.

"I had never done that before," she said. "Two years ago, I fell from a horse and I broke my knee. And after that I thought I could never ride again. And Lucio and I decided that if I had to quit, we would both quit. But he didn't want to quit completely. And then, since we love animals so much, we wanted some animal that we liked, and we thought of the leopard. And we got them very small. We didn't know exactly what we were going to do. Because we don't really treat them like animal trainers do. They're more like pets for us. You know, some animal acts, they say, 'Don't make a pet out of the animal.' But I think we do. And now we like them. Now we want to buy more animals. We want to buy a black leopard, and we're going to try to put the baby into the act. I wouldn't put more than four in, uncaged, because it would be dangerous. Too much tension. I'm tense now because one is a little bit more— I wouldn't say vicious, but she—she's aggressive."

I asked Gilda if she remembered the town where she broke her knee. "Yes," she said. "It was some town in California." She thought a while. She could not remember the town. "I remember the lot, though," she said.

"I don't want to butt in," said Lucio, "but they don't understand when it's slippery, when the grass is wet and so on. That's how she got hurt. The horse slipped, and she fell off and came down."

Where were your children born?

"Tino was born in Sarasota," said Gilda. "Armando was born in Canton, Ohio."

What show was that on?

"It wasn't a show. It was closed. We were laying off. The Cristiani show had closed. It was a bad year."

"There was dissension in the family," said Lucio. "We had a friend in Canton, and he wanted to put a show out. It was October. And when we closed, he said, 'Come over here.' So we went over there, but the story of the show slowly disappeared. But in the meantime Gilda was going to have the baby. So she had the baby in Canton."

"It was snowing outside, I remember," said Gilda. "It was

such cold weather. I remember sitting in the apartment and watching the snow come down. And I would say to myself that a month after the baby was born I would start practice again. And Armando came, and right away I put myself on a diet, and I was riding again after a month."

"And then," said Lucio, "we went out with my brother's show. Pete put out the Cristiani-Wallace show that next spring." I told Lucio that I had seen him in that show. "We were pretty good," he said.

I remembered differently. They were excellent.

THE PARTY

The fifty-eight miles from Thorndale to York took us through Pennsylvania Dutch country, or, at least, through pseudo-Pennsylvania Dutch country. HEX SIGNS FOR SALE, said a billboard. WELCOME TO THE EIGHTEENTH CENTURY, said another. The motels, gasoline stations, fast-food joints, drive-in movies, and mobile-home lots had been decorated to look like something they weren't. The motels called themselves "inns," but they were just motels.

There were beautiful little blue flowers along the roadside, and it was an almost crystal-clear blue day. The countryside was deep green, and the corn was growing taller, and from the rises you could see church steeples sticking out of the trees where a town grew. We crossed the rocky Susquehanna and rolled toward York. It was Saturday, and it felt like a Saturday.

The lot was between a cluster of shopping centers, but it was behind some buildings, and the big tent was hardly visible from the road. The performances were to be at two and eight o'clock, and in between the Robert Dover Tent of the Circus Fans of America was going to hold a party for the show. Circus fans were all over the lot while they set up the Big Top.

An hour before showtime a fan knocked on the Cristiani trailer. Gilda came to the door; she was trying to sort the laundry, start a meal, and get ready for the show. "Remember me?" the fan asked. Gilda didn't, but she was polite about it. "You want to play a game of chess?" asked the fan. He had a chess set in his hand. Gilda looked confused. She said she really didn't have time today. "*Last* time you said you liked to play chess," said the fan. Gilda repeated her apology. The fan walked off and soon was knocking on somebody else's door.

Linda Chandler had been back in the sideshow bally since the day after her painful burn. She still had the big bandage on, and she made no effort to hide it on the platform. Bob Mason got the tip assembled around the platform, and he introduced Miss Linda Our Snake Charmer, and he said:

"Yesterday she placed her hand down into a cage containing six giant jungle snakes. She was trying to remove one of them when two or three of the others attacked her, viciously biting her arm and requiring a quick trip to the hospital. Fortunately, our snakes are boa constrictors. They are not poisonous, but she will tell you the bite is very, very painful . . ."

The workingman named Okeechobee came back on the lot, and the others welcomed him as if he had been a long-lost rich relative. Okeechobee, a thirty-seven-year-old man with striking light blue eyes, never worked too hard, but he was always good for a laugh around the Big Top crew. The men were honestly happy to see him back on the lot after his three days in jail.

What had happened, Okeechobee said, was this:

"I ran out of gas, and I was parked on the side of the road. We was moving from one town to another—I don't remember which ones. It was about seven, seven-fifteen in the morning. I just pulled off the side of the road. Me and Pongodies was settin' there, and we decided, well, heck, what about it, and he took a sip and I killed the whole pint. I figured I had about three hours to wait until they'd be back for us.

"And here come the man. Well, he carried me in. Driving while intoxicated and no driver's license. I spent three days in jail and they carried me to court. The judge fined me three hundred dollars and thirty days for DWI. I like to died. Then he turned right around and he fined me two hundred dollars more and thirty days in jail for no driver's license. That's five hundred dollars and sixty days.

"He says, 'I'll tell you what I'll do. Since you're traveling with the circus like you just got through saying—' I had explained that I had sore legs and sore feet and didn't want to drive in the first place, but they were short of drivers and needed some help, so I volunteered. 'Well,' he said, 'I'll cancel the sixty days. And if you'll stay till tomorrow morning and pay your fine, I'll just cut the fine right down to two hundred.' So he cut it down to two hundred and let me out the next morning, and the circus was good enough that they sent the money order. They wired the money down."

I asked Okeechobee, whose real name was Velden Dean Carroll, where he was from. "Well, originally Texas," he said. "I'd call my home base Lubbock, Texas. The plains."

The men said he drank a lot of wine.

"Well," he said, "about half a gallon a day."

Is that bad or good?

"Well, in some ways it's bad, and in some ways it's good. I don't *average* a half gallon a day. Like today I might drink a fifth. My specialty is white port."

Would you be better off if you didn't drink it?

"I wouldn't think so. Sure wouldn't."

You mean it helps you function?

"Well, with sore legs and sore feet, like now, I'm drinking heavier than I would normally. I drink a pint and go to work and not worry about it."

How'd your legs and feet get sore?

"Well, just bumping and bruising. Running into stakes in the dark. Not taking care of them. Get a bruise on my leg, not take care of it, not keep the dirt out of it. When I get off work I'm tired and I go to sleep, instead of washing it. Not taking a bath."

When you were a little boy, what did you want to be when you grew up?

"A musician, believe it or not!" Okeechobee laughed. Whenever he laughed, which was often, his face became actually radiant.

"I had one year of college as a music major. Texas Technological, in Lubbock. I farmed seventeen years. Irrigated farming in west Texas. Got hailed out two years in a row and said to heck with it. The hailstones blew my crops away two years in a row. So I sold my debt off. Sold insurance three years. And I just turned into a tramp, and I'm tramping around. I've traveled with the circus four months and enjoyed every minute of it.

"In Okeechobee, I was picking oranges when the circus come along. Eight months of that is enough. Climbing trees, carrying a twenty-two-foot ladder. That's enough. It don't pay too good. Course, I was making more there than I am here. But I don't have to work as hard here as I did there."

Can this really be an easy life?

"You can make it easy, or you can make it hard. If my feet weren't sore, it'd really just be plumb easy. See, you work four hours in the morning putting the tent up, work an hour and a half, maybe an hour and forty-five minutes at night tearing it down."

How many times have you been in jail?

"Five. All of them drunk charges." He laughed.

You're not *proud* of drinking, are you?

"No, I'm not proud of it. But I can't see the harm it does. When I get too drunk, I just go to sleep. I don't get out and cause bodily harm. I don't believe in fighting. No violence. Man walk up and knock me on the ground right now, I'd just get up and laugh at him and walk off. Now, I would protect myself in self-defense, but outside of that—I believe in doing right with people and being honest about it."

What's your philosophy about life?

"Well, in a few words, I can just say *be honest*. When a man asks you to do something, tell him you'll do it, and go do it. Just do your honest day's work, get an honest night's sleep—course, that's kind of hard to do around here."

How much do you make?

"Right now I'm making forty a week and room and board."

How much of that forty do you spend on wine?

Okeechobee

"Uh, outside of what cigarettes I smoke, I guess the rest of it I spend on wine. Well, I'd say getting a haircut and shaving soap and washing clothes, too, which is not much. Subsistence don't cost a whole lot. But I do my drinking, and they know it."

Is the circus a good place for somebody like you?

"Well, if you like to travel and move around, it is. I get itchy feet. I don't like to stay in one spot. I couldn't hold down a *steady* job. I guess this is about as steady as I'd want to go. But you're still on the move. You're in this town today and you're over there tomorrow, and you're liable to be back in Florida this winter, and then next year you're liable to come back up here and do the same thing all over again.

"It's frustrating at times. And we get mad. A bunch of men that live around each other all the time, occasionally

somebody gets mad. And you get a grudge against this old boy
or that one, but the next five minutes you're out there working
right beside him and you just don't think about it. You don't
worry about it. It takes a certain amount of—well, I can't coin
the word, but—you just have to have a good attitude. A *for-
giving* attitude.

"You got to forgive a lot of things. And people. And you
got to forgive the weather, too. I don't worry about the bad
weather. You just get out there and get wet, and you get the
sniffles next morning, and you just take a little Vick's salve
and rub it on your nose and keep on going, because it'll die
down. I just drink another pint and forget about it!" He
laughed again.

Jim Raab was not only the promoter for this portion of the
show's tour through Pennsylvania; he was also an active circus
fan, a member of the Robert Dover Tent, which was giving
the party for the show in York. Raab had been booking towns
for Hoxie in Pennsylvania for eleven years, and he recalled,
as we were waiting for the party to start, that back then it was
a tiny show, seating about a thousand people, "and it had one
elephant and maybe two acts." Raab said he was sorry Hoxie
couldn't be here for the party.

I told Raab that some of the people I had talked with
about Hoxie seemed to think of him as a father figure. Did
he feel that way?

"That could be, somewhat," he said. "But primarily I
think of him as a cut above—above anything I can think of.
He's a great man. I remember one day in 1964. I was in Pine
Grove, Pennsylvania. And Hoxie and his office manager were
sitting in the office one afternoon after a performance, counting
tickets and putting them into bundles of one hundred. And
I said, 'What are you doing?' He said, 'Why, we're bundling
these tickets up to send to the next town.' I says, 'You mean,
Hoxie, you don't print new tickets for each town?'

" 'My God, boy,' he said, 'look at the expense that would
be involved.' It was this saving pennies, saving, cutting corners
every place that he could, and he put the money back into the

show. And that's the way he operated. The tickets just had the times and 'Hoxie Brothers Circus' on them. No date, no sponsor, no town. It was just a stock ticket. They had about fifty thousand of them made for the season and they just rotated this same number of tickets.

"I finally convinced him that he could print tickets with names and dates for about four dollars a thousand. And we modernized and started to do that.

"You know, Hoxie is about the only living circus title around. I mean, there's no Clyde Beatty any more. And the Ringling brothers are all gone. There's no such people as Sells and Gray, and no Carson and Barnes. But there is a Hoxie, and he's a living trade-mark. He's a real personality. He's always tried to do everything right and honest. And I think that's taken him a long way. People remember that. He doesn't try to beat anybody out of anything. He may be a hard businessman, but he doesn't beat anybody out of anything."

The fans' party was held in the cooktent. The performers and bosses changed into the sort of clothes they wore when they went out to eat, and a few of the workmen washed up, and they filed by the tables that were covered with food. For the workmen, some of the food was quite familiar: bologna sandwiches and baked beans, sloppy joes, cold cuts, coffee. There was a nice cake that said "Welcome Hoxie Circus."

A congressman was there, and he made a little speech to the circus people, most of whom did not know who he was. He had ridden Myrtle in Spec in the first performance.

There was also a Methodist bishop on hand. Fred Corson, of Harrisburg, was the past presiding bishop of the World Methodist Council, and he was also a circus fan. "I am a very great circus fan from the earliest time that I can remember," he said. "I grew up in a little town, Millville, New Jersey, where about the only excitement during the year was the circus coming to town. And I've seen all the old ones." He named a lot of them; it sounded like Bert Pettus remembering the days gone by. "I used to see them all," he said.

Bishop Corson said he had particularly good feelings about

The cake in York

the Hoxie show. "I've come to it for several years," he said. "And I think that Hoxie is a very able circus man. And I think he manages his circus well, and he won't stand for any trouble in it. And I think that is the secret of his continuous success. He isn't here today, is he? He's been sick, I know. But he's a fine man."

"If you weren't doing what you're doing now," I asked, "would you like to be a circus person?"

"If you'd asked me that seventy years ago, I'd of said, 'Yes.' But not now. I'm seventy-eight now, and I just think I couldn't stand the pace. But seventy years ago it was different. I'd go to the circus and then I'd come home and I'd climb the back fence with a circus whip in my hand and pretend the fence was a horse, and I'd do all the acts."

Is there anything that circuses and God's work have in common?

"Well," said the bishop, "I've never seen a dirty thing in a circus. I've never seen anything in a circus that I'd be ashamed to take my wife to or that I wouldn't want one of my children to go to."

LIKE
A CATHEDRAL

The show crossed the Delaware Memorial Bridge into New Jersey on Saturday, July 27, and played its first date there in Thorofare. It was almost like the start of a new season. Along with the assumption that New Jersey was an inordinately circus-minded place, there was the acknowledgment that the people ought to get a little more for their money and that there ought to be more ways for them to spend it.

Hoxie arrived on the lot, hatbrim up, and talked with Gary Jacobson about building an elephant ride—a square metal scaffold with a deck across the top and with stairs leading up and down. A child would climb the stairs and then be at the proper height to climb onto Myrtle's or Bonnie's back for a brief ride around the front yard. The ride would cost a dollar. Gary thought it was a fine idea, and he went to work building the scaffolding, but Hoxie felt he had to show him how to do it properly, and Hoxie ended up doing a lot of the work.

Hoxie was everywhere—checking tears in the canvas, looking over the rolling stock, suggesting ways to make the sideshow platform look better, and then, when people did not immediately put his suggestions to work, doing it himself. The sides of the animal trucks, which formed the banners for the sideshow, and which depicted some scenes that were not seen in the sideshow, were being repainted, this time without the scenes. Hoxie hired Jim Hand, a show painter, to letter the words "Hoxie Bros. Sideshow and Zoo" over the sides of the trucks in enormous letters. Jim had been doing this for Hoxie for twelve years.

The refurbishing went on for several days, and Hoxie continued working as hard as ever. Betty Tucker said the reason was New Jersey. "People in New Jersey love the circus," she said. "They don't just bring their kids to the circus and leave them, the way they do some places. They come with them. It's like a picnic here. They take the whole family."

I asked her about Hoxie's health.

"Well, he's mean and ornery again," she said, "so I guess he's getting a little better. But he doesn't behave like I want him to. He gets out there and does this kind of work when he's got all those people here to do it for him."

"I just don't like to see things left tore up," said Hoxie. He was repairing a sagging portion of the sideshow platform. "And that goes for anything that's broke around here. If we bought it to begin with, that showed we needed it, doesn't it? If it gets broken, either replace it or fix it.

"So I come around here, and I try to get everything fixed up that I've got around this show, and then I won't have any problems. I've worked every day since I been here, since Thorofare. I'm just getting the thing cleaned up and painted

Jim Hand lettering a truck

up. Got a new sound truck, and the trailers have been painted, and they're painting the office wagon now. And by tonight this thing will look a lot different. The old saying is, you know, 'Paint will cover a multitude of sins.'"

I asked him how it was working out, having two shows on the road. Was he really taking it easy and letting other people do the work? (Obviously he wasn't, at least not here.)

"No," said Hoxie. "I do a lot when I'm around the Lewis show. I've got the thing operating pretty good now, and it's making a little money. I don't care who you are, or what you're doing, if you're in this business, and you don't watch it like a hawk, it'll never take care of itself. And any time a man can set down with a cocktail in his hand and think he runs a circus, he's crazy, and I don't care *who* he is."

I asked him if the season had been a good one so far.

"Oh, yeah," he said. "*All* of them are good. Just some of them are better than the others. We're gettin' by. We manage to eat, and to get from one town to the other, and we work for the inn-surance and gasoline people. That's all we do anyway."

The show was playing generally along the Jersey coast, where the vacationers were. In some places, the crowds came to watch the tent going up and pretty much stayed around all day, filling the Big Top at night. In other places the attendance was spotty. The circus people blamed it on the economy, which was not in the best shape that year. There was a general air of lassitude, not just about spending money, but about everything: for one thing, Richard Nixon was still in the White House, lying his head off, and everybody *knew* he was lying, and the whole country seemed to be rolling along more slowly than usual. There was a languor about the American people that was hard to put your finger on, but that was there nevertheless. People still went to the circus, especially people in New Jersey, and, really, especially people in the New Jersey seaside resorts; but no longer could you count on them to fill the house twice a night every night.

The show was leaving Margate early one morning, after

a very successful night there, and one of the young workmen
was shepherding the trucks through a toll plaza, and one of
the trucks crushed his leg against the toll booth. It was not a
serious injury, but it was painful. I heard about it on the car
radio. Later I mentioned it to Hoxie, and Hoxie said, "Did
they say what town we were playing today?"

The foreign students had been with the show for several
weeks now, and they had formed distinct impressions of it and
of America. Generally speaking, the French students had lost
no time becoming critical of the United States. It is a facility
that the French seem to have in abundance. The students from
the other parts of Europe appeared to be more tolerant.

Yves le Fur, a student in the plastic arts at the University
of Paris, was nineteen years old. He said he had signed up for
the summer in the United States "because I thought it would
be a rich experience to meet some people, to change from
town to town, to see another country, a different continent."
He said he had concluded that "the United States I don't like.
The way of life I don't like."

"The people are not together," he said. "The country is
too large. For example, in the villages. The villages are very
big and the people can't meet each other. And there are no,
as in Europe, no little streets or places where people meet each
other every day to talk, to drink, or whatever—the life of a
village.

"If I walk in the street I can't see nothing—only cars. People do not walk in the street. I am alone in the street if I walk."

Yves worked in the Big Top, and he had done some truck
painting in anticipation of Jim Hand's arrival, and he had
butchered cotton candy. "I prefer to sell cotton candy because
you are with people then," he said. "You see the eyes of the
children, and if you see the eyes of everybody, the eyes of
everybody become the eyes of children. They are like children's
eyes. Everybody—old man, old woman—they are changed. In
the circus it can be like a cathedral—something rich, and full
of colors, and very big.

"I think I shall be marked by the circus. Marked in my
brain. The material of the tent, the boards, the colors, the

blues and the reds—and there is a spirit of the circus, something which is both artificial and instantaneous. It is like a *feast*. And afterwards, at night, when we come down, the feast is over. And you know how sad it is when the feast is over. The papers—the plastic bags and everything that everybody leaves on the ground. They show that the feast is over. But you know there will be another feast tomorrow.

"And in the morning, you make something virgin. And it's always the instant, you know. We live all the time in the instant. We make something new, and some people will leave, and some people will die, and the day after it is the same. And for the performers, the performance is everything. You take the performer out of the circus, out of the Big Top, and he is somebody completely different than he is in the circus. Very interesting."

Peter Nellemann, from Denmark, was studying law. He worked with the elephants. He had been to the United States before, on an exchange program that had placed him for a year with a family in Rochester, New York. They were upper middle class, he said, and "now I have seen the other end of it. I have seen the low end. A lot of people work here because it's better to live here than it is to live in the gutter. These people are much nicer and much better than you would expect. When I told my friends that I wanted to work in the circus, I was told that there were a lot of dirty and nasty people there. And they *are* dirty, but there's a natural explanation for that. They're not that nasty. Usually they're kind."

Jan Bronkhorst drove the new sound truck around in Sea Isle City, letting the residents and the vacationers know that the circus was in town. "It's fun, doing the sound truck," he said, "because that way you get to know the way a lot of cities are built. I get a kick out of the enthusiastic children at the side of the street, jumping up and down and yelling, 'Circus, circus! I'm coming tonight!' It's interesting."

"You know," he said, "every day I'm surprised at how nice the circus people are. That's one of the things that keeps me here. If it had been just business people who only cared about making money, I think I would have left a long time ago.

It's surprising how human they are, in the context of what other people are like. And still, somewhere in the back of their minds, they're there just to make money. I guess most of them like the circus world also, and everything that surrounds it— traveling and everything. That's the *reason* they do it.

"But if you travel with a circus for a while, you grow a little cynical. You start caring about fewer things. You start caring about just your own business. You have more times where you say, 'Let it go, let it rest.' I guess you kind of limit your input for your worries. Your attitude toward other things gets a little harder. Otherwise it's hard to survive. In a way, it's a shame. But I can understand that you grow into it after a while.

"Like that guy who got his leg hurt in the toll booth. I felt bad about that, but I felt there was hardly anything I could do about it. You feel a *distance* with these people, you know. You work together, and you travel together, but there's not this clan feeling that exists in one family. It's not like a family where people know each other very well and they've been together a long time and help each other and everything."

Was it perhaps a defense mechanism that circus people worked out because they knew there would be a certain number of tragedies, a certain amount of hard luck?

"I think that's true," said Jan. "Because if you *do* care, you die of a heart attack. I guess that's the way show business is. In a way, it's a very efficiently organized place. People limit their interests, their cares and their responsibility, to a certain area, and they only work on that, and they get that finished. Everybody has a certain job, and it forms one big circus."

Has your philosophy changed as a result of being here?

"What I've learned, I don't think I've had time to let it sink in and blend with my other thoughts. It will change me; and it will make my experience richer. It won't change me radically, but it will enrich me. But it will take a while. I don't have any time to sit down and think. No time at all. You either work or you're tired or you go out with some other people. There's hardly any time for yourself. There's no place you can go and sit by yourself. Those places are hard to find."

Magaly on her trapeze

Villas was a two-day stand. It was a tiny town on the southern tip of New Jersey, but enough people came to justify the two days. It was a date some of the circus people might as well have skipped. Anita Fornasari, the mother of the musical clown family, hurt her arm. And Magaly Rosales hurt herself seriously. She was climbing the rope to get to her trapeze when a metal ring holding the rigging broke. The trapeze fell to the ground, striking Magaly on the head. She fell unconscious in the Big Top.

The sponsor in Villas was the local rescue squad, and its members swarmed around Magaly when she regained consciousness in the back yard. They took her to the hospital. There were no broken bones, but Magaly was badly shaken up. She stayed in the hospital overnight and then returned to the show, but she did not work again for more than a week.

Five of the students left the show when it was in Villas. Four of them were French. John Hall said a boardwalk concessionaire in Wildwood had promised them jobs at higher pay.

The circus put up a sign at the main entrance, announcing that it was in the market for more workingmen.

"You know," said Phil Chandler, "my philosophy is that everybody should do what they're happiest at doing. Whatever gets you through the night, that's my philosophy.

"Take a look around you. There are so many miserable people working in offices, factories. They work fifty weeks out of the year for two weeks off just to travel around, when we get to do it fifty-two weeks a year. Like my father—he was that way. Don't misunderstand me. I don't *knock* people because they have office jobs and factory jobs. Somebody's got to do it. I just thank God that I'm able to do what I do, and that I'm still able to earn a dollar or two and put food on the table. But my philosophy is just do what makes you happy. Because you only go around once. And you play *that* right, and once is enough." He smiled broadly. He was sitting in a lawn chair in the midst of a field of elephant dung.

It's not important, is it, that you be a magician or even a ringmaster? It's that you be in front of people?

"Right. Just so long as I'm in front of the public. I guess you'd call it an ego trip. But magic is my first love. You could say that with this show I'm being paid for announcing and giving them the act, or you could say I'm being paid for the act and giving them the announcing. But I like it. I think it's fun. I'm just sorry that sometimes the audience doesn't come along with me on my trip of fantasy and make-believe. They're missing so much by trying to figure out how I do what I do. If they'd just let themselves *go*, and let themselves be a kid, they'd have more fun.

"Mandrake the Magician told me, a long time ago—and this was part of his routine that he used in his night-club act—he'd say, 'Every child should see a real live circus and a real live magician.'

"I've remembered that throughout the years. That's the reason I wear evening wear in my act. A lot of times I may be the first magician a kid's ever seen alive. They've seen pictures of them, and maybe on television, but none that they can reach out and touch. And you'd better look like what they envision. Not some guy in a business suit or a tuxedo. I'm in the evening wear. That's how it's pictured in every picture you've ever seen of a magician, right?"

I asked Phil when he had started.

"Oh, Christ," he said. "I've been doing shows ever since I was eight years old. For money. My first wife used to say, 'Jesus Christ, weren't you ever an amateur?' I'd say, 'No. I can either do something or I can't do something.'

"When I was a kid I started doing magic and puppets. I used to do club dates, like for the Lions Club, or Kiwanis, or the Cub Scouts. And this was all for money. Of course, I played a lot of free ones, too, because a very wise man once told me, 'When you're young like this and getting started, get as much exposure as you can. Play everything.' I worked for free, for five dollars and ten dollars, and I used to get really big twenty-dollar dates and *really* big thirty-five-dollar dates. But for a kid starting out, you have to start small. That's how you learn to control people. I remember when I was a kid—those damned birthday parties where the mothers used to call and I'd say, 'Well, how old are they?' And they'd answer, 'Well, they're just at that cute age.' And I always wanted to say, 'What age is *that*, madam?' Because then I hated kids, being one myself.

"All that was in Dayton and surrounding territory. Then I played the ghost shows in theaters. What I did was basically magic. I played those for seven or eight years prior to 1968 or '9. And then buried-alive shows, and then a girl-in-the-ice show, and then I really hit the circus thing heavy after 1969. A lot of Shrine circuses, which I liked, but some of the jumps were killers. They think nothing of jumping maybe eight hundred, nine hundred miles overnight.

"I was with a circus right after I got out of high school. It was the Great Fred J. Mack Three-Ring Circus. Fred Mack was a potato-chip manufacturer who I guess was sort of a circus fan. I was on concessions then, running the floss joint." He meant the cotton-candy place. "And then after that I played a lot of Shrine circuses and Grotto circuses, and in 1969 I was asked to come over to the Hoxie show for the last ten weeks

because the other illusion act they had hired had blown. So
that's when I first met Hoxie and, you might say, fell in love
with the show and became generally enthralled with Hoxie,
he himself.'"

When you were a little boy, were you different from other
little boys?

"Definitely. I was always having shows. Back-yard circuses. We had a finished attic. At one end of the attic I built
a stage, with draw curtains, and I stole my dad's Christmas-tree
lights for overhead lights. And the photofloods that my grandfather used to have, I put them up as footlights. We'd have
variety shows and magic shows up there, and charge kids money
to see it, and we had popcorn and Kool-Aid for sale.

"My parents didn't go along with this. My grandmother
was the only one who did. She was the only one who really
ever encouraged me to be in this business. I can't say that she
said, 'Go out and do it,' but any time I wanted to have a show,
she ran the concessions. She helped clean up the mess afterwards, too.

"I never went to college. I got as far as the twelfth grade
in high school, but I didn't graduate. I was a summer-school
regular. Arithmetic was my main problem. I couldn't get out of
school fast enough. If I'd gone to summer school that summer
of my twelfth year, I would have graduated. But that's when I
joined the circus. In fact, I left school two weeks before gradua-
tion time just to rejoin the circus. I thought, 'Fuck you, I'm
never going to come back home in my life.'"

Have you been possessed by the devil lately?

"No, not lately. But I will tell you about one time when
I was. About two years ago, when my divorce was in progress, I
was really going out of my tree. Doing some pretty wiggy
things. And I met this girl and started dating her, and she was
very much into the religion thing. I don't mean *sickeningly*
with it. But she attributed the things I was doing and saying
to Satan.

"She was of the Pentecostal belief. And she says, 'I think
I can help you.'

"I said, 'What do you mean?' She says, 'Well, by a prayer

chain, where you have three or four people praying for you.'
I mean, I was really mixed up. I didn't know whether I was
afoot or horseback, or whether to shit or go blind. As divorce
will throw anybody into. I mean, I was really wigged out. And
she said, 'Satan is inside you and he's causing all these things.'
My life wasn't right. Everything I did turned to shit. And she
says, 'It's the devil inside of you that's causing it. If you want
us to, we'll pray for you and cause the devil to leave.'

"You'll say I was playing with something like *The Exorcist.*
I didn't know what the hell an exorcist was at the time. Maybe
this was a mild form of exorcism. At any rate, we were over
at my cousin's house—a cousin I'm very, very close with. We're
almost like sister and brother. And Peggy, the girl I was going
with, was a friend of this cousin. So they started to pray for
me. I'm sitting there in this chair and they're praying for me,
and you have to confess all of your sins. Everything. Verbally.
And don't hold back. You can't hold back one thing.

"And I'm sitting there and I'm talking, and they're praying
for me, and this is the God's truth—I felt something start like
at my toes, and it was like a heat. The fieriest heat I have ever
felt. Just like I stuck my feet in *flames.* But it was inside. It
was like when Linda burned herself. I felt this come up through
my legs and body, and like exiting through the back of the
neck." He demonstrated, with his hands, the course that the
heat followed. "It felt like a whirlwind or a tornado.

"And then it was gone. And after they were done praying
for me, I said, 'I had the strangest feeling.' And they kind of
looked at one another, and they kind of smiled. They had been
praying for Satan to leave my body and to put my hands into
the hands of Jesus.

"The only way I can say it is I felt as though all of my
problems were relieved. Gone. And that what would happen
would happen. And I told them about this feeling, and they
were kind of chuckling, and they said, 'Well, you might say
you've had Satan leave your body. And any time you feel Satan
is close to you, all you have to say is, "Satan, go away or I'll
wash you with the blood of Jesus." And that's what Satan's
afraid of, and he'll go away.'

"You can call that exorcism or whatever, but, believe it or

Phil

not, after that, in the following weeks and months, everything seemed to go all right. I had everybody on my ass. Bill collectors, the start of my divorce, my family, people who I knew— they were just like the hounds baying at the fox. But ever since that happened, everything just seems to have gone right. It's the strangest thing I've ever had happen to me. I didn't know what the hell to think. They say everybody's got to believe in something. I don't know. You can call me crazy, but . . ."

What do you think it was that created the heat?

"I don't know what it was—whether it was Satan or whatever it was—but the heat was real. It was as real as I'm sitting here. I've never had anything like that happen to me before, and I hope it never happens again. But it was real."

Presumably, you could keep it from happening again by not having any sins to confess.

"True, true."

How are you doing at that?

Phil laughed. "Well, every now and then, Satan and I, we play games. Got to have a little excitement in life. He'll tempt me to do something and I'll do it. Other times I won't. But I know how to control him."

THE RAIN ENDS

New Jersey seemed to pass by quickly. The solstice was long gone now. Although the really hot weather had just started with the beginning of August, and therefore you spoke about the real summer's being here, the days were getting shorter and there was no way to deny that fall was coming. The show would stay in New Jersey for almost two months, until the last day of September, but it seemed much less because the jumps were so small, the towns seemed so much alike, and the people were so much the same.

Old people left, and new people left, too, and a lot of new people came to the show and stayed, and life went on. Magaly Rosales recovered and went back to her trapeze. Lucio Cristiani continued complaining about the condition of the riding ring, but he also continued his superb work. Armando and Robin Anne Chandler sort of fell in love with each other, as eleven-year-olds sometimes do, awkwardly (by grown-up standards) for both of them. Armando juggled his practice rings higher and higher when he knew Robin Anne was watching, and Robin Anne, a beautiful child, with long blonde hair the color of Armando's, stood and watched in the pretty costumes Linda made for her, and she was not at ease, because she did not fully understand what was going on, but she did it anyway, from instinct. Some people might say the instinct was what society taught little girls to do, but it was also a fact that it was the way the race—and circus families—was perpetuated. The parents approved. Lucio, who in the thirties and forties had had to chaperon his sisters on their dates with handsome young men and not-so-handsome old circus owners, said she was a fine child. Phil said he would have given anything if he had been born a Cristiani. Life went on.

Lucio looked tired, although you would not know it in the Big Top. I asked him if he was.

"Oh, I don't know," he said. "I might get tired sometimes, but you don't get tired for a long time. See, I never left this business, but I have friends that did, and they did get tired. But then they get lonesome. Now they confess that they get bored. I know a few who have businesses. One's got a restaurant and the other one's got a store that sells clothes and so on. And they all say that they miss the show."

Do you plan ever to retire?

"I couldn't even if I wanted to. I suppose I could quit working, but with the kids so young, I go with them. I don't think I'll ever be actually retired. Probably for a while—for a month or so—but then I have to move again. No, if my health holds out, I'll be moving all the time. I live for my kids now."

Lucio and Armando: "I live for my kids now"

"But I have *some* ideas," said Lucio. "I would like to have a circus of my own, for instance. The only thing is it takes a little financing. It's like finding a partner or two. If they're interested, I might go ahead with it. I got all the plans drawn up down in Sarasota. It's a little different. The tent would collapse into a trailer. You hook it up in the morning, and you go. You get where you're going, and you unfold it from the trailer, and you pull up your poles and so on, and it goes up in about forty-five minutes."

And if you were running the show, you wouldn't have to worry about the condition of the ring all the time?

"No, you don't have to worry, because you work on Celotex." Celotex was an insulating board, ordinarily used in houses, but it was also a fine flooring for bareback acts. "You put the Celotex on the back of the trailer, and that forms the stage, the ring. The ring is mounted like a platform, and it never touches the ground. You never have to worry about the uneven ground."

Jim Percy and his family were among those who arrived in New Jersey. I wondered almost immediately what his weakness was, because he was hard to figure out. He sold tickets and drove trucks and operated the sound truck from time to time, and his wife, Mary, played the organ in the band, and his teen-aged kids worked either in the band or on props. It took me a while to find out that he was a Lutheran minister, and that the circus was his church.

"I have a call from the Lutheran Church in America," he said one evening, as we sat in lawn chairs, "to serve as a pastor to show people." Jim puffed on a cigar. "This has been going on about four years now. It's what we call in our church a 'tent-making ministry,' which is sort of apropros for a circus, but it wasn't meant in those terms. It comes from the concept of Saint Paul, who was a tentmaker and who would not take money from any people he worked with.

"He made tents to support himself. And so, about four years ago, our church came up with the possibility that there may be certain areas in our world where a man could serve as a pastor but not be supported by the people he's serving, mainly because it can't be a congregation in any real sense. So that he has to make his own way—something like Saint Paul did, just going out and serving wherever he can, whenever he can, but earning his own way.

"Anyway, I work at whatever I can do around the circus. I've been doing this now for four years. I was with Circus Kirk, which is a youth circus sponsored by the Lutheran church. I worked with an indoor show called Children's Magic Circus for a few years. Then I went to Royal Wild West, up until this year, and then I came to this show."

What do you do?

"Just like everybody else, I'm doing what I have to do. I work the sound truck. My boy and girl and Mary are serving in the band. Another boy is working props. Wherever else we can fit in, we'll work and earn money. Wherever there is a need, or wherever there is an interest in a minister, I'm there to serve. Last show I was on, we had services on Sundays when we could. We had communion many Sundays, when it was possible. It was nondenominational. I'm Lutheran because I hang my hat there, but to me, denomination is meaningless. We're all in one world, trying to serve the best we can.

"Even Christian–non-Christian is not a term that means anything to me. I've dealt with Moslems and Muslims and the Jewish people. Any way I can interpret God to anybody, in any form, I'll be happy to do it. When Magaly fell the other night, I put on a clerical collar and went to the hospital with her. Sometimes a man in a clerical collar can make contact with the personnel in a hospital that a layman can't. I've gone to jails with people.

"I'm able to do a lot of my work with people by jackpotting with them. As soon as they know I'm a minister, sooner or later they're going to ask me something about it, and want to talk about it. Sometimes negatively, sometimes positively. I don't care which one. I'll take it either way."

How do you measure your effectiveness in a place like this?

"I don't know," said Jim. He took a long draw on the cigar. "I guess that's up to God."

Jim Percy

Surely you must worry from time to time about whether you're being effective or not. You've got a ready-built cathedral here, but not necessarily a congregation.

He laughed. "We call it a tabernacle. Right, there is no congregation. I'm not out to make Lutherans out of anybody, or even Christians out of anyone. I'm here just to serve as an emissary—as someone who knows *some*thing about God, from my training. Something about the Bible. Something about human relations that maybe others don't have the knowledge about.

"I served in parishes in western Pennsylvania for seventeen years, so I'm not new at it. I'm forty-four. I was ordained when I was twenty-four, so you can figure that's twenty years I've been in this. And the effectiveness in the parish, of course, is measured by how many children you baptize, how many members you have on the rolls, and the offerings, of course. Now, none of these things do I have now. I *have* baptized people on a circus—adults. I've had people ask me when they were loaded would I baptize them, and I say, 'Fine, when you're sober we'll talk about it.' And then they forget about it. Once in a while they'll come back and talk to me seriously about it. I've baptized infants. I've married people—people who met on the show and they wanted to be married and they knew me, so they called me and asked if I would marry them, and I was very happy to.

"I do these things. But the exact way that you measure a parish—how many members you gained this year and how many you lost, and so on—I can't do that, obviously."

Do the people on the show seem to appreciate your being around?

"I've only been here a week," said Jim. "I don't approach people as a minister. I come in saying, 'I'm working on the show same as you,' that's all. I also happen to be a minister, if they ask. I think, like the two women who were hurt the other day, and who went to the hospital, they seemed very appreciative of my being there. That's the only real point where I can say I had some specific religious function."

Do you think you might have regular church services here?

"That will be up to the people who are here," he said. "I don't press that issue. It's available. If a few people are interested, we'll do it. I can have communion with two or three people. My family and a couple of others would be all that would be necessary if anybody wanted it."

Would the logical place for that be under the Big Top?

"Sure. But I've had it anywhere. I have had services in the Big Top most of the time, but if they're busy there, we can go out in the back yard and have a service anywhere."

The layout in Ocean City was like most of the beach dates: the lot was a sandy area just off the main road that ran the length of the beach, and it was difficult for most of the residents and tourists not to know that the circus was in town, because most of them passed it once or twice during the day on their way to the beach or the market.

Just before the first performance started, they made a special announcement. Thomas Waldman, the mayor of Ocean City, took the microphone and announced that the city was giving Hoxie a special award—an engraved chunk of its boardwalk—in recognition of his showmanship and in appreciation for his bringing the show to Ocean City through the years. The band played "For He's a Jolly Good Fellow," and the crowd applauded. Afterwards, Hoxie said, "I think that's terrific, that a city will take its own boardwalk and do that." He was obviously very pleased.

At the second performance, Lucio walked around the track, doing his drunk routine before entering the ring and riding the horse, and Leo was standing by the front door. Leo mocked Lucio a little, staggering and hanging his head to one side. It was not completely play acting on Leo's part; he had spent a good part of the afternoon in an air-conditioned bar next to the lot. Lucio watched Leo for a moment, and then turned to the crowd and said, "He's not kidding."

That night, after the show was over and while they were taking the Big Top down, Phil Chandler sat in his trailer and drank a beer. He said something was bothering him, and I asked him what it was, and he said it was his consumption of alcohol. "I'm particularly worried about how early in the day I have that first one," he said. "You know, I believe in whatever gets you through the night, but this could be a problem. Maybe I'll solve it, though. I think I will."

The rain started about six o'clock on the following morning, as the trucks were moving to Beach Haven. It was a Wednesday morning, August 7. On the radio, there was nothing but talk of Richard Nixon's troubles. Nobody on the show seemed interested in them, though. They had classified him long ago as a crook, a downtown artist of the grift.

The rain was chilly, the sort of rain that strikes the coast sometimes in the summer. If you were there on vacation, you would feel that you were being cheated out of your time on the beach, and you would stay indoors and read old magazines by the weak light and wish that you could have a fire in the fireplace, except that there was no fireplace. By the time the trucks arrived in Beach Haven, a short jump up the coast, it was a bona fide northeaster. The rain was coming down at a thirty-degree angle, getting people wet no matter what they wore. They got the sideshow tent up and the workmen stood beneath it, dodging the leaks from the canvas above, joking about the weather and trying to stay out of it. They had the centerpole up, and the stakes were laid out on the ground around it, but the Big Top did not go up right away. Bill Hill

Setting stakes in the rain

peeled a lot of money off the roll he always carried and sent a man to a hardware store to buy rain suits for the workingmen. The man returned with more than a dozen bright yellow suits, made in Taiwan. The men put them on and went to the cooktent, which was up now, and they ate and drank hot coffee, and then started hammering the steel stakes into the ground. The stakedriver was not working because its mechanism was too wet.

It was Hoxie's birthday. He was sixty-four years old today, and he was working as hard as anyone. John and Lisa Hall gave him a fifty-peso Mexican gold piece.

A workman who had joined up the night before came with more or less the clothes on his back. He wore a pair of fairly new brown-and-white wing-tipped shoes, and they were ruined five minutes after he walked out into the rain and mud. Some of the puddles were half a foot deep by noon, and it looked as if there could be no show today.

The performances were scheduled for four, six, and eight. The night before, someone had made Leo a present of a case of beer, which he had drunk in its entirety, and this morning he had obtained a pint of booze from a liquor store, and he had drunk that straight down. Now he stood in the rain with the elephants, looking as if he were a part of them, and of course he was.

I caught myself revising my half-baked theory about the immortality of the Big Top. It really was the elephants who were immortal, who represented the world. They were always there, even when the canvas was not up.

Slowly they got the stakes in place, and they unrolled the soaking canvas and laid it out. Gradually the tent took shape, high in the middle where it had been hoisted partway up the centerpole, high on the edges where the sidepoles were in place, drooping around an inner circle where the elephants had not yet set the quarterpoles. The men gathered around the centerpole to stay dry. Bill Hill sent out for a quart of liquor, and when it came he put it next to the centerpole and the men took snorts from it to warm themselves up.

The cook came around with a big pot of hot coffee. Leo

Leo that morning

turned down the coffee, but he walked straight to the quart, took a long shot of it, started walking back toward his elephants, spun around, and fell flat on his ass in a huge puddle. He flailed at the air for a moment with his bullhook and then passed out. Two men carried Leo off to the bull truck to sleep it off, and Gary Jacobson picked up his bullhook and finished the job of setting the quarterpoles.

The rain stopped at four o'clock, at the time the show was to start. The puddles of water slowly receded into the sandy earth, and the performers walked through them on their way in and out of the Big Top. The show was only half an hour late in starting.

Lavallette was the next town, another beach town, farther north, toward New York. The air was clear and the ground was dry, although there were occasional puddles left over from the day before. The canvas went up on schedule, and the stiff breeze started to dry it out. Leo was back with his elephants.

At the second performance that night, Phil Chandler interrupted the show briefly with an announcement. "Direct from our newsroom here at the Hoxie Brothers Circus," he said, "we hear that President Nixon has just turned in his resignation, and it is official: the President has resigned." The audience applauded and screamed. Even some of the circus people were touched by the gravity of the announcement, although later they could not remember the name of the town where they had heard it. Way back in my mind I saw a picture of Bert Pettus, wherever he was now, as he learned the news.

A SPECIAL BREED

The dates along the seacoast ended along about the middle of August, and the circus went farther north and inland, into the Jersey suburbs of New York City. At times it was within eyesight of the skyscrapers of Manhattan Island, but the show never crossed the river. King Charles's arrows went back and forth, and sometimes they crossed each other as the show made short jumps among the rabbit warrens of northern New Jersey.

Some dates were straw houses; some were terrible. In Bayonne, New Jersey, on September 4, the advance sale was fifty-two dollars. Last year, Bayonne had been a good date. This time it set an all-time bad record. Nobody knew exactly why, but the cause was vaguely attributed to "the economy."

Johnny Walker said it was all part of show business. "Two years from now I might be on the bum," he said. "I'm making money this year, and I might not make it next year. You never know. You never get too big in this business. Even the owners know that." I asked him if that made him insecure. "Well, there's nothing else I know," he said. "So it doesn't matter whether it makes me insecure or not."

"This time of year," he said, "you get like a little dog. Get to biting a little. You know, your temper. Hot weather and all. And you know the season's ending."

On Labor Day the show was moving from Roselle to Bayville, and a tire on the office trailer went flat. The tire rubbed against the wheel well, and the friction started a fire. The office trailer burned to a cinder. Inside was the financial and promotional heart of the circus: insurance records, publicity, picture files that John Hall had built up over the years, card files on nine years of sponsors, address books, sound equipment. "It was more or less a real calamity," said John. "Of course, you have to roll with the punches."

In Irvington, the police came on the lot with a message for Magaly Rosales. Ordinarily, messages were transmitted to circus people by an archaic system that involved looking up the route, addressing your letter to a town several days down the line, and mailing it to the person, care of the circus, care of general delivery. On every day that the post offices were open, someone from the office would check general delivery for any mail.

If you needed to get in touch with someone on a show in a hurry, it was necessary to look up the route and then to call the police in that day's town. You told the police there was an emergency, and you asked if they would please go to the lot and deliver the message. Many times it was not an emergency at all, but it was about the only way to get a message delivered in a hurry. Western Union was no longer good for this, and hadn't been for years.

In this case, the emergency was real. Magaly's father's circus was playing in Mexico, and a hurricane had roared through nearby. The winds had collapsed the Big Top, and the workmen had put it back up. The winds had come again, and Magaly's father, Raoul Esqueda, had gone inside to see how his tent was taking it. While he was inside, the tent had collapsed again, and one of the quarterpoles had struck him on the head. He was seriously injured, but he was alive, and they had taken him to a hospital.

Magaly, who had recovered from her own injuries only a few days before, immediately left the show and flew to Mexico with the baby. By the time she got there, her father was dead. Ruben stayed behind with the Hoxie show, doing his foot juggling. Magaly did not come back. Ruben seemed very lonely.

When the show got close to New York City, the Chandlers

unhitched their trailer and drove over to Manhattan for part
of a day. Linda bought an outlandish assortment of wigs, including a chartreuse Afro that really looked weird.

The lot in Parlin was a shopping center. But it turned out
that the merchants didn't want the Big Top next to their delivery doors, and a city official who came to the lot sided with
the merchants, and the circus had to show in the open, without
the Big Top. The performers did not like this, but neither did
they go into fits of rage. They accepted it the way they accepted rain and wind.

We got a truckload of dirt to put in Ring Two so that the
Cristianis could work their horses on the asphalt. Lucio got a
hoe and started spreading out the dirt, carefully removing
little stones that could hurt the horses' feet. "One thing about
a horse act, you see, is that it's a little rough, but you get a
little more money to pay for the trouble," he said. "It's like
everything else—the supply and demand. The horse act is
trouble, so a lot of people want to stay away from it. First of
all because they don't like animals. And secondly because it is
too much trouble. So there aren't too many on the market.
So the demand is bigger and the money is better." He worked
away at the soil.

"Maybe we're a special breed," said Lucio. "You take any
normal human being, and you tell him that he's going to live
with very little water sometimes. He don't take a regular bath.
And regular sleep. And regular eating habits. And sometimes
you're in dirt, and sometimes in mud. And that's your job. The
normal human being would ordinarily refuse. But we do it.
We do go on, and we do the same thing every day. We don't
have accommodations and all that. And in spite of all that, we
keep going. Now, you wonder why. I believe we are a special
breed."

Phil Chandler walked up. I asked Lucio if it was possible
for someone not from a circus family, someone such as Phil,
to be a member of the special breed.

"I don't know," said Lucio. "There must be some kind of
a percentage that has got *exhibitionism* in them. They want

Linda and her wigs, and her own hair

attention. They love the spotlight." Lucio's eyes glistened.

Phil smiled. "You hit it, Lucio," he said. "Bingo!"

"That's my belief," said Lucio. "But it affects us all. Take my wife. She complains about that ring. She says, 'Oh, I'm not going to do anything tonight, the ring is so bad.' Then when she hits that ring, she risks her leg. She gets on the horse and dances like nothing was a problem, because she's a ham, see?"

Are you a ham?

"Oh, yes. I admit it. See, if I would see a psychiatrist or a psychoanalyst who could explain it better, I guess they would explain something that I cannot explain. But I believe we are a special kind of people, that nature put us over here to go around and make circuses all over the country."

He stared at the inadequate layout on the shopping center lot. "Only I wish we would not make the circus on a place like this, without the Big Top," he said.

You don't like performing outdoors without a tent?

"Absolutely. It's a completely different feeling. You feel that there's nothing around you. If you've been outdoor without the tent all the time, and then you go under the Big Top, you feel different, too. The ring looks smaller. Everything looks different. Now, when you go from under the tent to outdoor, the way we do here today, it's worse. The point of balance is not there.

"You see, when you ride the horse, you go instinctively. And then you suddenly ride in the outdoor, without the Big Top, and you feel *loose*. It's like you've been wearing a belt all the time and all of a sudden you feel like you're not wearing the belt.

"It's a feeling. It's an intangible. Something that you cannot explain, but you just feel strange. It's a different thing that I don't know what it is. But I feel strange, like I'm loose. It's like the Big Top has been holding you in place. Even the animals feel strange."

Always, in New Jersey, new people join the show as workingmen, and always many of them are young men. One of them had seen the show in his home town, Middlesex, and when Phil had made his announcement about people staying to help tear down, he had stayed and made three dollars. The next day, when the show was in Parlin, the boy, who was sixteen, hitchhiked over to the lot and came on full time. "I like the work," he said. "It's better than working out." He said he wanted to go to Florida. "All I want is to be able to swim on Christmas Day in Florida." he said. He had shoulder-length hair, and he was a nice-looking young man; almost too nice and innocent-looking and clean to be joining a circus as a workman.

"I worked with my father a while," he said. "He's a metal worker. Every day, he drills three holes in three thousand pieces of metal. He sits in a chair that has no back.

"Here it's different. It's not like going to the same old shopping center. I used to come home from school, put my dungarees on and all, go to the same old shopping center, see the same people every day. It wouldn't matter what time it was, or whether it was raining, sleeting, snowing, hailing, hurricane, there were still the same people sitting there doing the same things, saying the same things. I'd go there just to talk to somebody. It was better than sitting in my room and looking at the ceiling. This is a hell of a lot different, boy."

Robert Chandia had joined in Edison. He did not work very hard, but he was tolerated because he acted so crazy. He was widely assumed to be brimful of pills and chemicals and illegal organic products. A couple of times, when the audience was not around, he took off his clothes and streaked. Phil Chandler called him "Lenny" because he reminded him of the late Lenny Bruce. In Parlin, I asked Robert Chandia what he thought of the circus.

"We're thirty-five thousand feet below the surface of the earth, man," he said, "and we're in the magician's hat. We're that small." He indicated with his fingers a height of about one and one-half inches. "Right inside of space, right? And when the people come up the ramp at night, this is a spaceship. To myself I feel it is. A circus spaceship. I've never seen the outside of it.

Robert Chandia

"I feel myself flying in it, with the master controls, and feeling like the outside atmosphere, like the wars we have to go through to reach these destinations, the ramps that the elephants pull us on at night and, shit, pull the trucks through the mud and all that garbage? Who's tying the ropes up? Like green men, about half an inch big, bringing our tent up, through each space we go to."

He smiled broadly, but it was a smile to himself alone.

And Big Al. Alan Fiske. He was a teen-ager, skinny and not too clean. He had run away from his parents, and then they had moved to Canada, and he had no home to go to and he didn't even know where his parents were, he said. Why they called him Big Al, nobody knew, because he was not big at all. A doctor might find some evidence, even, of malnutrition. Big Al worked at the Big Top, and at props, and at sideshow, and he occasionally screwed something up, but they let him stay because he was always kidding around.

And Cowboy. Melvin Goakey. He was nineteen. He worked stock in the sideshow. He had decided on the spur of the moment to join the show when it was in Rensselaer. "I live as my ancestors did," said Cowboy. "From one day to the other."

What kind of ancestors did you have?

"My father is three-quarters Cherokee. And my mother is a quarter Sioux. So that makes me about half Indian."

Cowboy quit school when he was sixteen, and he started driving a truck for his father. He left home after a fight with his mother.

You ran away with the circus, which is something a lot of kids dream about. But you did it.

"Oh, yeah, but so what? You see a lot of movies where the circus is all glory and no work, and you see a lot of kids wanting to join the circus for that reason. I think the first day I thought the same thing. But after that I found out different.

"I thought at first, you would get to see all these big actors, and it was really quite a thrill. I think I'll remember that first day the rest of my life. But then I found out the actors were just people, like everybody else. But I think I'll remember that first day. Everything was new to me, and I thought it was all shining stars and glory, and it wasn't, and it really surprised me."

In New Jersey they put up a new sign in front of the marquee. This time, it held out the promise of Florida in the wintertime.

In Guttenberg, the tent was set up in a public park, next

to an athletic field. Evel Knievel had failed, a few days before, to jump his rocket ship over the Snake River, and on the
athletic field some boys had built ramps out of sheets of wood
and they were jumping them with bicycles. Every once in a
while a boy would fall and skin his knee, but they built the
ramps higher and higher, anyway. All day long and into the
night the kids rode over the ramps.

There was a rumor that winter quarters this year would
not be Miami, but that it would be someplace in central Florida, near Orlando. There was another rumor that the reason
for this was that Hoxie was going to build a year-round circus
park near Disney World, and that this was the cause for the

change in winter quarters. I wondered if that was the big proposition Hoxie had hinted at back in the spring.

Leo had heard the rumors. He said he was thinking of leaving the show.

"I might stay and I might leave," he said. "I might go to a kiddie circus."

Forever?

"Another season, anyways."

You don't like this circus any more?

"I'm sick and tired of working with elephants."

How many years have you been working with elephants?

"Twelve."

What makes you sick and tired of them?

"Just sick and tired of working with elephants, that's all. Get sick and tired of *seeing* them."

If you worked for a kiddie circus, what would you do?

"European Ferris wheel. Down in Florida. The *warm* part of Florida."

You know about the new winter quarters?

"Yes. It's too goddamn cold in Orlando. The daytime, it's warm. But at nighttime you freeze. Central Florida."

What makes you sick and tired about the bulls?

"Looking at the bastards."

What's wrong with the way they look?

"Just sick and tired of looking at them."

Do you suppose you know everything you need to know about elephants?

"Nope. Never will. They're smarter than we are."

Okeechobee said he had cut down to a quart a day. "It got *to* me," he said. "It was going to make an old man out of me fore my time, so I just cut it out. The first seventeen years wasn't bad, but the last twenty, boy, it's been holy heck." He laughed.

I asked him if he missed his earlier life.

"Yeah, I really do. I really do. In a way. But I'm enjoying traveling now."

But doesn't every town look pretty much like every other one when you're traveling with a circus?

"Well, you get to see places—like the other day, I passed a place where they made ball bearings. I'd bought them before. I always wondered where they came from. Well, I passed the place and I got to see it."

You actually get a kick out of things like that?

"Oh, yeah, yeah. You look over yonder and you see this, and you look over there and you see that." He was pointing to the north and south of the lot, and on both sides there were inconsequential scenes, or at least they were inconsequential to me. "Somebody will come up one of these days and go to talking about something or someplace, and you can say, 'Well, I've *been* there.' It's kind of a sense of achievement, I guess you'd call it."

In the first performance at Guttenberg, when it came time for the bareback act, Lucio walked the horse around the ring once, looking down at the rocky ground. Then Gilda rode around once on the horse's back, and their eyes met for a moment, and Lucio shook his head. Phil announced that there would be no riding act that night because of the condition of the ring.

"This life is all right," said Lucio, after the first show, "but when you get to this time of the year, you long for the home life. For a while, anyway. You want to relax for at least three or four weeks. Don't think of nothing. Lie down and don't think of getting up to go to the next town.

"When you put in about five, six months, you need what the people outside the circus call a vacation. We call it a rest. I think we would appreciate that, especially now." He looked very tired.

"It is a physical tiredness, and I think you get mentally tired, too. It's all that moving, and the traffic, and the truck and horses and so on, and you sometimes have a flat and you're in the middle of the traffic and so on. And other things happen, like right now I need a blacksmith and I don't know how to get one. They tell you they will come and they don't come. And you need a vet, and you don't know which one to pick. It's a cumulation of things, you know. It doesn't bother you for a while, and then later on you start to say, 'My God, why should I do that?' And it builds up in you until you say, 'Gee whiz, I like to go home, I like to lay down and just forget about the whole thing for a while.'"

King Charles was angry again, or perhaps it would be more truthful to say he continued being angry. He had been having trouble with the station wagon Hoxie had bought him for the arrows, and he had wanted the show's mechanics to work on it, and John Hall had told him that was not the mechanics' job.

"I still say the same thing," said Charles. "John Hall is good in his office. He's very good in the office. I respect him for it, for his ideas and everything. But in the back yard he's not worth a damn. Even the lowest man on the show disrespects him in the back yard.

"I've been on circuses now for thirty years. Thirty years I've been on the circus. Ten years ago I quit and went into night clubs, which I'm doing this year. I've decided. I'm going back into night clubs.

"And I'll tell you this. For six months, the circus might be what you call a lifetime—of knowing people, and meeting people, and forgetting people. And whenever the circus is about to close, when it has a week or so to go, the circus gets real shitty. Understand me? The circus gets as shitty *as can be*. Guys all the year are promised free wine and rock-candy springs when they get to winter quarters. But when the circus is over and they're finished with you, they're finished. And the last two weeks of the circus, they start *showing* you that you're finished. In thousands of ways. When the show is winding up, you really see the ass of the circus.

"If you come back to this circus next year, you'll see a lot of new faces. It's just like living a lifetime of six or eight months. So just figure up, out of thirty years, how many lifetimes I've lived here—tragedies I've seen and happiness I've seen. Some people I've worked with one season, never heard of them again, I don't know if they're living or dead. I guess they feel the same about me. I think I'd like to go back into the night-club circuit."

4 HOME RUN

THE ELEPHANTS

Pennsville was the last town in New Jersey. The show played there on the last day of September, and it was none too soon for some of the old-timers. A couple of mornings they had waked up and found frost on the windshields, and that was too much for them. Gary started putting the bulls in the truck at night so they would stay warmer.

The season would end on Saturday, October 12, in Valdosta, Georgia, and then, on the following day, there would be the home run to winter quarters—wherever that might be. It still was uncertain whether the show would return to Miami or whether it would end up near Orlando. To the young workmen who had joined in the North and who had never seen Florida, it made no difference. Florida, in their minds, was palm trees and sand beaches and balmy nights and good-looking girls in bikinis. The old-timers knew better.

The jumps were longer, for the show had to go a great distance in a short period of time. It moved from Pennsville to Hancock, Maryland, and then to Harrisonburg, Virginia, and then there was a day open for travel, and then Thomasville, North Carolina. Some of the roadside stands that had had corn a few weeks ago were selling pumpkins now. Along the East Coast, the days were sunny and warm, and the nights were chilly. The weeds by the side of the road took on a brownish grey look, and you knew that the life was ebbing from them for another winter. The corn in the fields was brown and lifeless now, its gold plundered, its stalks ready to turn into next year's fertilizer. The sun was at a different angle, now, and suddenly you were aware that it was setting earlier. After Thomasville came Burlington, and that was the day the elephants got sick.

It had been a beautiful day, a Saturday, and for some reason the people in Burlington had really wanted to see a circus. Because it was a Saturday, there had been shows in the afternoon and at night, and both of them were straw houses. The term comes from the practice, in the old days, of putting straw on the ground for overflow crowds to sit on. The lot in Burlington was next to Interstate Highway 85, and so many people came to the afternoon show that traffic was stalled along the interstate while people waited to get off and into the parking lot. The audience for the nighttime show was almost as big.

"The elephants were fine this morning when I unloaded them," said Gary Jacobson that night. "This has been a disaster." It was obvious that Gary was thinking of how he had blown his golden opportunity to become a young elephant handler. "We had some hay that I considered not very good, but I thought it was edible. I watered them pretty good, put them in the sideshow tent, gave them three bales of hay each, and about an hour and a half later I went in and unchained Bonnie's back leg to take her out for the ride. She was shaking, and she shouldn't have been. Her mouth was slobbering, and there was some slime running out of her trunk. I thought, goddamn, she's caught a cold, going to get pneumonia and die on me."

As Gary spoke, the elephants, all ten of them, were lined up in the sideshow tent. Myrtle was vomiting a clear liquid, as was Hoxie. Almost all the elephants looked as if they were in great internal pain. Myrtle leaned forward on her legs as if she were trying to do something with her stomach. Bonnie tried to lie down every once in a while, and Leo yelled at her to get up.

"And then," said Gary, "I looked over and old Myrtle was doing the same thing. Then I saw *all* of them were doing it.

I thought, shit, they've got a virus and they're all going to die, and my great adventure on Hoxie Brothers Circus is going to come to a fucking screeching halt.

"The hay looked perfectly good. But we got a vet here, a hillbilly vet, and he diagnosed it as being wet hay. Not moldy, and not very wet, but wet to the point where it was poisonous."

Vickie said she had known something was wrong earlier in the day, when Bonnie refused to eat any cotton candy. "And that is her weakness," she said.

As soon as the elephants' troubles were discovered, the office started calling veterinarians. Mac Bradley, a fan from Roanoke, Virginia, found the vet. He had been in touch with the vet once before that day, asking if he could come to the lot and examine the horses. The show's horses, and Lucio's, needed certificates proclaiming them free of disease. They could not cross the state line into Florida without the certificates. When Mac called the second time, seeking help for the elephants, the doctor was away at a football game. His wife had him paged, and he came straight to the lot. His name was Carl Sellars, and he was by no means a "hillbilly vet." He just had a Southern accent.

Sellars observed the elephants. He was pretty sure they were suffering from monstrous stomach-aches brought on by eating bad hay, but he was not so sure about the treatment. He called an old friend at the zoo in Washington who had had experience along these lines. The two medical men conferred on the telephone, and it was decided that Sellars would give the elephants injections of antihistamines and then try to get them to eat a gruel made of bran mash. "The bran mash is more or less an alkaline thing," said Sellars. "They have an acid condition right now. We're trying to counteract it."

Was this likely to end in death?

"It's possible, but not likely," he said.

The owner of a local feed mill had gone downtown and opened up his store in the evening to get the bran. Everybody was being very nice about the elephants. I thought about

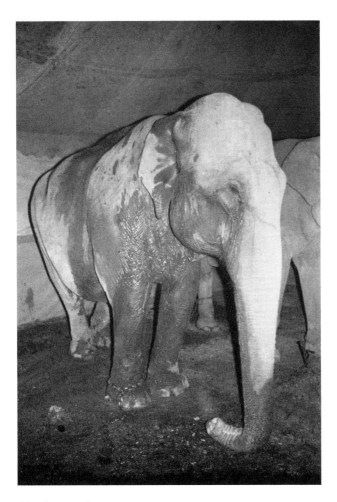

Myrtle in sickness

Bert Pettus and what he would be saying now. He would be trying to find the man who sold them the hay, no doubt.

"I don't claim to be an expert," said Sellars. "This is my hobby—exotic animals. I took a toe offen a lion at the mall Tuesday. Traveling lion show. And I had fun doing it. Things I don't know about, I like to learn. That's why I'm treating these animals tonight."

From outside, you could hear the band and Phil announcing the acts. The crowd never knew about the sickness, although I suppose some of them wondered what kind of circus this was, with no elephants. The bran arrived, and Gary and the vet mixed up a mash out of it and put it down for the elephants to eat. Hoxie went after it, as did some of the other babies, but Gary had to stuff it into Myrtle's mouth with his hand. Myrtle let it slop down her trunk.

Then eventually the elephants did eat it. They drank a lot of water, and the vomiting stopped. John Hall decided to leave the sideshow tent up overnight, so the elephants could stay inside and keep warm. "Losing one elephant is a big loss," said John. "But the possibility of losing ten is hard to describe. I would hate to put a word on it."

Gary and Vickie got their sleeping bags out of the bull truck, and took them and a couple of folding chairs into the sideshow tent. At one o'clock in the morning, when I stopped by to check on the elephants, I saw them there: Gary and Vickie were asleep in their bags, a Thermos of coffee between them. Along the sidewalls of the sideshow tent were the elephants. All of them were standing up, and Myrtle's skin seemed to have dried where she had been vomiting. A lot of the gruel was missing, so they must have recovered enough to eat it. The elephants swayed back and forth, their trunks like giant pendulums, as usual. Not far away, in the shadow of the lion cage, slept Leo. His bullhook was next to him.

Greensboro was the next town. It was a short jump. The elephants looked good in the morning, and they moved with the show, but Gary was careful not to work them too hard. The roads between Burlington and Greensboro bore the names of churches, names like Mount Hope and Bethel, and they were named that way because when they were built churches were an important destination. Now the interstate ran from one shopping center to another, one suburb to the next, and that was what was important now. For the first time since the North, now, you started to notice pickup trucks with gun racks.

Greensboro was to have been Bob Mason's last day as sideshow manager. He could not stay for the final days of the season, because he had to get back to Dayton and start producing magic for the Christmas season. "I have my own show to worry about," he said, "and I'm messing up all my

Christmas dates as it is. I *wanted* to leave back in September. And here we are into October. But I wanted to stick around as long as I possibly could, to help out."

But, in Burlington, Bob was coming off the interstate to make the turn onto the lot when his brakes failed. He had to make a sudden choice between swerving and going straight, and the choice he made was to swerve. The camper careened down the exit ramp and overturned. When it stopped, it was upside down.

"The first thing I worried about was my dog, Josie Belle," said Bob. "She was up front with me. I couldn't get my foot out. I was caught in the rigging there somewhere—the accelerator or the brake pedal or something. And they wanted to call an ambulance, and I'm hollering, 'Don't call an ambulance. Just pull on my foot and I'll be out of here.'

"So I got the seat belt loose, and my dog came crawling out of the wreckage. She looked all right. So I sure didn't want an ambulance. I had money in the camper, and personal belongings. And that's the first thing you start worrying about, once you find out you're okay, you know—your property."

Bob had the camper towed to a repair place, and he had to take the day off in Burlington and Greensboro. The camping rig was a total loss, but the truck itself was repairable. And now he was trying to get it into shape to make it back to Dayton again.

"That's always the thing," he said. "Getting the show back to quarters, whether it's your own or somebody else's."

One reason he felt so bad about the wreck, Bob said, was that it was costing him money. "It's like the average family," he said. "Although there are days when I make very good money, when it's all over and done with it's just a living. And I go to the grocery store just like everybody else, and I try to save few pennies here and a few pennies there. And when you have an accident, you think, 'Jesus, I've scrimped and I've saved, and I've done without, and now this.' So you just have to accept the fact that you've had a good-sized loss, and that's it. Still, it's tough.

"But you're doing something that basically you enjoy

doing. It's a challenge. There's no union. There's no *nothing* here. It's strictly a man on his own."

Vickie sat in the doorway of the sleeper on the bull truck, playing with Martin. Martin was a monkey someone had given her and Gary. Vickie had been completely absorbed into the circus now, or at least it looked that way. I remembered the time in Baltimore when she had been sitting on the embankment in the lightning storm. "You never did go back to your husband, did you?" I asked.

"No," she said. "When I said that in Baltimore I had just been on this show a week, and I was experiencing so many new things. I had nothing to do. We didn't have the elephant ride at the time, and I kept thinking that life with my husband would be *easier*—even if I didn't love him. But there were people there at home. There was Mom and Dad. Back then, I just didn't have anyplace to go, or anything to do, or really anybody to talk to. I think what I meant that night was that if I went home to my husband I would have my family, and my sisters, and the mobile home I lived in in Florida. I thought that maybe, by going back to him, I'd have it all back again."

Are you glad you stayed?

"Yes. I have some things to do now. I have my own little elephant to take care of—Betty—and I feed her and water her. And I help with the elephant ride, taking tickets, and I take care of Martin, and we picked up a couple of dogs the other day, and I'm pretty busy now. I didn't have any of that when we first came on the road. I have a place to live now, in the sleeper of the elephant truck.

"And I know how to keep clean now. We have a big bucket, and in warm weather we fill it up and put it in the sun in the early morning, and by late afternoon we have warm water. It's not *really* warm, though. And when it's cold I find the closest and cheapest motel. It depends on what the weather is. Sometimes it's very hard. For about four days there, it was real cold, and I had a bad cold, and I couldn't wash my hair, and I had to go buy a scarf to cover up my head because I was so embarrassed."

Vickie

Vickie had turned twenty since coming on the show. She was very bright and attractive, and she loved the animals. She talked with a delightful Southern drawl.

And you're happy now?

"Yes. Very happy now. Next year there's lots of things open for me and Gary. We'll be married by that time, and my divorce will be final. Gary and I will be married sometime this coming winter."

Is it necessary that you get married?

"No, no. As far as Gary and I are concerned, marriage doesn't mean anything at all. But my family is very strict, and I feel like I've hurt them enough by running away. As a kid I was into so many things. And it would make *them* happier if they knew we were married. If anybody can make it on a show with a guy, and living in the conditions that we've lived under for five months, they can make it. We've been in the worst, and it's getting better, so it's almost that we know now that we can make it.

"Most couples, they each have a different job, and they can go off in the morning to work, and they come home at night, and they have the night together. We get up in the morning together and we're together all day long. It brings a lot of conflicts. You just get tired of each other sometimes, and you just want to get away."

How do you get away from each other here?

"The only thing I've been able to do is go to the nearest shopping center and not buy anything. I just window-shop, look around, go sightseeing. When we were along the beaches I'd just take off and go swimming in the afternoon, just alone. But when you're on a crowded lot, it seems that *then* is when you need to be alone, because you're right at each other's throat. And that's when you can't be alone. So you just shut up and wait for the good lots."

The audiences looked diverse now, for the first time since the show had left the South four months before. Perhaps it was just my Southern prejudice, but the people in the bedroom communities in New Jersey and Pennsylvania and the farming towns of the Midwest had looked, for the most part, all the same. They seemed to be grey. They were like the middle-class condominium owners of Sunrise and Davie and Coral Springs. Now the people were more like those at Okeechobee: lower middle, a mixture of blacks and whites, still struggling against the soil, some of them, their confidence in the American dream not yet dulled by banks and tax collectors and politicians. The word "heritage" still meant something to them. Because they were close to the soil, they were still close to the seasons, and now it was fall, and that meant it was time to celebrate the harvest a little (it mattered not that the harvest was reaped now in a store full of kitchen appliances or a yard full of used automobiles, instead of a field full of cotton or tobacco, as it was in their fathers' time). And so they came to the circus.

In other towns, the retarded had come in special busses from their schools or hospitals. Here, they came from their real homes, because here their parents and their children kept them around; an obligation to be met. The audiences came: the crippled, more than you see elsewhere in the country; people in T-shirts with snappy sayings on them; people with glazed expressions as they left the Big Top; people without glazed expressions; people dressed in the latest fashions and in the oldest ones; women passing their prime but still dressed in beehive hairdos and short skirts and high boots, still proud of their legs; teeny-boppers who looked like teeny-boppers anywhere; teen-agers who looked to be as afflicted with malnutrition as the people in the photographs from the WPA years. People with stringy blond hair; people with crewcuts, still. There were a lot of fathers in semimod attire: muttonchops, sometimes neat beards. From Monday through Friday they worked for IBM and NCR, and they had to wear white dress shirts and conservative ties; on weekends, and on the nights when they went to the circus, they put on bright plaid pants and, sometimes, white shoes.

It was a Southern fall. The days were warm and bright, and the nights were cold. Football weather, where you sweat in the afternoon and then, when the sun drops behind the stadium, you get cold. People wore sweaters and car coats.

Margaret McGuire said the men were different here than in New Jersey. "Here they're gentlemen. In New Jersey they act like they've seen everything," she said.

A young workman named Edward Kizis, who had joined somewhere in the North, had shot two weeks' pay on a Polaroid camera and some film. He went around the lot, now, not working very much, recording the scenes that interested him and producing, sixty seconds later, faded and improperly exposed renditions of what he had seen. Mostly they were pictures of the other workmen standing with animals or against a backdrop of the Big Top, poses that looked like a hundred years ago. Kizis wore a cowboy hat and jeans encrusted with dirt, and he had long blond hair, and there were several teeth missing in front. I watched him for several days, and finally concluded that he was part of an advance party of film actors sent to the show by Federico Fellini.

▶

Life went on. The Cristianis had introduced their baby leopard into the act in Burlington, and they had been surprised at how calm it had been on the pedestal out there in front of thousands of people. It was almost, Lucio said, as if the cat had some sense of show business. The same cat had been very nervous about people in the spring, and it had jumped me and tried to bite my head off while Gilda had been walking it in some Midwestern town. I believe it was Logansport. A horse had been born in New Jersey, and they had named him Lightning. Now Lightning was making Spec.

Literally hundreds of people and animals had lent parts of their lives, and in some cases the rest of their lives, to the show this season. And a lot of them were not here now. They had moved on. I thought about Jeff, and Joe Hamilton, and Harry, and Junior, and Bert Pettus, and Gypsy Red, and Arnold Sherman, and the jaguar and boa constrictor, and I looked around and saw the people who were here now, and I thought, *A lot of the people think they know the circus, and yet they know only a small part of it.* I was sounding like King Charles when he said John Hall had not seen the circus. Who was left? The bosses were still here, and most of the performers were here (but Magaly was in Mexico), and Leo and Art Duvall were here, King Charles was here despite his bitching, and the elephants were here, and the Big Top was here. Super-chicken was still here. Hoxie was still alive. And I wondered if, on some day, nobody showed up to put up the tent and a circus beneath it, if somehow it wouldn't get done *anyway;* if somehow enough people wouldn't sort of appear from somewhere to do it. And in many cases, do their best.

Art Duvall had been demoted from one of his jobs, that of getting water for the show. I never learned the reason for his demotion. Art stopped showing up at the back door at about this time; unless a circus fan was handy, the performers had to open the door for themselves now. Cowboy was given the job of getting the water. He threw himself into the task, but somehow he never did as good a job as Art, with all his faults and griping, had done.

At the line-up for Spec in Greensboro, Leo stood next to his elephants, leaning on his bullhook. He was somewhat drunk. He talked to the elephants. "When I give you the signal," he said, "I want you to take a great big shit on Hoxie and John Hall." The elephants ignored him; they cast their trunks around the ground next to the back door, looking, as always, for something to eat.

Someone asked Bill Hill how he felt about the end of the season, and he said, "Gee, I wish it was just starting!" He was joking. "I'm looking forward to getting away from these idiots for six months," he said. Then: "I'm just kidding. They're all good boys. Just poor boys. I feel good about it. I'm tired." He said he would work telephone promotions in the wintertime. "I've got a lot of bad habits," he said. "I've *got* to work year-round."

The Chandlers invited the Cristianis to dinner in Greensboro, and they all squeezed around the little table, and Lucio proposed a toast to Phil "for doing such a good job with the back yard this year." The Chandlers had obtained a regional map of McDonald's hamburger joints, and almost every day now, when they were moving from one town to another, they stopped for lunch at one of them.

The show moved from Greensboro to Morganton, in the foothills, and as the altitude increased so did the signs of fall. There were trees that had turned, now, and many more that were in process of turning. Most of the run to Morganton was over an interstate highway, but King Charles made a long detour so the trucks could avoid a weight station. At one point, along about Statesville, ascension balloons appeared. There was apparently some kind of a meet that day, and the whole sky became full of huge balloons, drifting along in the cool, clear air. Some of them were far away on the horizon, and some of them came right across the road. The traffic slowed to watch them; even the intercontinental tractor-trailers slowed down. It was a case of seeing something suddenly that your eye was not prepared for. The balloons, I thought, were in the same category as elephants.

FOR THE
LITTLE KIDS

In Morganton there was a flap over the telephone promotion of the circus. Mearl Johnson had bought out the show on this leg of its trip, and he had set up the usual phone room and sold tickets the usual way. His telephone canvassers had told the residents that they could turn down the tickets, they could buy them for themselves, or they could pay for them and return them, in which case they would be given to deprived children. The deal had been worked out in advance with the local committee, the Morganton Jaycees, and everybody had seemed happy with it until a local banker had raised a fuss.

The banker had been quoted in the paper as calling the whole thing "a gyp from the word go." He had said the Jaycees had allowed Johnson to undertake the promotion while "knowing good and well they'll sell a thousand more tickets than they have kids." The Jaycees had denied the charges, but they were afraid that the banker's uproar would cut attendance. The president of the Jaycees also felt that the young newspaperman who had written the story had been "overly impressionable," and that he hadn't given enough of the Jaycees' side.

None of this bothered the circus people very much, but a couple of them recalled that they had seen, on their way through Morganton that morning, a number of massage parlors, and they were wondering what the public-spirited banker was doing about that. There were, in fact, an inordinate number of the parlors visible in and around Morganton. One of them, a cracker-box house hardly big enough for more than one person to get massaged in at a time, was called the Executive Massage Center, and it featured, according to a sign, an ALL GIRL STAFF.

The lot was a county fairground, with the usual stock barns and midway and a big open field where the Big Top went. Johnny Walker cast his eye around the place for a moment, and then he said this had been a part of his home.

"I grew up on this property," he said. "Before they made it the fairgrounds this was our property. Where we're standing now used to be the end of the cow pasture. It feels strange, being born and raised fourteen years here and all of a sudden come back with a circus. See that church over there?" A steeple was visible on a distant hill. "The Episcopalian mission. Me and my sister was the first ones baptized in it. Old fellow had a watermelon patch right down there." He pointed.

"Right along here, this was the cow pasture, and we had apple trees along a ditch we had at the end of the pasture. And in the pine trees, where the needles fell, and where you could tell where the rabbit pass was, you used to make gums and bait them with apples. You know the gum. It was a box with a trap door in the front and a string and a stick, a fork-ed stick in the middle. And the rabbit would go into the box to get the apple and he'd trip it and it'd close up on him, you know."

What'd you do with the rabbits?

"I'd skin them and take them to town. Some mornings I'd get four or five. Getting half a buck apiece for them."

Who'd you sell them to?

"Well, River Hill over there, we used to call it Nigger Hill, and we'd sell them to the colored people." Johnny laughed. "Traded mules with them and everything else. They couldn't get ahead of me. I sold a mule one time to the Davises, the colored Davises, and I knew they plowed gardens. Well, *I* plowed gardens in the spring, see, for the people in town. I'd get eight to ten dollars for it. I had a mule, and I caught him stumbling. So I wanted to sell him real quick. And I sold him to them for twenty dollars. He lasted three days. I had to hide out—they was looking for me.

"I kept saying, 'Look at the *teeth*, now. Look at his *teeth*.' And I was giving him the boot the same time, making him stand up. I figured he wouldn't last three hours, but he lasted three days.

"A horse trader traded *me* out of him. That's what got *me*, and I said *I* got to get rid of him, too. I used to go to auctions around here ever Wednesday and Thursday with a Davis that lived over there on Wilson Hill. A white Davis. Old man Davis was a horse trader. And there ain't no people in the world like a horse trader. They'll trade you out of your boots or anything. Regardless of whether you be their friends. There *ain't* no friends when a horse trader's trading with you."

Are you glad you left Morganton?

"Yeah," said Johnny. "I don't like Morganton. I like the fast-moving people better. The fast-stepping people."

Jim Percy got back with the sound truck and took a break in a lawn chair in the shade. The temperature was in the eighties, and it was a lazy fall afternoon. He lit a cigar.

"There are two words that fit the religious world and also the circus world," he said. "One is *fantasy* and the other is *celebration*.

"Fantasy is daydreaming—building castles in the air, right? That's the circus world. Fantasy is also an extremely important part of religion. The other thing is celebration—people gathering together just to enjoy, to be happy. To be exuberant about something. That, too, is religious, and it's also circus."

I recalled that one of the foreign students had called it a "feast."

"Yes," said Jim. "Feast—celebration—fantasy. That's good. I like that. Those two words, celebration and fantasy, have always struck me as being what's happening. These people are coming in and they're celebrating together. It's something you can't do on television. If you're watching television it's a private thing. You'd got to get into a *crowd* to celebrate. One person doesn't celebrate. It takes hundreds."

I told him that I supposed one of the reasons he was here was the idea that the circus could learn something from religion. Was it not also true that religion could learn something from the circus?

"I always say that I learn as much from them—or maybe more—than they learn from me," he said. "There's an easygoing attitude about circus people. I remember Jesus said, 'Be not anxious about tomorrow.' Circus people, for all their bitching, are not anxious people. They just go from day to day and expect that the Lord will take care of tomorrow somehow.

"They're not uptight about property, particularly. They're more concerned about people, and the relationships between people. They're earthy. They're tied to nature a lot closer than the average person in the twentieth century. And I think I learn from them.

"I've been selling sideshow tickets, you know, and I hear people who go into the sideshow say, 'It stinks in there.' And my reaction is that it stinks more in Newark, New Jersey, than it does in the sideshow. Those people don't notice that. *This* stink is an *earthy* stink. This is part of nature. This is the way the world is. This is animal dung. It's more natural, somehow. And I learned that from these people.

"And the family—the concept of the family. The family is a working unit. Not dad working and supporting every other member of his family, but the whole family works. Everybody contributes to the family good. Circus kids, for the most part, are the kind of kids you can be proud of. You can say that these are working, contributing members of the society they live in. How many other kids can you say that about?

"Their attitude toward even God is kind of easygoing. It's kind of a 'the Lord will provide' attitude. They expect that things will work out somehow. They're not uptight about tomorrow. These are some of the things I've learned."

It was getting to be late afternoon, and in the background Claude Pasauer was warming up his horn.

▶

John Weathersby had been offered the job of boss canvasman if he would come back next year. He was an obvious good
choice, because he was extremely competent and intelligent,
he knew every bit of the work, he was equal to any responsibility they placed on him, and he had a sense of humor about the
whole thing. He was twenty years old.

I asked him if his father, King Charles, was really going
into night clubs.

"I don't think so," said John. "It's something he says every
year. I think he's stuck here at home."

When John was a child, his father used to bring home
pictures and stories about the circus season. John remembered
that the pictures always showed "sunny days and green grass,"
and when he was old enough he started working in the summers himself. That's when he learned about the rainy days and
mud. He was afraid, now, he said, that being boss canvasman
next year would give him too many headaches. "Got to have
somebody above me," he said.

Aren't you really acting as boss canvasman right now?

"Well, Johnny Walker takes off every once in a while, and
I do it on my own. He's supposed to do most of the stuff that
I do now. I don't mind doing it. If there's nobody else there to
do it, I'll do it, just to have a show for the little kids."

For the little kids?

"Yeah. Little kids got to have a circus. It kind of burns
me up when the circus doesn't come to *my* town. You got to
have a circus. Shit, you can't see an elephant every day. You
got to go to a zoo, fifty, sixty, maybe a hundred miles away.
And where can you see a lion or a leopard? Or a camel? No,
man, you *got* to have a circus."

That night in Morganton, the young reporter who had
written the story about the banker's allegations came to the
show with his wife. John Hall talked to him a while, and
Johnny Walker told him about being born and reared in Morganton, and people generally tried to show the reporter that
the circus wasn't as bad as some people thought.

There was no profit for the show in convincing him of this,

since we would be gone tomorrow. The reporter took it all in, and he wrote down a few notes on a program, and at one point he said, "I guess a lot of these people are mad at me."

Johnny Walker said, "No, nobody's mad at you. You just got tooken in by the people downtown, that's all."

Early in the morning, moving from Morganton to Laurens, South Carolina: There was heavy mist on the ground, and it turned the grass white as if it had snow on it. I stopped at a luncheonette, and the waitress wrapped up two bacon-and-biscuit sandwiches for me to eat on the road, and she filled the Thermos and handed it to me, and said, "You kill something, be sure and bring us some." She thought I was a deer hunter. It was a part of the country where waitresses told their steady customers, "Yawl be good now," and where the customers replied. "I'll try," and then the waitress said, "Don't do nothin' I wouldn't do." Maybe the expressions are just stock ones now, and don't mean anything any more. I hoped that was not the case.

On the road, the signs that warned of curves and intersections all had bullet holes in them. Twenty-twos, from someone's adolescence. There were lots of Bar-B-Q places, and Orange Crush signs, and ice machines that said Serv-Ur-Self but that were locked. And an amazing number of cinder-block structures out on the highway that were beauty shops.

A lot of the trucks broke down on the way to Laurens. It was not all that bad a jump—some hills, and not much interstate—but the age and abuse of the vehicles was telling now, in the last week. Someone jokingly said, "Maybe we ought to end the season," and someone else replied, "Yeah, a week ago."

The lot in Laurens was a fairground, too. Posters showed that we were running about two weeks ahead of the annual county fair. The fairground was rotten-looking, with peeling paint and clogged urinals in the men's room, but nobody seemed to be fixing it up.

Here it cost fifty cents for the elephant ride. It had cost a dollar in Jersey. Gary said the reason was people were poorer here.

One of the young workmen got a letter from a young woman in his home town asking where she should send the baby. She had just discovered she was several months pregnant.

In the sideshow, Phil Chandler was explaining why Linda, who had just finished being the snake charmer, was about to become the Electric Girl. "Now, everyone in the circus has two jobs," he said. "And Linda's other job . . ." Leo, who was dressing the elephants off to the side, heard this, and said, "What's *my* other job?" Linda had lost weight during the season, and she looked great.

At the end of the first show, a woman holding an infant came up to Phil and asked him if he would autograph a coloring book for the child. "I want Angie to have it when she grows up," said the woman. Phil really laid it on during the coloring-book pitch. He talked for five minutes about the qualities of the book, which was pretty ordinary, and he even tried to sell the fact that it had a blank flyleaf. "You can use the page," he told the audience, "to paste or tape in pictures you've taken of the performers and the animals." Then, when he was finishing, he suggested that the audience buy not one, but two of the books—the extra one for "little Willy, who couldn't be here tonight." We used to make up awful obscene jokes about why little Willy was detained. People bought a lot of the coloring books.

Big Al was back. He had been reported as having blown the show, but the report had been untrue. As soon as he had been listed as missing, people had started talking about how much they liked him. "We can't get along with him," said Okeechobee, "and we can't get along without him. Big Al is a hard-luck story from word one. He's just like a nail in a tire over there that makes it go flat. But he's welcome around here. He's okay."

On the road from Laurens to Anderson, we saw the first cotton of the year. There were only minute signs of fall here. The ivy-looking cover crop that the state had planted along the roadsides to stop erosion had grown unabated, and it had climbed over whole trees and telephone poles and it threatened

Big Al

even to cross the roads. There was still erosion on the roadsides, and it was bright pink clay.

Sometimes you would meet another car on the highway, and the driver would wave. In one way, this was a very friendly part of the country; in another, it remained deep and dark and mysterious and brutal. It reminded me of Mississippi during the civil-rights movement. If you had out-of-state license plates, you were especially careful about how you drove. There was a different kind of justice here. But there was also a road sign that said A NEW LIFE BEGINS FOR YOU WHEN JESUS IS YOUR LORD. And brands of gasoline you never heard of before, and pecan groves, and very many Doctor Pepper advertisements.

The route slip had said that Anderson was next to a shopping center, but it had neglected to say that the lot was a former golf driving range, and that it was on a steep slant and it was full of gullies and waist-high weeds and brambles. Anderson was well known as a bad circus town, and nobody knew why the show had decided to play it this year. It was an atrocious lot. When the Chandlers arrived, Phil swore this would be the lot where he would dump his holding tank. Everybody's temper turned to awful as soon as he pulled in. I asked Lucio if he would do his riding act here, and he said, "Oh, you *always* do your act in the last week."

The show people went to the shopping center as quickly as they could, to stock up on groceries and to do the last wash of the season. In one of the supermarkets there was a section labeled "Gourmet Foods," and it contained canned refried beans—the staple food of some of the poorest people in the world—canned tortillas, and canned catfish stew.

The committee arrived and disclosed that the advance ticket sale totaled sixteen dollars. One hundred and forty-eight people came to the first show, and ninety-five came to the second one.

The bear stole the false teeth of one of the butchers.

When Lucio came in as a drunk in the second performance, Phil took the microphone and said, in mock surprise, as usual, "Sir, what are you doing in here?" Lucio replied, "I don't know."

That night, Vickie opened the door to the bull-truck sleeper and looked outside. Her face was white, and she looked sick. I asked her what was the matter.

"I had a miscarriage this morning," she said. "I was two months pregnant." She had been crying. It had happened in a ladies' room in an eating place. Gary called Vickie's father in Florida, and he made plans to fly up and get her and take her home. When she was well again, they agreed, Vickie would rejoin Gary in winter quarters. The airline schedules were bad, and Vickie's father had not arrived by the time it came to move out of Anderson the next morning. Gary had to move with the elephants, so he took Vickie to a restaurant and left her there, in her car in the parking lot. Her father knew where she would be. The show left on schedule, and Vickie stayed behind, waiting for her father in that parking lot.

Athens, Georgia, was next. The roads were deeper and darker now: faded 7-Up signs, no longer green; a sign spray-painted on a piece of plywood saying FARM FOR SALE. Many failed gasoline stations, their brand names efficiently stripped away by the home office. More cotton fields, now; more women with enormous beehive hairdos from the fifties. More historical markers; the South is big on historical markers. Farmhouse mailboxes held up by lengths of chain that were welded into curves; in the towns, black yard men doing their work on white yards. The spool truck broke down thirty miles out of Athens and had to be towed in.

A good old boy from the fire department came by to inspect the show in Athens. He asked me where the hoochie-coochie show was. I told him there wasn't one.

"Gol-dang," he said. "I was hopin' there'd be one. There was a *good* one at the fair we had last year." I started to explain the difference between carnivals and circuses, but he wasn't listening. "This old gal, she had this anaconda, you know, the goddamn thing was sixteen feet long, and she stuck his head *up herself,* you know, and then be damned if she didn't take it out and stick his head in her *mouth!* Woo-eee! That was the goddamnedest thing you ever saw!" He was getting carried away talking about it. He was really disappointed that there was no hoochie-coochie show with the circus.

A man came on the lot carrying a fiberboard suitcase. He wore a dirty T-shirt with a Harley-Davidson advertisement on it, and black pants and boots, and his hair was in ringlets. He said he wanted to go with the show to Florida. He said he had been working carnivals, but that circuses weren't all that different. They hired him and put him to work with the elephants. He picked up a bullhook and started telling the elephants what to do. Sue slapped the hell out of him with her trunk. She lifted him all the way off his feet and sent him several yards through the air.

Both performances in Athens brought pretty good houses. Between shows, Big Al bought a candy apple and gave it to one of the Cristianis' horses. During the second show, when he should have been playing his horn, King Charles set his trumpet down and said, mysteriously, "It's a mighty long road that has no arrows." And the next day we headed for Valdosta, for the end of the season.

VALDOSTA

Friday was open for travel to Valdosta. A lot of the trucks broke down as they went the length of Georgia, but there was nothing the mechanics couldn't fix. The truck that Okeechobee was riding in broke down about halfway, and Okeechobee and the fellow he was riding with went to a coffee shop and waited. "Of all the places to break down in," said Okeechobee, "he *would* pick a dry county."

The last half was interstate, and the cars had license plates from the North, and they were headed, as we were, to Florida. The scenery was all interstate Stuckey's. As we approached Valdosta, the usual arrows indicating "slow down, get ready for a turn" were missing, and at the very last exit I saw a foolish-looking state highway employee tearing down some of the arrows and changing others, to make the show go straight to Florida instead of turning. He was grinning stupidly. I changed the arrows back. I felt hatred for the towner.

It was a fairground again, but this time the lot was huge and grassy, with plenty of room. The grass was tall, but by the time the show had been there two hours it was matted down, and it looked as if the Big Top had been there forever. The elephants loved the grass. A hundred yards away there was a water pipe coming out of the ground, and Armando Cristiani set up a portable plastic swimming pool and filled it. Gary walked the elephants over to the faucet, and he dis-

covered that Myrtle was broken to a garden hose. That is, she
knew how to pick the hose up with her trunk and stick it into
her mouth. "You never stop learning about these animals,"
said Gary.

Hoxie was on the lot. His hatbrim alternated between up
and down. He asked Art Duvall to make sure all the truck cabs
were cleaned out. Art was perhaps the dirtiest human being
on the show, but he went to work with a fury, as if he were
trying to make up for the demotion from the water truck.
When he finished, there were little piles of trash beside each
truck. Most of them were made up of nondescript clothes and
bottles, but in one of them there was a single baby shoe.

Mike McGuire delivered the mail, and Lucio had a report
from the vet in Burlington. The blood test on the white horse
had come back positive for swamp fever. "But she's in heat,"
said Lucio, "and sometimes that throws the readings off. But
we can't cross into Florida with her. We'll have to leave her
in Georgia until we get a negative report." He went off to
make arrangements for boarding the horse in Valdosta.

When the Big Top was up, Linda and Phil put up her
trapeze, and Linda put on a costume she had been working
on all season, and John Hall came and watched as she au-
ditioned her single-trap act. John said he liked it. He invited
the Chandlers back next year, at more money. The Chandlers
were very happy.

"I just noticed Art Duvall," said King Charles. "See how
he looks. He knows what the winter will be. Art realizes what
winter quarters is. And it seems like even the new guys who've
been here their first year in the circus business, they seem to
know it's all over. All the fun's over now. And today *winter*
begins.

"Just look around. Watch. Just observe everybody. Even
the performers, when they came they had great expectations.
They were going to do so much in this limited time of six and
a half months. They haven't accomplished it."

Have you accomplished anything?

"Not what I should have," said King Charles. "I've learned
a lot—or should I say I have realized what I've been knowing

all the time. Out of all the years I knew I was wasting on circuses, I finally realized it now. I know how futile and useless it is.

"You know, out of all the times that you have heard me curse the circus out, you haven't heard me say a bad word about Hoxie Tucker. I've learned how to be a gentleman from Hoxie Tucker. Hoxie Tucker has never mistreated me. The whole trouble is with John Hall. There have been a lot of guys coming here, workingmen, and you know what their salaries are, and these fellows were promised bonuses and everything. Hoxie never promised *one* of them a bonus. Whenever Hoxie *do* promise one a bonus, he gives it to you. But all these fellows, now, they're looking for bonuses, which I don't think they'll get. I was talking to that old man over on the animals, and I said, 'What are you going to do for the winter?' He says, 'When I get my bonus, I'm going back to Harrisburg.' And I almost cried, because I know there won't *be* any bonus."

Just then the man who had joined in Athens, the man with the Harley-Davidson T-shirt, walked by. He asked King Charles if he knew where he could get some food. The cookhouse was closed.

"I pity you," King Charles screamed. The man was surprised. "You ain't nothing but a fucking *victim*, man. And I *pity* you. I ain't got nothing but pity for you." The man looked confused. He turned slowly and walked away.

Hoxie's hatbrim was down now. It might have seemed that he would have little to worry about on the last day, but he had plenty. He had the problem of getting the show back to winter quarters. He already had given up on any hope that he could avoid weight stations going into Florida. And he had reluctantly decided that winter quarters would be the site near Orlando. But he was not happy with the decision. His real inclination was to head back to Miami, but his daughter had prevailed on him to stay at Orlando. It was obvious that she was trying to keep him close by so she could help keep him from having more heart attacks.

I asked him if it had been a good year.

"Got everything but money," he said. "It's been all right. No complaints."

Was there a special feeling that he had on the last day?

"No. The last day is just as important to me as the first one. And I know that after it gets home, in two weeks everybody'll be wishing it was back out. But I know *I* won't. I got too many other things on the fire right now."

Was the circus park near Orlando one of them?

"Yes, that's right. And that means I need more equipment and animals, and so I bought another circus the other day. Barnes and Dailey. Fair-sized. And I bought two new elephants. And I got four more coming, besides that.

"It's going to be a permanent park, year-round, out there next to Disney World on some property we have there. And besides that, the show'll go on the road next year just like always. But I need extra animals and stuff for the park, which I'm buying as I go along, and we've accumulated quite a few in the last month." He said the park would be a joint venture between him and his daughter and son-in-law. He did not seem very happy about the park idea.

With the economy the way it is, don't you have to be out of your mind to be doing something like that?

"Absolutely. But if the economy comes back, and I've got it all there and got it paid for, it belongs to me. So that's my thinking. John'll be in charge of it, in the wintertime, at least.

"You know, John always wanted to be a manager. And I think he's had his fill of it now that he's done it a couple of years. I don't think he'd take a circus now if you gave it to him. And don't *ever* let a guy tell you you can be a nice guy and run a circus."

You mean you've got to be a mean son of a bitch like you?

"I'll agree to that."

I have this secret feeling that you're not really mean.

"I'm not mean. But people got to *think* I'm mean in order to get things done right. And that's just the way I operate. I operated all my life that way."

‣

A black dog walked onto the lot in the afternoon. It looked almost exactly like the Chandlers' dog, D.O. It walked from trailer to trailer, accepting handouts and staring at the Cristiani leopards. When Phil blew the five-minute whistle, and the performers and animal handlers lined up for Spec, the dog lined up with them. It was afraid to go in, though. Even on the last day, there was someone who wanted to join the show.

King Charles again, during a break in the first performance:

"Wouldn't it be great if all the people that we had known during the year were here? Gypsy Red and Tuba Jeff, two of the musicians, they're not here. Everybody that come on the show and started with it. They all joined in good faith, and it turned out to be bad faith and they left." And then King Charles went off into one of his speeches about the cookhouse and John Hall. "All circuses are run the same way," he said. "A circus is a circus. It's a product. It's a *thing*. And you have to run it that way, and there's a miserable side to it, and the poor workingmen do catch the miserable side. And next to the workingmen, I would say the musicians catch it . . ." And then King Charles started telling about how the show had refused to reimburse him for a dollar-and-thirty-five-cent long-distance call he had made several weeks earlier.

He had been putting up arrows, he said, and he had run across a weight station that no one had known about. He had routed the show around the station, and he had called back to the lot to make sure they knew about the change. "If they'd of gone through that weight station," he said, "it would have cost the show thousands of dollars. And they refused to pay for that phone call. Hell, they wouldn't even pay me for the chairs I bought for the band. Paid thirty-five cents each for them at a Salvation Army store, and they won't even pay for *that*." And then he picked up his horn again and played a few notes, and the elephants entered the Big Top.

John Hall, standing in the front door before the last performance: "A season is like a life. It struggles to get born in the spring, it lives during the summer, and it dies in the fall."

And what kind of a death is it?

"It's kind of a sad death for the people who're involved. Because it's something that you've worked hard to create all summer. You struggled and lived with it. And it comes to an end in the fall. And it makes it a little sad."

Linda rode Prince through Spec for the last time, and when they came out of the Big Top she kissed the horse. She was crying.

Inside, Phil welcomed the audience. He explained that it was traditional in a circus, on its closing night, for some of the performers and others to engage in a little foolishness. "And I should tell you this is our closing night," he said. "But I guarantee you one thing. You will see the entire circus performance, plus a few little extra added goodies thrown in."

The performers all seemed to be wearing their best costumes. "They're called 'comeback costumes,' " said John Hall. "They wear them and hope they'll be asked to come back next year." The major acts, like the Cristianis, would not be invited back next year under any circumstances. They liked to move from show to show, year to year, and it was understood that the show, too, would not want to take the same feature acts back over the same territory in the next season. But, still, the Cristianis had on their best costumes, too.

The second show went pretty much as usual, except that at the end, for the motorcycle act, Jorge Del Moral came on in a woman's leotard and with a frizzy black wig and enormous breasts. Just as he was settling himself on the trapeze for the trip to the top of the centerpole, Hoxie walked in, stared at Jorge for a long moment, walked a third of the way around the ring, stared more closely at him, and walked back out the front door. His hatbrim was way down.

And then the motorcycle came down. Phil reminded the audience that there would be another sideshow performance. King Charles lifted his horn in a signal to the other musicians, and they played "Auld Lang Syne."

And the music ended, and the show and the season were over. The workmen came in to tear down the rigging and take out the props. The performers stayed around the back door, saying goodbye. "Adios, muchachos," yelled King Charles from the bandstand. "In all finality. It is all finality. Adios, mu-cha-chos. It is all fi-nal-i-ty. A circus without an arrow down the road is a mighty damn long road.

"But they won't be long for me *no more!* I'm not gonna *be* no more!"

John Weathersby drove the fork-lift, with its huge, ele-phantine tires, through the back door toward the heavy props, to pick them up and put them on the truck. His father held up his hand, and John stopped the fork-lift next to the band-stand. Charles picked up the band's folding chairs and put them, one by one, in front of the fork-lift's tires. John ran over the chairs, flattening them like pieces of paper.

"I wasn't compensated for them, and I bought them," yelled King Charles. "I don't need 'em *any more!*"

Big Al saw what was happening, and he joined in the spirit of the thing. He picked up a heavy steel stake and a sledge hammer, and he walked over to Charles's seat, which was lying flat on the ground, and he drove the stake through the heart of the dead chair.

Hoxie sat in the office trailer, angry as hell. I asked him about the end of the season.

"I don't give a goddamn whether it *ever* starts again or not," he said. "How do you like that? And that's just the way I feel about it. I don't care if it *never* starts again, as far as *I'm* concerned. I don't care if it *never* starts again. No part of it. And I'm telling you the truth."

As I walked away from the trailer, I felt, more than any-thing else, hurt that Hoxie had reacted that way. I felt em-barrassment at hearing him say those things, and I felt sorrow for him. But I thought I knew why he had done it. Hoxie wanted to die under canvas, just as he had said back on re-hearsal night. But there were forces at work to slow him down a little, to prolong his life, to insure that he would not die under canvas. There was the projected circus park, which, theoretically at least, would keep him in one place, close to his daughter, who wanted to save his life.

And there was the fact that the season was ending, and there would be no more canvas for a while. The season was dying in the fall. Hoxie was a man who belonged under canvas, who had been under canvas for most of his life, and he hated to see it come down.

"I'm going to miss Prince horse," said Linda.

"I'm going to miss Lucio talking to his cats in the mornings," said Phil. "But we'll see these people eventually, sooner or later." They moved out early the next morning, bound for Dayton.

Ruben Rosales left early in the morning, too. He estimated that it would be seventeen hundred miles before he got to Magaly and the child. The Cristianis left a little later, after putting their horse in a boarding farm.

King Charles, on his way to his car, passed Hoxie. Hoxie said he had wanted to give Charles a three-hundred-dollar bonus, but that Charles's behavior the night before had made that impossible. "Hoxie," said Charles, "you weren't going to give me that money anyway. If you were going to give it to me, you would have given it to me before. Or you would have given me that dollar thirty-five that you owe me." The two men walked away from each other. King Charles left for Ville Platte.

Slowly, the back yard emptied. By ten o'clock in the morning, Sunday, October 13, the performers were gone. But the Big Top stayed up. Bill Hill had decided to leave it there until the morning sun dried it off. Otherwise, it would mildew during the winter.

Inside, the props were gone, and the seats were gone, the rings were gone, and it was just the Big Top and the poles and a few ropes hanging down. Beams of sunlight came through the rips and tears, focusing themselves on the green grass below. Already the grass was starting to spring back up, and in a day or two nobody would ever know that a circus had been here.

The black dog that had joined the show yesterday walked

cautiously through the back door and toured the empty track, sniffing and exploring.

It was a long time before the morning mist cleared, and the Big Top, with its insides empty, looked like a ship without any of the people or crew or cargo, without any decks and ladders and lashings and direction. It looked now, more than ever, like a sail in the mist.

WINTER QUARTERS

Winter quarters was in the lake and citrus country, in the center of Florida. It was quite a few miles away from Orlando, and it was almost two miles from the nearest paved road. You drove along a sand track past thousands of orange trees, and then made a turn in front of a pasture and went through a gate, and that was winter quarters. There was a swamp next to it. In the pasture was the carcass of a World War II navy training plane, its wings forever crippled. A lot of trucks got stuck in the sand coming in. The elephants pulled them out.

One of the teenagers who had joined up in New Jersey was outraged. "It's fucking *crazy!*" he shouted. "This is a joke, right? We ain't s'posed to be here, right? In the middle of fucking nowhere? Man, I'm leaving tomorrow."

Are you still going swimming on Christmas day?

"Yeah, man. I don't know where. But not here, man. Not in the middle of the orange groves, man. You got to be crazy."

Robert Chandia looked at the crippled airplane in the pasture. "There goes our spaceship, man," he said. "It just crashed."

I heard, from the ground beneath our feet, a tiny whir-ring noise. It was a small rattlesnake. Later, the men found alligators in the swamp. The elephants loved it. They sprayed water on themselves and then rolled in the black sand.

Hoxie came in at night. He was still in a foul mood. He did not give the orders for the men to be paid. Many of them had been expecting to get their money, but there was a lot of work that had to be done first. Hoxie chewed out some of the workmen. He had seen two of them in a circus truck stopped at an eating joint along the road, and he threatened to beat their asses if he ever caught them using trucks for their personal purposes again. He told the cook that there would be no evening meal that night. "Set up the kitchen for a good breakfast tomorrow," he said.

Bill Hill heard this, and he intervened. "Hoxie," he

said, "he's got those hamburgers all thawed out. Why don't we go ahead and feed them?" At this, Hoxie seemed to mellow a bit. He agreed. A little later, he was telling the cook to make sure that everybody got plenty to eat.

John Hall watched all this, and it bothered him. Lisa said he had discovered that he was suffering from a bleeding ulcer, and that it was bleeding profusely now.

The next day, they paid the men, and most of them left. By eleven in the morning the highway that ran by the orange grove was covered with men with their thumbs raised.

Big Al was one of them. I asked him where he was going. "I don't know yet," he said. He was headed north. The man in the Harley-Davidson shirt stood by the entrance to the grove and hitched south. Two hours later I saw him again. He had gone two miles farther down the road.

Back behind the orange trees, Leo was watering the elephants. Vickie was there, with Gary. She looked well and happy. Art Duvall had claimed an old run-down shack as his home. Margaret Ann, Maureen McGuire's little girl, was walking around with nobody to play with. The Percys had parked their trailer in the pasture and were trying to figure out how to get the teen-agers in the local school. Some of the workmen were starting to call Jim "Preacher" now, and he did not mind the title. It might mean that eventually he could hold services in winter quarters. Superchicken walked around the place, checking it out with his aged, but sharp, eyes.

"This place is okay," he said.

Are you going to stay here?

"Yeah, I think I'll stay around a while."

Will you go out on the road next year?

"I don't know. Honestly, I don't know. You know, in the spring of the year, you get that itchy feeling. And when you get that, next thing you know, you're looking for a circus."

POSTSCRIPT

Hoxie decided to stay in central Florida, although he disliked the idea. The circus park was scheduled to open in November, 1974. It did not. The economy, and other problems, kept it from opening on time. Hoxie sold some of the equipment and animals that he had been accumulating.

Junior, on the lot at Circus Vargas:

"Well, I was approached by Clifford Vargas a couple of weeks before Hoxie opened, and the offer that he gave me was so terrific financially that I looked at the salary with Hoxie, and I looked at the salary with Clifford Vargas, and financially I doubled my salary by coming over here. He gave me a new truck for my trailer, and I started out with seven hundred and fifty dollars a week. Now it's up to eight fifty. I'm the boss canvasman here. The Big Top here is one hundred and sixty-one feet wide and three hundred and eighty feet long."

Why, though, did you leave when you did—the night before Hoxie started on the road?

"Well, I don't know. It was just that the decision was in my mind. I knew if I was going to make a move, this was the time. I didn't know why I didn't go before, before the night before the show opened. I was just wondering, should I go with Hoxie, or should I go with Vargas? Then I stopped to realize, all these years in this business—animal training and putting up the Big Top, and mechanic and everything —and then I realized that, back in the older days, when I was a younger kid and everything, it was more a *fun* game than money. And now, to me, it's a business. And I figured business is money.

"And I figured if I'm going to make something, or do something, or have something in this business, I have to go where the high salary is at. And I figured I could better myself by coming to Circus Vargas. Hoxie and I—we was friends. But it was a job. And I figured, you know, that I had been over there going on six years, and I figured I could better myself by leaving. That was the whole idea."

What about the fact that a year before, in Sweetwater, you had gotten hit by the cats?

"I never gave that a thought."

Are you going back into the arena?

"Oh, yes. That lives with me every day. Every day I put up that Big Top, ever week I get paid, I always try to put a few dollars away and say, this is what I want to do— to buy my own animals. And through the will of God, if possible, I'm going to do it again." On the wall of Junior's trailer there was a framed picture of him in the arena with Hoxie's cats.

"No. I'm not afraid of going back in. It was just that the longer you stay around one of these shows, the harder it is to make them understand that time changes, that prices go up, and everything else. And they begin to figure that the longer you stay there, they *own* you."

Did you ever find out who murdered your wife?

"No. I called last year, and they gave me this story about how it happens all the time in New York. They haven't heard anything, but I should keep in touch. This is going on what, now? Three years? So I figured, well, if I *did* find out, what would it mean? It's not going to bring my wife back.

"You know, you never live that down. It's hard to explain it to someone unless it happens to them. You know, they can say, 'Oh, gee, I'm sorry.' They have the sympathy. But this is something that I hope no other person has to experience.

But then I figure, well, we all have to go that road, you know. But you have to ask yourself—I don't know whether you ever asked yourself this—you have to ask yourself, *What is the purpose of life?*

"I can see a person living until they're sixty, seventy years old. And whatever they've done in life is terrific. You say, 'Well, he lived a lifetime.' But then you say, 'Do you know this person who just got killed?' 'Oh, how old?' 'She was twenty-four years old.' What was the purpose of life from the beginning to twenty-four years?

"You know what I mean? These are the things that I wonder. For what? What was the purpose of twenty-four years of a human being living? What was the purpose of that life? I don't guess nobody has the answer. This is just a thing that comes up."

Slim, who was beaten by Stash in Davie, Florida, never filed charges against Stash, according to the police, although Slim told everybody he had.

Joe Hamilton called me several months after the season ended. He said he had left the show because he had had a relapse of the malaria he had gotten in Vietnam. He said he did not know why he had called the cab in Charleston and headed for the bus station. "There was the inclination, I think, of heading back home," he said. Joe said he spent more than two weeks in the hospital. He did not recall saying anything to the cab driver about the driver's license bureau, and he said he never saw Bob Brown that night.

King Charles did not return for the next season. Leo stayed with the show, just as everybody had known he would. Phil and Linda Chandler got their buzz saw and worked with it over the winter on indoor dates, but they were eager to go on the road again the following spring.

John Hall signed up new acts during the winter, and he kept me posted by telephone and mail about the coming season. Gary Jacobson was not hired to work the bulls again.

The elephants made it through the Southern winter in fine style.

Hoxie, too, survived the winter without serious illness, although he had to go into the hospital for an operation just as the new season opened. Superchicken stayed. The new tent arrived. It was red, white, and blue, but you knew that before long it would take on the color of mud.

My work was over. I had set out to write a book about one season in the life of a tented circus. I suppose I had wanted to get something out of my system. Exactly what it was, I was not sure. I knew only that it had something to do with one Saturday morning many years ago, when I was about six. My father had taken me to see Ringling Brothers' Big Top going up, out at the fairgrounds, and we had wandered into the back yard and stared at the people there and we had wondered how they lived.

I had held that picture clearly in my mind all the rest of my life, especially when a circus came to town, and finally I had gone out seeking it again. Now, I knew I had finished my work. I had lived and slept in the back yard, and the people had been kind to me, and they had allowed me to live in their world for a while. And now the season was over, and I could let the circus go.

But then came the January thaw, and after that the cold snows of February. It is impossible to go through the month of February in the North without thinking of spring. I knew that before long the trees along the turnpikes would be turning their subtle shades again, and that the forsythia was not all that far away, and that down in Florida a circus was getting ready for another season. On one of those February days, when the brown snow was rotting on the streets and when the sun had been away a long time, I called Hoxie and we talked about the new year. He was tired, he said, and he was still mean, and he was still working for the gasoline and inn-surance people. The show would go out in March again.

We said goodbye, and Hoxie said, "When you coming?" And I ached for it, and I knew that some of us can never let the circus go.